POLITICS in the PEWS

THE POLITICS OF RACE AND ETHNICITY

Series Editors Rodney E. Hero, University of Notre Dame
                   Katherine Tate, University of California, Irvine

Politics of Race and Ethnicity is premised on the view that understanding race and ethnicity is integral to a fuller, more complete understanding of the American political system. The goal is to provide the scholarly community at all levels with accessible texts that will introduce them to, and stimulate their thinking on, fundamental questions in this field. We are interested in books that creatively examine the meaning of American democracy for racial and ethnic groups and, conversely, what racial and ethnic groups mean and have meant for American democracy.

*The Urban Voter: Group Conflict and Mayoral Voting
Behavior in American Cities*
Karen M. Kaufmann

Democracy's Promise: Immigrants and American Civic Institutions
Janelle S. Wong

Mark One or More: Civil Rights in Multiracial America
Kim M. Williams

Race, Republicans, and the Return of the Party of Lincoln
Tasha S. Philpot

The Price of Racial Reconciliation
Ronald W. Walters

Politics in the Pews: The Political Mobilization of Black Churches
Eric L. McDaniel

POLITICS

in the PEWS

*The Political Mobilization
of Black Churches*

Eric L. McDaniel

THE UNIVERSITY OF MICHIGAN PRESS
ANN ARBOR

Copyright © by the University of Michigan 2008

Published in the United States of America by
The University of Michigan Press
Manufactured in the United States of America
⊛ Printed on acid-free paper

2011   2010   2009   2008   4   3   2   1

A CIP catalog record for this book is available from the British Library.

Library of Congress Cataloging-in-Publication Data

McDaniel, Eric L., 1976–
     Politics in the pews : the political mobilization of Black
churches / Eric L. McDaniel.
          p.   cm. — (The politics of race and ethnicity)
     Includes bibliographical references and index.
     ISBN-13: 978-0-472-07046-6 (cloth : alk. paper)
     ISBN-10: 0-472-07046-0 (cloth : alk. paper)
     ISBN-13: 978-0-472-05046-8 (pbk. : alk. paper)
     ISBN-10: 0-472-05046-X (pbk. : alk. paper)
     1. African Americans—Religion.   2. Christianity and politics—
United States.   3. African Americans—Politics and government.
I. Title.

BR563.N4M336   2008
261.7089'96073—dc22   2008017465

To my mother, Nedra L. McDaniel

CONTENTS

ACKNOWLEDGMENTS

I could not have completed this volume without the help and support of numerous people. First, I thank my dissertation committee, Dianne M. Pinderhughes, Paul Quirk, Todd C. Shaw, and Michael Pratt. Other people have assisted greatly in my intellectual growth. Wilberforce University has provided a unique and unforgettable experience, and I am grateful for the guidance provided by others at the University of Illinois. I also acknowledge help and support from Harwood K. McClerking, Corrine McConnaughy, Brian McKenzie, Irfan Nooruddin, and Ismail K. White. Frank Baumgartner, Jim Granato, Errol Henderson, Vincent Hutchings, Katherine Tate, Nicholas Valentino, and Hanes Walton have provided support and guidance through this journey. Many people associated with the field of religion and politics, including David Campbell, Fredrick Harris, Lyman "Bud" Kellstedt, Geoffrey Layman, and Corwin Smidt, have inspired my work.

At the University of Texas, I thank my colleagues—Zoltan Barany, Jason Brownlee, Jason Casellas, Chris Ellison, Gary Freeman, Terri Givens, Ted Gordon, Ken Greene, John Higley, Andrew Karch, David Leal, Patrick McDonald, and Daron Shaw—as well as wonderful graduate students Mary C. Slosar, Laura Sylvester, and Heidi O'Keefe for their research assistance.

I am extremely grateful to Jim Reische at the University of Michigan Press, who has supported this project from beginning to end, as well as to the anonymous reviewers whose comments have allowed me to create a book of which I am truly proud.

I could not have completed this book without financial support from the University of Illinois's Department of Political Science, the University of Notre Dame's Erskine A. Peters Fellowship, the Society for the Scientific Study of Religion, the Religious Research Association's Constant H. Jacquet Research Award, the University of Texas, the Center for African and African American Studies at the University of Texas, the Public Policy Institute, and the National Science Foundation.

In addition to professional support, I have received emotional support from my family and friends. My mother's unrelenting faith has allowed me to accomplish more than I ever thought I could. I thank my grandparents, James and Irene Hamer and Lloyd and Mildred McDaniel, for their constant support. I also thank Bridget Floyd, Jermaine Hamilton, Marcia Philpot, Meagan T. Speight, and Robert L. Yarbrough, just a few of the family members who have pushed me through. I thank Bishop C. Garnett Henning, who has been a father to me and is the inspiration for my work. I cannot forget my friends Shannon Bonds, Eric Ford, Harvey Gipson, Alan Jackson, and Carl Smith, all of whom have served as stress relievers.

Finally, I thank my wife, Tasha Sian Philpot, who has proven me unworthy of someone as exceptional as she is.

Introduction

The service at Red Memorial[1] progresses like most Sunday services in Black churches. Classic hymns are sung, and the members appear relaxed but focused. The choir loft is full; the congregants are spread throughout the front half of the church and have a joyful attitude. They clap and sway to the music during the choir's and clergy's procession into the service. Rev. Red, the pastor of the church, keeps the members upbeat by having them sing a Caribbean hymn that she learned while on vacation. Along with this spiritually uplifting service, however, Rev. Red wants to deliver a serious message. After the morning announcements, she stands in the pulpit and greets the congregation as she does each week, yet this week her message is different. She does not focus on meetings or other issues related to the operation of the church. Instead, she reminds her congregation that Tuesday is Election Day and makes sure that they understand the importance of voting. She does not allow the fact that this is an off-year election to diminish the need for her congregation to vote. She states,

> Often African Americans in particular do not vote on the off-presidential election. We tend to vote only for presidential elections. So as a result, the persons who make the decisions and the laws that directly impact us, we seldom vote for.

She further notes the city's various problems and how citizens need to make sure that roads and water services are maintained at high quality.

Reverend Red is relatively new to this church, so she treads lightly. While she does not tell her congregation for whom to vote, she does offer hints:

> You better vote right and [for who] is going to do the greater blessing for all of the people and particularly for your own issues. . . . If we have a Republican president and a Republican-controlled Senate and a Republican House, and a Republican-controlled Michigan . . .

As she says this, however, a member of the congregation yells out, "Vote Democrat!" Rev. Red responds,

> It's not just about economics, it's about war. It's about localization, school, criminal policy, and part of what makes this country halfway decent is the fact that we have checks and balances. And I would feel the same way if it was all Democrats. . . . I don't want . . . one party to have total control of all of the decisions that are made in this country.

To assist her congregants in making the "right" decisions, she informs them that a voter information guide developed by the denomination's local ministerial alliance is available. The list details the candidates whom the members of the ministerial alliance have determined to be the proper people for the positions they are seeking, based either on face-to-face meetings or research.

Regardless of the issues or candidates, Pastor Red once again stresses the importance of voting. She asks how many congregants are registered and how many plan to vote. To leave the discussion of political participation on a high note, she tries to mobilize her congregation by way of an African American church ritual, call and response:

> REV. RED: *Everybody . . .*
> CONGREGATION: *Vote*
> REV. RED: *And vote right.*
> CONGREGATION: *Vote right.*

As a parting reminder, one page of the church's Sunday bulletin contains only a single word, "VOTE."

On this Sunday, Red Memorial made strong attempts to mobilize its members and inform them about political issues. The church has become a haven for political activity, with a political identity adopted and embraced by both the members and the pastor. As a result, Red Memorial is a politicized church. It not only informs its members of political events but also works to mobilize them so that they can use that information.

Parallel discussions about the upcoming election occurred in other churches throughout the United States. In addition to addressing members' spiritual needs, religious institutions often facilitate congregants' participation in the political arena. The Black church in particular has a historical legacy of political activity, especially during high points of racial conflict in the United States. However, church-based political activism is not a given. Not all churches or even all Black churches are politically active. What, then, determines whether a church will answer the call to engage in politics? This book answers that question.

Documenting and analyzing church-based political activism is nothing new. Historians, sociologists, and political scientists have long been fascinated with the idea of politically active religious institutions. This research shows that religious institutions play a vital role in American civic life (Verba, Schlozman, and Brady 1995). In general, churches aid in fostering skills that can be used in the political arena (Verba, Schlozman, and Brady 1995; Wald 1997). Within political science, scholars (Brown and Brown 2003; Brown and Wolford 1994; Calhoun-Brown 1996; Guth et al. 1998; Harris 1999; McClerking and McDaniel 2005; Tate 1993; Wilcox 1990b) identify a special class of churches known as political churches. In addition to building basic civic skills, political churches actively engage their members in the political process by mobilizing them for political action and providing information about issues and candidates.

But while the extant research notes the importance and impact of political churches, scholars have neglected to examine why churches choose to become politically active. After all, the primary goal of churches is not to facilitate political activity. In the past, church-based political activism has been treated as a constant, static state—either churches are politically active, or they are not. However, church-based political activism is better understood as a process than a condition. A failure to recognize this distinction has led to disagreement over just how effective churches are at pursuing political goals. Specifically, debate exists about whether churches serve as political opiates or as political as well as religious institutions.

Visualizing this debate requires looking no further than the controversy surrounding the Black church. Black churches have been viewed as the most politically involved of all religious institutions (Harris 1999; Harris-Lacewell 2004). While the civil rights movement arguably represented the pinnacle of Black churches' political engagement, these churches have served as the crux of Black political activity since their conception. Gabriel Prosser, Denmark Vesey, and Nat Turner used churches to plan their slave revolts (Harding 1969). During Reconstruction, Black churches served as centers for the political training of newly freed men and women (Raboteau 2001). As Blacks moved from the rural South to urban areas in the North during the Great Migration, Black churches became the hub for the political careers of individuals including New York congressman Adam Clayton Powell Jr. Even in contemporary politics, African American presidential candidates such as Jesse Jackson and Al Sharpton have used church networks to mobilize supporters (Walton and Smith 2006).

Despite the Black church's historic political legacy, it has fallen silent during some critical times in Black political history. For example, many observers note that Christianity was first introduced to slaves as a means to keep Blacks docile and disinterested in disturbing the status quo. Others note that many free northern Blacks also remained out of the abolition debate. Even during the height of church-based political activism, the civil rights movement, only a minority of the churches were actively involved. For example, no more than 10 percent of ministers actively supported the Birmingham boycott (Charles Payne 1995). Furthermore, McAdam (1982) shows that while Black church organizations were active in the movement, their level of activity paled in comparison to that of student organizations.

Consequently, scholars argue that the Black church has not lived up to its potential with respect to helping Blacks achieve equality within American society. According to W. E. B. Du Bois, one of the major champions of the Black church, its structure and achievements demonstrated "the ability of the civilized Negro to govern himself" (2000, 22). Yet Du Bois also criticizes the church for spending too much time focusing on otherworldly issues instead of addressing social problems (1990, 2003). Gunnar Myrdal concludes that the Black church was out of touch and "remained conservative and accommodating" as others in the Black community were protesting their condition in life (1962, 876). Much like Du Bois, E. Franklin Frazier (1974) notes the central role of the Black church in the development and advancement of Blacks, but he also believes that the Black church failed to advance Black social growth. In Frazier's view, the Black church "cast a shadow" over Black intellectual life and was responsible for "backwardness" on the part of Blacks (1974, 90). Frazier argues that the authoritarian nature of the Black church, with one man in charge, prevented its members from furthering their interests. Finally, Adolph L. Reed Jr. (1986) argues that the belief that the Black church has fostered Black political participation is a "myth," agreeing with Frazier that the church's antidemocratic nature prevented it from serving as an effective institution for politically mobilizing individuals.

How can these two realities of the Black church coincide? The process by which churches become politically active is quite dynamic, and heterogeneity exists both within and across churches. Not only does the number of churches that engage in politics vary, but so too does the level of political activity within a single church over time. As a result, scholars can reach vastly different conclusions depending on when and where they observe these institutions.

Therefore, determining why a church becomes politically active requires looking at the context in which the church exists. Specifically, a church becomes politically active when four conditions are met: the pastor is interested in involving his or her church in politics; the members are receptive to the idea of having a politically active church; the church itself is not restricted from having a presence in political matters; and the current political climate both necessitates and allows political action. Failure to negotiate agreement among all of these factors inhibits a church's ability to enter into the political arena and sustain political activism. Furthermore, because none of these four factors remains stable over time, the level of political activism of churches remains in constant flux.

Current attempts to understand why Black churches have or have not engaged in politics center primarily on clergy, with scholars such as Frazier and Reed asserting that church members have little say. Although pastors have considerable power in directing their churches, members play an important role in determining whether a church becomes politically engaged. The pastor is a necessary part of church-based engagement but is not alone sufficient. Du Bois, for example, argues that a pastor is subject to church members' wishes, describing the pastor as a "mayor" or "chief magistrate" who rules according to the "dictates of a not over-intelligent town council" (2000, 21). Similarly, Myrdal concludes that the church has been accommodating not because of a mandate from pastors but because the people preferred that it stay that way. Thus, understanding why churches choose to become politically active requires attention to members' attitudes and interests.

In addition, I offer a theoretical framework for understanding church-based political activism that accounts for the role of other factors, such as the organization and the environment. Even while criticizing the Black church, both Myrdal and Du Bois note that organizational structure and the sociopolitical environment worked to suppress church action. Myrdal points to the many churches with low resources that became indebted to White patrons to survive. Consequently, these churches hesitated to criticize racial injustices. Moreover, Du Bois (1990) compares the more radical northern Black church to the accommodating church of the South, noting that northern Blacks were granted more political freedoms than those in the South. Du Bois argues that for southern Blacks to prosper, they had to remain silent about wrongdoing. Any attempts to address these improprieties would engender retribution. Thus, regardless of the wishes of pastors and members, church-based political activism is subject to organizational constraints and the environment in which it exists.

At most, the various accounts of church-based political activism focus on one or two of these factors but do not examine how all four simultaneously shape a church's decision to become politically active. By taking a more holistic approach, I provide a deeper and more nuanced understanding of church-based political activism. I begin this task in chapter 1 by explaining why religious institutions have been and remain a critical feature of American democratic politics. I then revisit the central question guiding this study: How are political churches created and maintained? Drawing on political science, psychology, and sociology, I contend that the level of political activity undertaken by a church is a function of its pastor, members, organization, and environment. Further, I explain why the Black church provides an excellent test of this theory.

Chapter 2 qualitatively assesses the extent to which this argument holds. Using data collected from several churches in Detroit, Michigan, and Austin, Texas, I document the ebb and flow of political activity of contemporary Black churches as they adjust to the changing environments in which they exist. I demonstrate that each of these four factors represents a salient piece in the progression of church activism. Pastors may serve as the catalyst for church action, but they are limited by their members' support. In addition, both pastors' willingness to call for action and congregational support are shaped by the constraints of the organization and the environment's need for action.

Having established a broad picture of the process through which a church becomes politicized, I use chapters 3–6 to demonstrate that in addition to contributing to the political activity of a church, the four components of church-based political activism are mutually reinforcing. Chapter 3 places the political engagement of the Black church within a historical context by documenting how the institution responded to slavery, Reconstruction, the Great Migration, the civil rights movement, and other significant periods in U.S. history. Chapter 3 illustrates how the geographic and sociopolitical environment influenced pastors' and members' negotiations of the proper role of churches in politics. In this chapter, I show that the Black church was most active during times when political activity was necessary but other avenues for political action were few. In contrast, lulls in political activity occurred in areas in which either Blacks were prospering or the cost of political engagement was prohibitively high as a consequence of rampant oppression and violence.

Chapter 4 shifts the focus from the environment to the organization, examining how factors such as resources, culture, and process guide church-based political activism. Using survey data from several sources, this chapter demonstrates that variables including membership size, geographic location, the pastor's educational level, and whether the church adopts an Afrocentric point of view significantly predict the social and political engagement of churches.

Chapters 5 and 6 discuss the two key actors, clergy and members. Chapter 5 evaluates which types of pastors are most likely to see the political identity of the church as salient. Using quantitative and qualitative data, I find that pastors are more willing to engage in church-based political activism when they (1) have an interest in politics and (2) have congregations that permit their churches to be used as vehicles for political activity. Again drawing on both quantitative and qualitative data, chapter 6 examines members' attitudes, demonstrating that support for church-based political action is conditioned primarily on whether congregants believe that their religious needs are being met. Since the church is above all a religious institution, any activity seen as prohibiting the church from achieving its principal goal is not sanctioned. In addition, congregants are receptive to political activity by their churches when they have an interest in politics and perceive a lack of sociopolitical justice in their environment. Theology, denomination, and geographic location are also important determinants of congregants' receptivity.

Chapter 7 summarizes the previous chapters' findings and their implications and discusses areas for future research. I speculate about how the Black church is likely to react to issues that have not yet reached the

Black agenda. In addition, I contemplate how mobilization attempts from outside organizations such as the Republican Party are likely to affect the political activism of the Black church. Finally, I discuss how this project's theoretical framework can be used to explain the political engagement of other religious institutions and other nonexplicitly political organizations.

CHAPTER 1

The Political Transformation
of Religious Institutions

Although intrinsically apolitical, religious institutions have consistently engaged in politics throughout American history. Scholars have long noted that many of the key ingredients that shape political behavior can be found in religious contexts (Berelson, Lazarsfeld, and McPhee 1954; Tocqueville 1945). Places of worship help shape political attitudes and mobilize individuals for political participation (Huckfeldt, Plutzer, and Sprague 1993; Rosenstone and Hansen 1993; Verba, Schlozman, and Brady 1995; Wald 1997; Wald, Owen, and Hill 1988). Churches, synagogues, and mosques provide a regular meeting place in which individuals interact and discuss public events and affairs. These institutions also present an image of what the nation should be and motivate members to become politically involved. As a result, connection with these institutions leads to a strong increase in political engagement (Brown and Brown 2003; Brown and Wolford 1994; Calhoun-Brown 1996; Guth et al. 1998; Jamal 2005; McClerking and McDaniel 2005; Tate 1993).

Moreover, in the twenty-first century alone, the political engagement of religious institutions can be seen at all levels of government. A growing number of religious groups have chimed in on contemporary political issues. In such areas as placing the Ten Commandments in government buildings, advocating bans on gay marriage, or adding creationism to textbooks, the intersection of religion and politics is becoming evermore salient in the American political landscape.

Given that religious institutions seek primarily to address the spiritual needs of their members, how and why do such institutions trans-

form themselves into political organizations? A religious institution becomes a political organization when it incorporates politics into its
identity. That is, politicized religious institutions decide that politics is
an important means of achieving their overall goals. In attaining this
end, four conditions must be met. First, leaders must advocate organi-
zation-based political engagement. Rank-and-file members must also
agree that it is appropriate for the organization to delve into politics.
The organization itself must facilitate and sustain political activity. Finally, the context in which the organization exists must be amenable to
political action.

I test my argument by focusing on the Black church, an ideal case for
studying this phenomenon. More than any other U.S. religious institution, the Black church serves as a symbol of religious political action. The
substantial variation in Black churches' levels of political activity and mobilization offers insight into the broader variation in political participation across religious entities. In addition, the dynamics that explain political activity within Black churches provide a useful starting point for a
broader understanding of the role of religion in contemporary American
politics.

While scholars have not ignored Black churches as political institutions, a coherent theoretical conceptualization of what constitutes a political church has not previously emerged or been tested. Researchers
typically examine the behavior of members of these organizations instead of the organization itself. Accordingly, extant research provides an
understanding of political churches as political mobilizers (Brown and
Brown 2003; Brown and Wolford 1994; Calhoun-Brown 1996; Harris
1999; McClerking and McDaniel 2005; Tate 1993; Wilcox 1990b) but
cannot speak to how the church exemplifies a politicized organization.
Even the institutional studies fail to define clearly what signifies a political church. In his study of church social activism, Billingsley (1999)
speaks of activist churches but never defines them. Lincoln and Mamiya
(1990) discuss politically active churches but differentiate them from
other churches only by their actions—that is, whether they participate.
Thus, this study integrates behavioral and institutional studies of the
Black church to paint a more detailed illustration of a politicized church
that captures its nature both within and outside of the electoral context.
This approach provides a better means of assessing if and when civic institutions can repair breaches in American democracy.

DEFINING A POLITICIZED CHURCH

For the most part, conceptualizations of politicized or activist churches have been vague. Researchers tend to define a politicized church as a church that is politically active. Calhoun-Brown (1996) provides the most direct definition of political churches: churches that "provide an environment in which politicization can take place" (941). She further explains that these churches "communicate political activity as a norm" and that the political activity is "facilitated by the institution itself" (942). Tate (1993) argues that these churches provide a setting that encourages political knowledge and skills (95–101). These definitions describe a political church in terms of its activities but say nothing about why, when, and how these activities become part of a church's repertoire.

Rather than being defined in terms of its outputs, a politicized church is best understood as a church that holds political awareness and activity as salient pieces of its identity. A church's identity encompasses a set of characteristics that members feel are central, enduring, and distinctive (Albert and Whetten 1985). An identity establishes the focal or core set of attributes that denote the essence of an organization (Ashforth and Mael 1996)—for example, an organization's mission statement. With respect to a Black church—or any church, for that matter—the main objective is to facilitate salvation. The essence of a church is to save souls.

In realizing this identity, however, churches may come to identify with other activities as well. Many organizations are hybrid organizations, meaning that they possess multiple identities (Albert and Whetten 1985). Like individuals, organizations identify with multiple activities or roles. Members of a church will recognize facilitating salvation as the core attribute of the organization but may also see a connection to political awareness and activity as an attribute of the church and choose to adopt a political identity. Similar to Olson's (1965) and Wilson's (1973) analyses of the creation of political organizations, the political identity of a church should be understood as a by-product of the church's attempt to advance its central interests. The adoption of this political identity leads to the creation of a political church.

Possessing multiple identities allows the organization to take part in a wider array of activities and services. In the case of a religious institution, adopting a political identity enables the church to engage in both secular and spiritual activities. Multiple identities, however, can also lead to role conflict and overload (Pratt and Foreman 2000). Churches must determine how much political activity they can take on without sacrificing their primary mission and/or depleting their resources.

While multiple techniques for managing identities exist, churches mainly choose to aggregate their identities as a way of striking a balance between religion and politics. Pratt and Foreman (2000) define aggregation as the retention of multiple identities by creating an identity hierarchy.[1]

The identities of the church are prioritized—the core elements of the church's identity will be ranked at the top, while the additional identities will be ranked in the order of importance to the church's immediate goals. Churches already have a primary identity—facilitating salvation. As long as political action comes secondary to the central goal of the organization, internal strife will be avoided.

Thinking about the process by which a church becomes politicized in terms of a struggle to manage multiple identities helps provide an understanding of why quite a bit of variance occurs in political activism both within and across churches. Aggregation of identities requires a large amount of capital. It requires the organization to disperse resources to multiple programs (Pratt and Foreman 2000). The political identity of most churches is expected to remain at a high level of the hierarchy—that is, the church is expected to remain politicized—for a relatively short time. Churches with greater resources are expected to hold political identity as highly salient more often and for longer periods of time than other churches. However, no church can perpetually sustain political activism.

CREATING A POLITICIZED CHURCH

But what initially leads a church to recognize politics as part of its identity? Establishing an identity must be understood as an iterative process of negotiations between leaders and members (Scott and Lane 2000). Thus, a politicized church represents the end result of the negotiation process between the leadership and members as they decide whether to adopt a political identity. As figure 1 demonstrates, however, other factors influence this negotiation process. While the pastor and members are the key actors in the negotiation, the negotiation is also shaped by the organization itself as well as the environment.

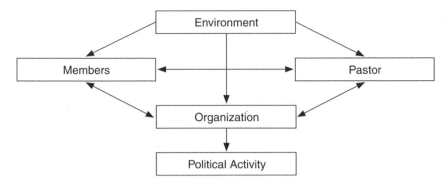

Fig. 1. Model of the creation and maintenance of a political church

Pastor

Like any other organizational leader, pastors become elite figures because they provide "a face to the organization" (Scott and Lane 2000, 47). While pastors' first duty is to serve as spiritual leaders, many are also administrative leaders. Pastors are involved in all facets of churches and their direction.

If a church is a politicized organization, pastors become political elites. Zaller (1992) describes political elites as "persons who devote themselves to some aspect of politics or public affairs" (6). Kingdon (1995) discusses elites in terms of policy entrepreneurs, describing them as people with a "willingness to invest their resources—time, energy, reputation, and sometimes money, in the hope of a future return" (122). As church leaders, pastors behave as activists and incur the initial costs of politicizing the organization. Historically, clergy have taken on the role of the activist to achieve some political goal. Clergy have used the power of their pulpits to affect public opinion and to rally their members and communities around particular issues. Generally speaking, clergy facilitate the connection between religion and politics (Beatty and Walter 1989; Smidt 2004).

During the twentieth century, clergy clearly used their resources to change the American political landscape. During the Prohibition movement, for example, clergy used their authority to lobby not only local governments but also the national government to ban alcohol. Clergy also used their influence during the 1960s and 1970s to pursue social justice issues, such as civil rights and opposition to the Vietnam War (Findlay 1993; Hadden 1967; Quinley 1974). More recently, evangelical clergy, a group that had historically remained outside of the political realm, have become involved and now exercise a strong presence in policy making (Guth et al. 1997, 1998). These evangelical clergy channel their messages to confront a variety of issues, including morality, education, and the environment (Crawford and Olson 2001; Jelen 1993).

Black clergy in particular have historically taken on the role of political elite. As the primary symbol of the Black church, the most independent Black institution, clergy have been called on to employ their resources to influence policy. During slavery, Black clergymen such as Richard Allen, Daniel Payne, and Henry Highland Garnet were ardent abolitionists (Harding 1969; Pinn and Pinn 2002). Nat Turner, a Baptist minister, led the Southampton slave revolt (Greenberg 2003). Many of the first Black elected officials in the South during Reconstruction were clergy. Clergy in the Black Methodist and Black Baptist denominations also lobbied government to help protect the rights of the newly freed men and women (Hamilton 1972; Pinn and Pinn 2002). Later, C. H. Mason, the founder of the Church of God in Christ, was arrested several times for protesting U.S. involvement in World War I (Sanders 1996). In the post–World War II era, Adam Clayton Powell Jr. used the Abyssinian Baptist Church in New York City's Harlem to create a political power base that provided him with a great deal of influence in Congress (Hamilton 1972; Wilson 1960). The prime example of Black clergy serving as political elites came during the civil rights movement, when Black clergy used their influence to mobilize their members, transforming attitudes so that parishioners recognized the need for political activism (Harris 1999). Both Aldon Morris (1984) and Charles Payne (1995) recognize pastors' influence as one of the reasons why people joined the movement. Black clergy also used their resources to provide meeting space and to raise funds for organizations such as the National Association for the Advancement of Colored People (NAACP) and Southern Christian Leadership Conference (SCLC).

Today, Black clergy remain important as political elites. The Reverend Jesse Jackson's presidential campaigns in the 1980s showed that clergy could use their status to recruit support (Tate 1993). Furthermore, George W. Bush has made several attempts to appeal to African Americans by recruiting Black clergy. Most recently, the presidential campaign of the Reverend Al Sharpton attempted to rekindle some of the same activities associated with the Jackson campaign (Walton and Smith 2006).

Members

Members too play key roles in the organization. They comprise the lifeblood of a church, resembling stakeholders in a corporation. Members are the church's capital, providing financial resources as well as labor. Because churches are voluntary organizations, they depend strongly on members' support. If congregants choose to reduce their support, either in terms of financial contributions or labor, the church will be harmed. Thus, although the pastor serves as the face of the church, without the support of the members, the organization will crumble. Pastors and members therefore must work together to develop the church's identity.

Black clergy have an image of independence, but like other political elites, they are constrained by their constituencies. Members of the U.S. Congress are accountable to the people in their districts; pastors are responsible to their congregations. Several studies demonstrate that clergy have less independence than was earlier believed to be the case: during the social movements of the latter half of the twentieth century, White liberal clergy clashed with their congregations. Quinley's (1974) study of activist clergy in California during the 1960s describes the consequences of the activism: many pastors faced decreased giving, membership losses, and in some cases removal. Campbell and Pettigrew (1959) find that White ministers who supported the integration of the public schools in Little Rock, Arkansas, faced a great deal of opposition from members, which led to decreased attendance and funds. Hadden (1967) records similar findings at the denominational level: when the "new breed" of socially liberal Presbyterian clergy came into contact with socially conservative congregations, the denomination faced substantial losses. These instances are not confined just to that era. Jelen (1993) documents the admitted failure of one White clergyman to address racial issues in a town with a strong Ku Klux Klan presence because he feared the repercussions from his congregation. Similarly, Guth et al. (1997) find that pastors who believe that members or potential members disapprove of political activism either refrain from participation or lower their levels of participation.

Black clergy have also encountered these limitations. During the civil rights movement in particular, many clergy faced opposition from members of their churches. Ture and Hamilton (1967) document that some Black clergy resisted joining the movement at least in part because of congregants' sentiments. Hamilton (1972) documents cases of clergy who wanted to be active but could not gain the support of their congregations. One young Black Episcopalian minister, for example, wanted to be politically active, but his largely West Indian and African congregation did not relate to the issues he sought to address. The congregants ridiculed him for his actions, and he consequently discontinued his political activity to prevent conflicts in the church.

Other works show that congregation members can also serve as catalysts for clergy activism. Chong (1991) argues that selective incentives, such as prestige and reputation, were used to bait clergy into joining the movement. Charles Payne (1995) documents how the women of churches in rural Mississippi pushed their pastors into the civil rights movement to protect their children. Payne also details how in some cases, crowds of people chided their clergy for not taking part in the movement:

> Pillars of the community were being denounced by name, ridiculed as cowards and hypocrites before God, and audiences of four or five hundred people were cheering and stomping. Deacons and church mothers sat in those audiences and laughed along with everyone else. (198)

Lee (2003) finds that congregants at the Second Baptist Church of Evanston, Illinois, removed their pastor because they felt that he was not responding to their call for activism. Finally, Harris (1999) argues that Blacks' overwhelming support for church-based political activism explains why Black churches are more active than White churches.

Regardless of whether political activity is initiated by church members or the pastor, one point is clear: the existence of a political church requires a consensus on the part of the pastor and the members. The creation of an environment that allows for political communication and mobilization requires the commitment of the entire organization—both members and pastor.

Organization

Beyond the members and the pastor, the nature of the church itself has some bearing on its ability to engage in political matters. Various aspects of the organization—specifically, resources, process, and culture—can influence the attitudes and actions of the members and pastor. An individual church's resources are the various forms of capital it possesses (McKinney et al. 1998). Several studies show that churches with higher levels of resources are more likely to be socially and politically involved (Billingsley 1999; Chaves 2004; Lincoln and Mamiya 1990). For example, Charles Payne (1995) notes that financial stability played a strong role in determining whether Black churches chose to become involved in the civil rights movement. Just as resources are important for individuals (Verba, Schlozman, and Brady 1995), they are also important for organizational-level political participation. A person in poverty would not be expected to make campaign donations; similarly, storefront churches should not be expected to hold political rallies. In both cases, the individual and the organization lack the resources or capacity to take part in that type of political activity.

Process relates to an individual church's rules and policies regarding decision making and actions (Dudley 1998). For example, some churches have specific rules guiding political involvement, such as bylaws stating that political leaders may not speak during services or forbidding the church from making political statements. Additional operating procedures may govern actors' levels of influence in the church's decision making. In some churches, pastors have sole decision-making authority, while in others they have no role at all in the decision-making process.

Organizational culture is defined by the practices and traditions of the group's members (Hatch and Schultz 2002). Organizational identity tells us who we are, while organizational culture tells us how we do things (Hatch 1993; Pratt 2003; Schein 1984). Each individual church has its own culture developed through the church's history, symbols, and rituals (Ammerman 1998; Becker 1999). Because churches regularly bring people together and foster social networks, members of churches may develop a shared worldview (Ammerman 1998; Becker 1999; Wald 1997). As new members and clergy enter the church, they learn this culture. Attempts to change a church's culture can lead to strong conflicts (Becker 1999; Hamilton 1972; Warner 1988). One conflict that many churches face involves worship services. Churches have specific methods of conducting worship services. Members want to hear certain songs and practice certain rituals and may expect that services will not exceed certain time limits. Moving away from established practices may lead to disgruntled members. Many churches have faced a great deal of conflict over changes to the worship service because these changes did not reflect the church's usual way of doing things.

Culture is also important for understanding the negotiation process. Churches that have traditionally stayed out of political matters should be expected to remain out. Becoming involved would change their culture. Conversely, churches with histories of political involvement are more likely to continue this involvement. For example, any pastor of the Abyssinian Baptist Church in Harlem should be expected to continue its tradition of community activism. The combination of the reasons for the church's founding—racial discrimination (Hamilton 2002; Pinn and Pinn 2002)—and Powell's activities should lead to the expectation that any new pastor will be socialized into this culture of church-based political activism.[2]

Environment

The final and arguably most important component of the identity negotiation process is environment, which affects a church's members, pastor, and organization. Churches are social institutions that exist within social contexts comprised of various forces. While a church may affect its environment, it is also influenced by the prevailing forces within this context (Eiesland and Warner 1998). Changes in the environment can affect how an organization identifies itself (Albert and Whetten 1985; Dutton and Dukerich 1991).

In decisions regarding political activity, the political environment is particularly important. Specifically, a discussion of church-based activism is incomplete without an examination of perceived threats to the interest of the members of the church and the local community as well as the opportunities for political activism provided by the environment. Historically, Black Americans have been a resource-poor group. Legally restricted by slavery and Jim Crow, Blacks have had few outlets through which to work for political, social, and economic equality. This legacy remains in contemporary politics. First, African Americans have not been integrated into America's political institutions—no African American has ever served as president, and only two African Americans have served as U.S. Supreme Court justices, for example. Moreover, "of the more than 11,000 persons who have served in the Congress, only 112 have been Black (107 in the House, 5 in the Senate)" (Walton and Smith 2008, 170). Second, relatively few interest organizations represent the African American community, and there are even fewer Black political action commit-

tees. Furthermore, compared to other interest groups, Black interest organizations are poorly funded (see Walton and Smith 2008, 117, for a
comparison of membership and budgets of Black and non-Black organized interests). Finally, even after the 1965 Voting Rights Act, registration and voting restrictions still systematically disenfranchise a significant
proportion of the Black electorate.

Given these barriers to traditional avenues of political participation,
African Americans have transformed existing institutions into political organizations. By using churches as means of organization, socialization,
mobilization, and participation, African Americans have realized some of
their political goals. Nevertheless, the ability to do so has not been constant. Historically, windows of opportunity have opened, such as Reconstruction, the Great Migration, and the Black freedom struggle. In these
instances, African Americans have entered the political arena using the
Black church. However, Blacks have historically been a marginalized
group, and this characteristic has been transferred to the organizations in
which they exercise membership. As Blacks themselves were restricted
from activism, their organizations suffered a similar fate. In some instances, the same barriers that have prevented Blacks as individuals from
participating politically have also constrained the activities of the church.

In summary, neither the organization nor its members exist in a vac-
uum. The outside world affects the decisions, actions, and identity of the
organization, its members, and its leaders. To become a political organization, the Black church must be located in an environment that not only
requires political action but also fails to place external restrictions on the
church's activities. Moreover, the church's leadership and membership
must agree that the church is the appropriate avenue for pursuing political goals. When all of these conditions are met, the church becomes politically active.

CONCLUSION

Citizens often find the cost of political participation too high (Downs
1957). Consequently, participatory rates in the United States tend to be
quite low. Without a responsive electorate, however, democracy is com-
promised. Maintaining a democratic political system requires reducing
the costs of political participation so that more voices can be heard.
Scholars have consistently found that contact with civic organizations
raises the likelihood that people will engage in politics. Therefore, it is

important to discern the circumstances under which organizations that are not inherently political can bridge the gap between their members and the political arena.

In what follows, I take up this task by examining how religious institutions become political organizations. Church-based political involvement is the product of an ongoing interaction of various factors. A change in any of these factors may trigger a change in the likelihood of engagement. As a result, levels of church-based political activism constantly fluctuate.

CHAPTER 2

Call and Response:
The Mechanisms of a Political Church

As discussed in the previous chapter, a political church is a church that holds political awareness and activity as salient pieces of its identity. Keeping members politically aware and mobilized is part of how political churches understand themselves. However, the political engagement of churches is not constant. Some churches may remain out of political matters, while others have higher levels of engagement. Still others continuously enter and exit the political arena. Arguing that the creation and maintenance of church-based political engagement is the outcome of a negotiation between the members and pastor that is mediated by the organization and environment, this study explains this variation in church activism.

This chapter provides an in-depth examination of several churches and illustrates how each church transforms and maintains itself as a political institution. Specifically, I use data collected from seventy-six interviews of pastors and members from seven churches in Detroit, Michigan, and Austin, Texas. The four Detroit churches were examined during the summer and fall of 2002, when the churches were responding to a statewide school voucher referendum and a mayoral election. The three Austin churches were examined during the fall of 2005 and spring of 2006, a time of local tensions related to police brutality, a statewide referendum on banning gay marriage, a mayoral election, and fears of gentrification.[1] I first discuss each church separately, examining how resources and constraints facilitate and impede social and political engagement. Next I link the similarities across churches to display the pattern in behavior.

Variation in political engagement stems from variation in the characteristics of the pastors, members, organizations, and environments. The pastors serve as leadership figures directing the congregation, but members also play a large role in shaping the church's direction. In addition, the interactions between the members and the pastor are constrained by church resources, process, and culture. Finally, all of the churches are affected by their environment. As these components change, they can change the church's level of political engagement.

BROWN CHAPEL

Brown Chapel is the least engaged of the seven churches examined. This church has been besieged by resource woes, an insular culture, and denominational constraints. Even though the church has a pastor who wants to be politically active, these limitations have slowed the church's political engagement.

Brown Chapel is a Methodist church located on the east side of Austin. The church has about 270 active members and has been in the Austin community for close to 150 years. Brown Chapel differs from all of the other churches because it is a predominantly Black church in a predominantly White denomination. Although the congregation includes a few younger individuals, most members are retirees. The members describe Brown Chapel as a "common" church and see themselves as a blue-collar congregation. Congregants also describe Brown Chapel as a "family" church because a significant portion of the church membership comes from a few family lines.

The pastor of the church, Rev. Brown, has served there for six years. Although he would like the church to become socially and politically active, he focuses primarily on providing stability.

> My preoccupation as a pastor has been to help bring some infrastructure to the church. I have been trying to work hard on setting up our office, setting up our procedures and policy, setting up our committees and organizations, and getting a handle on all the essential operations—anything that consumes our operation.

One of the church's key goals is financial stability. As one of the members stated, "For the last thirty years, we have been in bill-paying mode." On one Sunday, members of the finance committee had to solicit donations from the congregation to ensure that certain bills were paid. In addition to financial deficiencies, the church also lacks human resources. A core set of members does most of the work because others are unable or unwilling to volunteer.

This lack of resources has severely hindered the church's attempts at social outreach. As one member stated,

> Right now, outreach is suffering because we spend more time trying to pay the bills. And that's the reason we are trying to get rid of some of these debts—so we can do some outreach—what we are here for. But as far as the community goes, we do what we can.

Activities are limited not only by resource deficiencies but also by the church's culture. Because the church comprises several families and older individuals, it is very insular. As one member explained,

> If you notice the population at Brown Chapel, it is an older crowd, it is an older generation. And they are kind of set in their own ways. . . . I think it kind of goes back to being a family church where [people think], "Okay, we are going to take care of our own."

Many congregants cite the church's insular nature as a main reason for its failure to attract and retain new and younger members—members who might provide the financial and physical resources needed to energize the church.

Brown Chapel also has suffered through some severe conflicts between members. Rev. Brown noted that when he first arrived at the church, one of his key duties was to ease these tensions so that the church could advance. By helping members overcome past conflicts, he and the church could achieve more stability.

A further constraint to Brown Chapel's social outreach and political activism is the denomination to which it belongs. Both the pastor and the members point to Methodist guidelines as a reason for the lack of activism. They note that their denomination's discipline regulates their activities and that they must make sure that they do not violate these guidelines. As Rev. Brown stated,

> We are an incorporated church—incorporated in our denomination—and we are very careful about what we do and how we represent anything be-

cause we are representing the whole denomination. We try to be careful about what we say and what we represent. We want to make sure that we are always in keeping with our social principles and all of our denominational traditions. That is just our foundation that we try to adhere to.

Several members echoed this sentiment when asked about the church's political activism. They noted that each church within the denomination was expected to be like any other, with only minor variations.

In addition to limiting the church's activities, the denomination also provides many resources to Brown Chapel. The denomination has loaned money to the church, enabling it to survive. The denominational guidelines also place a great deal of decision-making power in the hands of the church members. A committee of members makes all decisions regarding paid personnel and has the power to refuse to renew the pastor's contract if they feel his leadership is lacking. Thus, while the denomination has constrained the church's activism, it provides much-needed financial resources and places the members on equal footing with the pastor in decision making.

A final constraint on Brown Chapel's attempts at social and political activism is its location in a fairly isolated area of Austin, which hinders the church's efforts to draw on the surrounding population for members. In addition, this location has hampered the church's efforts to reach out to the community. Despite support from both church members and the denomination, when Brown Chapel attempted to implement a program that would provide some assistance to Austin's homeless, the program floundered because the church was located too far from where the majority of the homeless congregated.

Despite these constraints, Brown Chapel has continued to engage in social activities. The church hosts health fairs and has developed a relationship with a youth leadership program. Both of these programs are relatively new, but the pastor and members hope that these efforts will provide a base from which to expand the church's social activities. The church also responded to Austin's influx of Hurricane Katrina evacuees by making donations to local food banks and working though the denomination to help those affected.

Brown Chapel has not been highly involved politically. The church at one time served as a polling station, for which the church received funds, but another facility has taken over that role. In response to fears of police brutality, a group within the denomination hosted a police/community relations forum at the church, but the church's involvement in that issue went no further. The church did not engage on such issues as the gay marriage amendment, mayoral election, and gentrification.

BLUE TEMPLE

Detroit's Blue Temple is a Methodist church with a congregation of eighteen hundred members, the largest in this study, although the number of active members is much smaller. The membership of the church is older and includes many retirees. For the most part, Blue Temple is a mix of blue-collar and white-collar individuals. Many of the members, including the pastor, live in suburban areas. Rev. Blue has served as the church's pastor for eight years and devotes most of his attention to church operations and the declining membership. The church has not effectively attracted young members, and deaths have begun to take a toll on membership and resources.

Along with their concerns about the church's future resources, many members noted that the church's culture was highly insular and resistant to change. The church has worked to bring existing members together through various activities such as having the cafeteria open during the week and hosting numerous lay groups and clubs, but these activities have failed to bring in new members. One member described the church as having a club atmosphere:

> We do things through clubs and groups and the clubs and groups do different things to raise money to strengthen our relationship with each other and things like that. And some churches don't have that many clubs and groups. Basically, Blue Temple is a club and group working church.

This inward-looking nature facilitates a close-knit membership but also makes the congregation somewhat set in its ways. The members are accustomed to a specific mode of operation instilled by a former pastor. One member felt that the church's resistance to change affected the worship service:

> With Blue Temple, they're more a tradition church. . . . They do allow the Holy Spirit to enter in, but sometimes I think sometimes we can be so struc-

tured, so rigid, that there's no room for the Holy Spirit to come in. Because everybody has to go status quo. And I think [at other churches], a lot of times the service is a little more freer and a lot more congregation participation.

Another member who had been at the church all of her life attempted to explain why the congregation resists change:

We're loaded with [people who think], "We always did it this way." We're loaded with that. Well, whenever you get a new person, . . . well, he didn't always do it that way or she didn't always do it that way. . . . You got to learn to change. . . . And it's hard on a new leader to come in and change Black folks. Because we always did it this way, and if we always did it this way, then why should we change?

Blue Temple has a tradition of staying out of the political arena. One member reported that the former pastor at times did not even acknowledge visiting candidates. Members openly stated that the church had historically removed itself from political engagement.

We've never had a lot of political stuff. Of course now we get speakers, we get visitors, we get political people come and say good morning and ask you to vote for them and all that kind of stuff in the pulpit.

In spite of this aversion to political engagement, Blue Temple has engaged in social activities. The church facility itself is large, with a community and day care center attached. Blue Temple has hosted several health care programs as well as summer programs for local children.

Even with the success of these activities, many of those interviewed argued that members do not support the continuation of social programs and cited three reasons: age, apathy, and the fact that many congregants live in the suburbs. As one member explained,

If you live way out in [the suburbs], that's a long drive to come all the way over here. But I think, to me, that if this is your church, then it doesn't matter where you live. I mean, if there's activity going on here and if you and if we're going to reach out to the community, I would think it would be worth that drive to come out here. Because not everybody's able to live out where you live.

Along with the members' lack of interest in political engagement, Rev. Blue has admitted that he is not as politically interested as he used to be. He attributes this lack of interest to several things, including being tired from his past activism, the lack of activism in his denomination, and the fact that his members have not called for activism. In his former church, Rev. Blue was highly active in protesting issues such as police brutality. At one time, he even ran for public office, but he no longer has the energy to take part in such activities.

Rev. Blue also notes his bishop's reluctance to engage in the political arena and his attempts to quell the activism of other ministers.

> Our particular bishop has suggested that we not openly support candidates. We have to respect his wishes. He feels that you put yourself in a position to be slandered if you back someone.

Likewise, Rev. Blue and Blue Temple did not become involved in the debate over school vouchers because of the lack of denominational interest.

> We don't react to anything. . . . Just prior to the new millennium, every denomination was putting together programs and challenges for the new millennium, and I was waiting for [our denomination] to hand out [something, but we got] nothing. You see what I'm saying? So I am on my own every time I get up before my congregation.

Although he did not take a public stance on the issue, Rev. Blue appealed to the congregation on the Sunday before the voucher vote. As one member recalled,

> I think the pastor had asked the congregation to basically vote your conscience but also to take into consideration that the school vouchers . . . would be a good thing to have, because . . . a lot of kids are not able to [go to good schools] and . . . it would have a big effect in terms of kids going to school. The reason why a child can't come to school is because his parents can't afford to give him lunch money or even buy supplies or something like that. [Vouchers] will come in handy.

Other than this appeal during service, the church did not take part in any other activities related to the voucher issue.

However, the church did engage in Detroit's 2001 mayoral election, holding a forum at which church and community members had the opportunity to talk to the candidates. Rev. Blue and the members took great pride in holding this event. As the pastor recalled,

> Prior to the election of the city officials, I had a political action meeting here and I had a lot of candidates. Kwame Kilpatrick was one, and it was just set up at the spur of the moment, but we had a good turnout. And I had more people tell me that was really great. [They said,] "I never attended anything like that. We need to have more of those." I was really surprised. Quite a few of my people came, and the different candidates got up and spoke, and my people said, "We've never been to anything like that."

Although Blue Temple does not have a history of political engagement, Rev. Blue noted that the members of Blue Temple were more supportive of his activities than members of his previous churches. Rev. Blue attributed the success of the political forum to member support.

> One of my members gave me the suggestion. And I said, "Oh, yeah." . . . All I heard were compliments, and there were a lot of candidates who came out. . . . Nobody complained, so all I heard were positive things.

Blue Temple did not engage in the 2002 gubernatorial and congressional elections, partly, Rev. Blue stated, because he had to remain neutral in his comments and activities.

> I have to be very careful of what I say because I know I have people coming from both sides. I don't try to tell folks how to vote, but . . . I make statements like, "Nobody can be a member of this church and not vote. You've got to vote." I don't know how many times I heard remarks from other people [who] say, "My pastor got up and tried to tell us how to vote, and he gone too far." I don't do that. Sometimes I want to, and I don't.

Nevertheless, several candidates visited the church, and the church provided its bus to take members to the polls.

WHITE CHAPEL

White Chapel has a considerable level of political interest by both the pastor and members. The church also has a history of being socially conscious, although it chooses to constrain its current political engagement. While the church possesses several of the components needed to create and maintain a political church, its culture mediates against political engagement.

Located in a Detroit residential area, White Chapel is a Baptist church with close to three hundred active members and has been known as a church of educators. Many of the city's school administrators have attended the church. According to the pastor, Rev. White, "I think per capita, this church may have one of the largest gatherings of retired schoolteachers and retired principals." A significant number of congregants have white-collar occupations—medical doctors, lawyers, and businesspeople, in addition to educators. For the most part, White Chapel is an older congregation, with what one member of the board of trustees described as a void in members between the ages of twenty-five and forty. Many of the church's primary lay leaders are older, longtime members.

Rev. White has been at the church for close to four years. He is the second pastor to serve since Rev. Ivory, who led the church for thirty-one years and retired in the early 1990s. Rev. White's immediate predecessor resigned after having conflicts with the trustee board. Although no disagreements appear to have arisen between Rev. White and the members, he seems not to have been brought in to change the attitude or operations but rather to assist in maintaining the church as it is. One deacon was very pleased that Rev. White has led the church to overcome past debt issues and expressed the general expectations for the pastor:

> I think he sort of melded into our philosophy. . . . He knows how we do things here.

The same deacon commented that the church focuses on worship, devoting only a limited amount of attention to social issues. The church's social focus for the most part concerns education. It allows a Head Start Program to use its building, works with local schools, and has implemented a lecture series for its members and the community. By gaining federal grants to help with food distribution efforts, the church has taken formal steps to adopt and implement social welfare programs.

White Chapel's members point out that their church is more structured than most Baptist congregations. The church's bylaws are very detailed and place strict guidelines on the pastor. For example, the pastor must have a master's of divinity degree, and the church does not celebrate such events as the pastor's anniversary. Until recently, the pastor's salary was capped at the equivalent of a high school teacher. Finally, there is a mandatory retirement age of sixty-five.

The church members prohibit political candidates from speaking during worship services. Many of the members believe that this stipulation is included in the bylaws, but according to one member of the committee that wrote the bylaws, it is actually an unwritten rule. Candidates may be acknowledged during the service, but they cannot address the congregation. After services, small forums can be held to allow members to become familiar with the candidates and ask questions.

These guidelines do not mean that the members do not want the church to be engaged. The members see no problems with providing information but do not want to be told by clergy or other congregants what position to take or for whom to vote, viewing this type of activity as properly limited to outside of the sphere of the church. This position is in keeping with the church's historical approach: Rev. Ivory was highly involved in political activity, but the members explicitly instructed him to separate his political work from that of the church. The members supported his campaigns but did not feel that his political activities should intersect with church activities, especially during the worship service.

The members focus more on taking care of the church than on political activism. One member acknowledged some of the Rev. White's work in local organizations but appeared more concerned with his educational achievements:

> He attends the meetings in the community. If there's something going on, he tries to find out about it if it has some ramifications in terms of the church. He has been involved in some personal study. As a matter of fact, since he's been here, he's earned his Ph.D., so he's active in that respect.

This attitude toward political activism by the church is reflected in Rev. White's concern about involving himself and the church in political issues. The pastor strongly believes that churches should be involved in political activity, but his own involvement has limitations. He cites the activities of Dr. Joseph H. Jackson, the former president of the National Baptist Convention, USA, who took a strong stance against the activities of the civil rights movement, as a cautionary tale:

> Sometimes we take positions out of our own experiences, and there's a danger sometimes of coming down on the wrong side of history.

More concretely, Rev. White recalls a recent event in the city in which a man suspected of shoplifting suffocated while being restrained by a security guard:

> My heart went out to that family. My heart went out to the security guard. Both of them were African Americans.
>
> The social, political activist sat right where you sat and said, "We need a mouthpiece. We need a preacher to stand up and do this and carry the banner," and [he] tried to feed into my ego. And I said, "Okay, what provoked the guard to go after this man in the first place?"
>
> It is sad that he died. It is sad that another brother went after him, but as a preacher I cannot get on TV, on the radio, and talk about how wrong, how unfair it is, and two weeks later the prosecution shows videotapes of him stealing.
>
> Now stealing—wrong. Restraining him so he dies—wrong. But I would rather have all the information. . . . [The activist] got offended and I never heard from him again.
>
> So what I'm saying is, I don't mind a scrap, but I choose them carefully because I want to be sure.

For the most part, the members agree with Rev. White's stance; however, some members feel that the church's approach to social concerns is stagnating. One member argued that the church has the ingredients to effect social change but does not deliver these services to the people. Other members described the church's conservative approach to worship as reflecting how it reaches out to the community. Several members linked the lack of energy in the service to the lack of expanded social activism, arguing that the church lacked "emotion" and "a fresh spirit." The pastor immediately preceding Rev. White was more emotional and brought in a new set of members, but when he resigned, the church lost many of the new members as well as some of the older members. These respondents believed that if the church retained this more energetic worship style, it would become more socially active.

Even though some disagreement exists regarding the way the church approaches political issues, the members are for the most part satisfied. One member expressed displeasure with the church's lack of political activity but acknowledged that she could pursue these activities through other organizations.

Even though the members did not push for political activism by the church, Rev. White was one of the pastors who led the opposition to the school voucher program. He did not directly address the issue from the pulpit, however. He kept his congregation aware of panels and town hall meetings on the subject, and he preached a sermon that touched on the subject by mentioning the need to protect the interests of the city's children. He chose to be so highly active on this issue as a result of his history in education, his lack of trust in those who backed the referendum, and the fact that many of his congregants were educators. Many church members strongly opposed the use of school vouchers. One member viewed vouchers as an attack on the teachers' union:

> I feel that the school voucher is an instrument that is being used by this Republican administration that we're in the middle of to destroy the public schools. [The governor] can't stand unionized teachers, and I was one of those critters—a teacher. And he has been trying to destroy the union, which he can't do 'cause they're too powerful, and since he can't do that, he will sponsor—support—this other stupidity called the voucher system, giving my public money—my tax money—to people who want to go to private school.

Many congregants seemed to share these feelings, as did the pastor, for the most part. However, one member neither strongly favored nor strongly opposed the voucher system.

> I think vouchers are great, and I think they're poor. It's according to the people who have to or want to use the voucher.

None of the members to whom I spoke knew how the pastor felt about the issue. A typical member's response when asked about Rev. White's views was, "I don't know. I never discussed it with him." Only one member I interviewed had some insight into the pastor's political views:

> I guess that he's not a conservative. I guess he's a Democrat, based on the various conversations that we've had and various things I've heard him talk about.

One of the members explained why this confusion might exist:

> We have a diverse group of people. I don't think everybody in here is kind of locked into some of these things. You have to be very careful about that. Some people will say, "Well, we're getting too political around here. We're

talking too much about politics. I came here to read the Bible," or whatever. . . . I think the minister does a great job with reading what's going on.

He might mention an issue. He would say we should register. We should vote. And he doesn't have any specificity to any of those issues. . . .

He may mention, "This is the wrong governor; we need a new governor," or something of that nature, but he doesn't ballyhoo any of them.

BLACK MEMORIAL

Much like White Chapel, Black Memorial has several of the components that lead to church-based activism. The church also has a significant level of resources, which has allowed it to take part in extensive humanitarian efforts. But the church is not highly engaged politically because the pastor and members see the church as an institution for assisting those in need through evangelism and social services, not for political engagement. While certain issues may spark their attention, overt political activity does not fit the church's culture.

Black Memorial is a Baptist church located on the east side of Austin. The church has an estimated six hundred members and has been in the Austin area for close to eighty years. The congregation represents a mix of ages and occupations, but most members are blue collar, as the pastor noted when discussing the recruitment of members.

I am a grassroots guy, so I don't always just go for the suburban mix. The Lord has blessed us to take them all different gambits, but we have people now in our membership who have Ph.D.s to what I call no Ds at all.

The pastor, Rev. Black, has been at the church for a decade. He and the members describe Black Memorial church as a "Bible-teaching" church, and all place a strong emphasis on evangelism and humanitarian efforts. The pastor points out that the cornerstones of Black Memorial's ministry are evangelism and social outreach.

The four cornerstones of ministry is that we minister to the masses, with the mandate message of mercy and music of the master. The first cornerstone is evangelism. Evangelism is the reason why our church exists. If a church does not evangelize to the lost, it is literally out of business before it even gets in business. The doors may be open, but . . . that's the reason why we exist. The second one is edification—that's the second cornerstone of ministry. It has to do with our teaching and preaching ministry. The third cornerstone has to do with extension, and that's what we do to reach out to others. What I am afraid of is that today that happens all too often, there is too much "in-reaching" going on. I mean, we know how to feed each other, we know how to fellowship with each other, feather each other's nest. We do all the things that give us the frills of being called a church, but we don't reach out. We don't do what Jesus did. . . . And the fourth one is exaltation. And so, with these four cornerstones in mind, is what makes us unique. We are committed to doing these things. Our church is evangelism, edification, extension, and exaltation.

This outlook reflects Rev. Black's tenure at Black Memorial, during which time the membership has changed drastically. When the pastor came to the church, the congregation was one-fifth of its current size and was significantly older. The church's changing demographics have brought benefits as well as difficulties. Both Rev. Black and church members noted that conflicts had arisen over changes in the worship service and church activities, and some members had left. However, he overcame these losses by bringing in new members, specifically focusing on families. The larger congregation has resulted in an expanded resource base, which has permitted the church to engage in a large number of humanitarian efforts.

Under Rev. Black's leadership, the church created a social assistance center and increased its focus on community needs. Members who predate Rev. Black's arrival tenure noted that the church had been traditional and insular, primarily a reflection of the former pastor and an older congregation. As one member explained, Rev. Black oversaw a dramatic transformation:

> Now that Pastor Black has come, being a younger pastor—I often say, "They must all go to the same Web site, because they all have this—how can I describe it—this desire to do more in the community, this desire to fellowship more with local churches, the desire to break away from the traditional, like hymns, songs.

Current members strongly value humanitarian efforts, highlighting the church's social assistance center as well as its other attempts to assist the community—for example, a back-to-school program that provides immunizations for children. Both Rev. Black and the members noted the church's response to Hurricane Katrina and its efforts to house several families as well as provide basic necessities to others. Rev. Black regularly pointed out members of the church who had evacuated from New Orleans and described how the church had helped them adjust to life in Austin.

The church also works to inform members and the community about health concerns. The church regularly hosts health fairs that offer educational materials as well as basic health care services, such as testing for high blood pressure, diabetes, and sexually transmitted diseases. At first, some members were reluctant to take such tests for a variety of reasons, but Rev. Black volunteered as the first person to take the test, doing so in front of the entire congregation to alleviate his parishioners' fears.

While the church has incorporated social awareness into its culture, political engagement has not been welcomed. Church members have organized a voter registration drive, and Rev. Black has encouraged his congregants to vote, but the church has inserted itself into few of Austin's political issues. Rev. Black expressed dismay that Travis County, in which Austin is located, was the only county in Texas in which the gay marriage ban amendment did not gain a majority of support. When asked about the renewal of East Austin and fears regarding gentrification, Rev. Black and the members noted changes in the community but reported no church activities related to the issue. This reaction or lack thereof is noteworthy because the church draws its members from a historically Black neighborhood.

When the issue of police brutality arose in Austin, several clergy and churches took part in protests regarding the issue, but Rev. Black and Black Memorial did not join them. According to Rev. Black,

> I discovered that in this culture, that in this day and age, marching in the street doesn't get the job done. You got to get to the table; you got to talk to the people doing business. And unless we're allowed to the table—and my philosophy is that if I am at the table, then my agenda is on the table. If you don't let me at the table, then that's another issue I have—is that where decisions are really being made? Are we at the table? Are the citizens actually speaking, or can [they] be heard speaking in the community? Are they being brought to the table?

Rev. Black noted that he has attempted to lobby Austin officials regarding events affecting his members and the local community, but he admits that many of these officials have not been willing to communicate with him.

The church was directly affected by issues of police brutality: a relative of one member was killed by the police. The church reacted primarily by attempting to help that member heal. Rev. Black and several congregants commented that although they were not happy about the deaths related to the police department's actions, some of the blame had to be placed on the actions of the victims. Several of the members noted that when Rev. Black discussed these incidents, he instructed his members on how to behave properly when dealing with the police.

RED MEMORIAL

As the introduction explained, on one particular Sunday, Red Memorial provided a vivid example of a political church working to engage its members by mobilizing and informing them. In recent years, however, this type of activism on the part of Red Memorial had not existed. At one time, the church had been a beacon of Black religious life in Detroit and was highly engaged. Nevertheless, changes in its local environment and internal turmoil led to steady declines in both the church and its level of political engagement. However, a revitalization effort coupled with a highly engaged pastor has resulted in Red Memorial's renewed politicization.

Red Memorial is a Methodist church located in a commercial part of the east side of Detroit. Most of its nearly three hundred congregants are older and have been church members for many years, with a preponderance of blue-collar parishioners and some white-collar members mixed in. As a consequence of the efforts of Rev. Red, who has been at the church for three years, the church is slowly starting to attract more young and white-collar members. Like Rev. Brown at Brown Chapel, Rev. Red was brought to Red Memorial to rebuild the church.

Red Memorial has faced difficult times over the past forty years. The church formerly was one of the city's premier churches, with close to one thousand members and the largest facility among the local Black Methodist churches. It took an active part in a variety of community issues. However, as the surrounding area shifted from residential to commercial, the church's membership declined. In addition, the church has suffered from a lack of consistent leadership. Since 1961, three pastors have died, while others have been removed for a variety of reasons. The rapid leadership turnover has cost the church many members, who have not been replaced. According to one longtime member,

We've had a lot of ministers, and all that changing of ministers, naturally you have change of style. Everybody has their own way of doing things, and everybody has their own vision of what the church is gonna be. And in that we lost a lot of members, just with the changes. Because . . . they just can't get used to new people. This year you are doing something this way, and next year you are doing something that way. So a lot of people just didn't like that.

When Rev. Red entered the church, her job was to provide stability and revitalize the church. She took steps to update the church in several different ways but started by making the church more open and active. The services led by Rev. Red are upbeat, and the congregation displays substantial energy. She also opened up the church for the members and the community to use outside of Sunday services. The church now hosts programs and meetings almost every night. The membership has grown, and the congregation is becoming younger and better educated. The church has shifted from barely surviving to becoming financially stable and socially conscious.

Although Rev. Red has revitalized the church, the fact that she is a woman did not sit well with some members, and some friction has resulted. According to one member, when church members explained to the bishop what they wanted in a pastor, Rev. Red met all the criteria except for her gender, but the bishop "just disregarded that and put her there anyway." Although most of the congregation supports Rev. Red and her vision for the church, a small contingent remains displeased with the idea of a female pastor.

Throughout her career in the clergy, Rev. Red has used the churches with which she has been affiliated to address political issues. At one of her former churches, she worked to pass stronger school bus safety laws when one of her younger members was killed in a school bus accident. She also worked with local officials on issues related to her church and community. This type of activism did not quickly transfer to Red Memorial. The controversy surrounding her gender made her more cautious about her activities outside of the church.

In addition to the gender conflict, the church also lacked the financial resources and human capital to expand. Rev. Red often found that introducing social and political programs to the church was very difficult. Because many of the programs she proposed were new ideas and the members lacked the skills needed to implement these plans, she spent an extensive amount of time preparing and informing them about the programs.

Also Rev. Red was an outsider, assigned to the congregation from another state. She consequently had to learn about Detroit and gain the trust of her members. At one point, a congregant told her explicitly not to focus on Detroit's shortcomings in her sermons. Despite its faults, the member explained, the city is the members' home, and they did not appreciate having an outsider regularly emphasize its shortcomings.

All of these difficulties factored into the church's lack of response to the school voucher issue. But Rev. Red noted that her opinions toward the school voucher issue were the main reason for her silence. While many ministers strongly opposed vouchers, she saw some good in them. Rev. Red has given serious thought to opening a school and sees the benefits of the voucher system, but she is also somewhat wary about the voucher issue's supporters—in particular, about the Republican Party's support for voucher programs. Rev. Red has held this mistrust for a considerable amount of time; she remarked that she stayed away from the issue at her former church because she could not stand in the pulpit on Sunday morning knowing that she sided with men she believed were racists. This sentiment kept her from being involved even though she saw both sides of the argument. She also remarked, as did Rev. Blue, that Black Methodist ministers have not historically been very active and that this pattern continues.

When Detroit had its mayoral election, Rev. Red became less cautious. She strongly supported the winning candidate. While her members never felt that she was completely open about her support, they knew whom she backed. Rev. Red notes that her support of the mayoral candidate has had some positive effects both outside and within the church. Because the candidate that she supported won, she has greater access to city hall. More important to her members was the fact that her connections with the mayor led to more publicity for the church. Rev. Red acknowledges that her congregants want the church to return to its former prestige. Although she does not describe this desire as the driving force behind the church's interest in reaching out to the community, she admits that it factors into the congregants' desire for more activism. As one member noted, the church has a history of engaging people in the political process:

> Red Memorial has always tried to make sure that the people knew what was going on and try to make sure that they would vote. Naturally, you cannot tell

people how to vote, but it was always suggested that they voted for the right thing.

Even with this fuel for activism, Rev. Red notes that members attempt to place constraints on her because of her gender. She acknowledges that they are very receptive on race issues; however, members are less concerned with gender issues. Rev. Red mobilized members to march in support of the University of Michigan's affirmative action policies, but gender remains outside the boundaries of her congregation's support. As she stated, "So for the race issues they understand it. For the sex issues, I'm out of place." A great deal of negotiating remains before she and the church can be in full agreement about the issues that the church will address.

GREEN MEMORIAL

Green Memorial is one of the most politically engaged of all the churches in the sample. The pastor is highly engaged in the city's political issues, and the church's membership expresses a significant amount of political interest. In addition, the church possesses substantial resources and believes it should have a spiritual, social, and political presence in its community.

Green Memorial is a Baptist church on the east side of Detroit with nearly fifteen hundred members. The congregants describe themselves as mixed in terms of social class; there are many who hold white-collar jobs, but the majority hold blue-collar positions. The church has a large contingent of middle-aged and older members as well as a significant number of young families and singles. When the current pastor, Rev. Green, arrived nearly two decades ago, the congregation numbered only four hundred. Members have taken a great deal of pride in the church's growth not only in size but also in prestige.

However, much like Rev. Black, Rev. Green initially faced a great deal of opposition to his proposed changes. Before he arrived, according to Rev. Green,

Green Memorial was a typical denominational church. Basically, churches in Detroit, with the exception of a handful, were all relatively small or medium-size, self-directed, community-based churches. Primarily they were there for purposes of fellowship, providing spiritual nurture for those who belonged to it and to greater or lesser degrees a spiritual presence in the community.

Rev. Green sought to establish a broader base for the church, arguing that it should be more accessible and should attempt to do more in terms of social issues. To facilitate these changes, Rev. Green reorganized the church's internal workings, replacing members of the board of deacons and changing the leadership of some of the church auxiliaries. These changes created great animosity toward him, but Rev. Green defended the reforms by stating that the present lay leadership could not implement many of his planned programs. Many of the deacons, he believed, were not willing to change their ideas of how the church should operate or were not prepared for the changes that needed to be made. Rev. Green and Green Memorial overcame these tensions because of changes in the congregation on two fronts. First, members' attitudes changed, and many congregants began to align themselves with his philosophy and agenda. Second, an influx of younger, better educated members proved more open to Rev. Green's ideas. The church eventually began to grow in prominence.

With expanding resources as well as members' support, the church has become increasingly socially conscious, engaging in endeavors that have helped establish the church as a central institution in the community. Green Memorial is in the process of building a new facility that will serve not only as a place of worship but also as a conference center, music hall, and theater. The church campus also includes a school. Finally, the church has created a drug treatment center that will remain open twenty-four hours a day.

Rev. Green and the church have engaged themselves in local political issues as well. Rev. Green views this engagement as part of his ministry; he argues that being politically active is a duty that he as a pastor must fulfill. Rev. Green works with the mayor's office as well as other municipal offices. From his early years in the city, he and the church have been engaged in local politics, supporting former mayor Coleman Young and working with several local organizations. It is not unusual to find local politicians at festivals and other church gatherings.

For the most part, church members have supported Rev. Green's activities. However, in some instances, the congregation did not provide its full support—when Rev. Green supported candidates of whom the members did not approve as well as when he did not support church members who were running for office. These differences did not cause any real conflicts: members felt that the infrastructure and future of the church were more salient than whom the pastor supported.

This philosophy was evident during the school voucher debate. Rev. Green actively supported the creation of the voucher system as a consequence of his long-standing discomfort with Detroit's school system—in particular, the city's high level of adult illiteracy. This animus toward the school system encouraged him to open the school at the church, and he saw both the school and the voucher system as means to help improve the city's educational system.

Rev. Green approached the issue by providing information not only to his members but also to the community at large.

> I really do not become bogged down in political politics as we know them. I take to my pulpit, I use my influence in the pulpit, via radio, through print material, through meetings here at the church, information and bulletins and so forth. I try to give as much information as I can to people to help them to make their own determination relative to political issues, including the voucher issue.

He did not know how all of the congregants felt about the issue but believed that most supported vouchers. He did not recall any opposition to his stance. Although some members saw other alternatives, these differences did not create any conflict. Several of the members I interviewed opposed the voucher system. One member cited a lack of faith in the policy, while another argued that private schools should not be a taxpayer burden:

> I was totally against that. Because I sent my child to private school. You know what I did? I paid for it out of my pocket, and I'm totally against [vouchers]. Schools getting paid from the state, taxpayers' money for your child to go to a private school. You want to go to a private school, you pay for that. Don't expect the taxpayer dollars to go that route. I am totally against that.

While the pastor and some of the members disagreed on this issue, conflict did not emerge because members were not certain of Rev. Green's position on the issue, a surprising circumstance given that he was one of the program's leading advocates. However, many of the members pointed to the fact that Rev. Green does not always state his position on issues. According to one congregant,

> Pastor Green always gives us the—"Here it is. Make up your own mind." He doesn't tell us, "You gotta vote for this person." He puts it out there, and you still make up your mind of who you're going to vote for. And I think that's the way it should be.

The fact that the members do not know whom he supports is very common. During the mayoral election, the pastor supported a candidate who many members believed was not fully qualified for the position. By avoiding any overt statements about whom he supported, Rev. Green prevented conflict. During the congressional and the gubernatorial elections, the pastor and the congregation appeared to support the Democratic candidates.

Rev. Green is free to take part in these activities because they are not members' greatest concerns. Because the church has flourished as an organization under his leadership, members focus on its spiritual and fellowship aspects. In addition, the support of Rev. Green's political activism as well as the activism on the part of the church members coincides with their acceptance of the church's expansive culture.

ORANGE CHAPEL

Orange Chapel is the most engaged of the churches in the sample. This high level of engagement stems from several factors. The pastor and members have a high level of political interest, and the church possesses a high level of resources and a culture of activism. Finally, the church is well embedded in its environment, which has made it attentive to any problems that may occur.

Orange Chapel is a Baptist church located on the east side of Austin. The church currently has about fifteen hundred members and has been in the Austin community for more than eighty years. Orange Chapel's congregation has a large number of individuals in high-status positions—several members hold high-ranking positions in local corporations or in state or local government. Despite the large number of members with white-collar occupations, the congregants think of their church as open to anyone. One member believed that the church attracted members because it allowed them to be themselves:

> We have people over there that are millionaires, and you got other people over here that are on social services aid. Everybody in the church accepts it, and there is no problem. You got a man singing in the choir, he is a district judge, and he has probably sent more people to the gas chamber, because of the case assignments. We have another man that's a U.S. marshal for southwest Texas, and we've got another man that's sat right behind [President George W. Bush] for two or three years.

The church also has substantial resources that allow it to play an active role in the community. Members have described the church as being "progressive." The church has historically been involved in the community. One former pastor was the president of the local chapter of the National Association for the Advancement of Colored People (NAACP), and another was highly involved in local and state politics. The current pastor, Rev. Orange, has led the church for fourteen years, during which time the church's level of engagement has increased.

The church has created a social assistance center similar to those operated by Black and Green Memorial. Rev. Orange has served on several local boards. When he was hired as pastor of Orange Chapel, Rev. Orange was expected to continue the church's tradition of social engagement. Rev. Orange's perspective in taking over the pulpit at Orange Chapel is different from the other pastors in the sample; he was a member of Orange Chapel before he entered the ministry, and he consequently sees himself as someone who embodies the culture of Orange Chapel:

> [The former pastor] was I think also seen as—and this may have been one of the reasons why my wife and I were drawn to this church—as that he had a social activism mentality. And so this church has had an image and a reputation of having members who have been socially engaged. Where I am now is really like the biblical model in the sense that I came here, I was a member, and I then moved from the pew to the pulpit. So I love this church. Although I grew up in a pastor's family and have been involved in the church, *I am of this church.* So in a lot of ways I represent this church's culture, and so I quite frankly believe that I may have gotten the church to a place where they believe that [activism] is expected.

Despite Rev. Orange's connection to the church, his appointment as pastor generated conflict. Several members were upset by the nature of his hiring. They wanted a higher-profile pastor and felt that due process was not followed. The dispute ultimately resulted in a legal battle that received national attention and caused the loss of a significant number of members. Rev. Orange believes that three years passed before that image of the church faded away, and the church has subsequently grown in membership and has expanded its activities.

With this conflict resolved, Rev. Orange implemented plans to bring the church together through its social engagement. While Orange Chapel has a history of activism, Rev. Orange noted that this activism involved individuals associated with the church rather than the church itself. He saw engaging the congregation in the community as his main task:

> Over the years, Orange Chapel attracted people who were engaged in the community, and that developed a view that Orange Chapel was an involved congregation. When I looked at it, though, Orange Chapel's reach as a body was not that involved other than through the individual members who were out in the community.
>
> One of the things that I have felt is a calling on my life was to engage Orange Chapel as an entity more into the community. So I developed ministries that reach out, held activities here that would make the church building available for the community.

Orange Chapel assisted in the creation of a neighborhood association to help revitalize the local community. Through this association, the church worked with the city and outside organizations to build a park, pave sidewalks, and tear down uninhabited houses. This relationship has also heightened the church's attention to the renewal of East Austin and the fears of gentrification. While the church has not addressed this issue outright, several of the members reported having conversations about it. The pastor and the members noted that this is a complicated issue with no clear solution, which may be why they have been slow to react.

Along with engaging the congregation in the community, Rev. Orange has initiated a focus on gender issues—specifically, domestic violence and female clergy. Rev. Orange's attention to domestic violence stems from his lasting interest in women's rights and his previous career as a lawyer.

I am actively involved in things like domestic violence, and I have taken public positions on that. And, I have been involved with . . . the domestic and sexual assault center here, and I might preach a sermon that deals with domestic violence because I think it's one of those issues that we ought to be doing. It's one of those issues we don't talk about in the church as a whole and in the Black church in particular. So you might find me talking about domestic violence in a sermon, but I will typically talk about that within the context of a relationship, and that's kind of how I elevate issues of—I seldom will take a topic and preach it that way. I usually will blend it with other things.

Rev. Orange noted that his method of discussing the issue and his ability to relate to his members represent the main reasons why he has not faced any conflict over confronting the issue of domestic violence. However, the issue of female clergy had the potential to generate major conflict.

Ordaining women is a contentious issue in Baptist churches, as many Baptists believe that only men should be clergy. Orange Chapel was one of the first Black Baptist churches in the area to allow female clergy. When Rev. Orange wanted to add a woman to the ministerial staff, he placed the decision in the hands of the congregation.

I preached a sermon on what the Bible—something on like what the Bible says of women preachers or something like that or women in ministry or something like that. And so I then shared that during a sermon one Sunday morning and laid out my processing of how I got the position biblically, because I knew that they wanted to know what I thought the Bible said about it. At the end of that, I asked them two or three questions—I forget all those details—one of which was whether or not you can support a woman in ministry. And in regard to this position that I am considering, "If the person who is offered this position is a woman, would you be willing to follow her leadership?" At the end of the service, I offered it to the congregation, and we had maybe four or five hundred people here that Sunday. . . . At that point, if the church had said no, I was going to respect that position. So they understood my position. And I would say maybe ten to twelve people could not support that, and so we went with [hiring the female minister].

This type of behavior on the part of Rev. Orange is not uncommon; several members noted that he was highly democratic in his decisions. One member commented on the professionalism with which church meetings were conducted. This respondent noted that just like his workplace, the details of the church projects were well explained and justified. Rev. Orange and other members noted that because the church has such a well-educated congregation, he has to conduct church business in this fashion. He could not dictate the programs of the church to the congregation; he needed their approval and support to implement the programs. As one member stated, Rev. Orange's leadership of the church was "management by persuasion."

The church has been highly involved in the various issues that Austin has recently faced. Much like Black Memorial, Orange Chapel used its social assistance center to help evacuees from Hurricane Katrina, several of whom have settled in Austin and joined the church. In reaction to controversies surrounding the excessive use of force by police, Rev. Orange spoke with several local officials, was profiled on the local news, and helped lead a march to protest the city's handling of the issue. For the most part, he did not bring these activities into the worship service. He would mention the work of organizations and attempt to recruit members to take part in these activities, but did not criticize the police department during the worship service. However, one Sunday he became so frustrated with the situation that he expressed his dissatisfaction to the congregation. The members were not bothered by his action, as several congregants noted their concerns about the issue.

One of the most interesting issues that the church addressed was the gay marriage amendment. Rev. Orange and his members are open to having homosexuals in their church. As one member stated,

> We are not concerned with somebody's sexual preferences. We don't make that our business. We don't judge you based on your sexual preferences, because we don't need to know that and we don't want to know that.

However, the pastor took the stand that marriage was between a man and a woman. He did not tell the congregation how to vote but explained his position and provided the congregation with a copy of a sermon by another minister that he felt explained his position on the issue. These types of actions on the part of Rev. Orange are not uncommon. Just as he does not force the church's agenda on its members, he does not force his political views on the congregation. During the 2006 mayoral and city council elections, Rev. Orange served as a senior official in one congregant's campaign. Most people in the church were aware of his role but noted that he did not campaign for the member in the church. Like Rev.

Green, Rev. Orange avoids conflicts with his members because he informs them of his position on issues but does not pressure the congregation to follow suit. The members repeatedly expressed that the church consistently kept its members politically engaged through mobilization or by making sure that they were informed of issues. This type of behavior has become an expectation, as evidenced by one deacon's response to how the church would react if Rev. Orange became less engaged:

> We would have difficulty with that. We would tell him, more likely, as he becomes older and he gets pushed back on his schedule, that he needs to bring some other ministers to do that—that is, going to pick up the load.

Table 1 summarizes the findings from these case studies. The remainder of this chapter will analyze these findings to provide a better interpretation of how political churches are created and maintained.

DISCUSSION

The preceding section illustrated how variation within each church shapes activism. Differences in the pastor, members, organization, and

TABLE 1. Summary of Political Activism and Characteristics of Churches

	Brown	Blue	White	Black	Red	Green	Orange
Activism	Low	Medium	Medium	Medium	Medium	Medium	High
Pastor							
Tenure	Medium	Medium	Low	High	Low	High	High
Social Focus	Low	Low	Medium	High	High	High	High
Political Focus	Low	Medium	Medium	Medium	High	High	High
Members							
White-Collar	Low	Medium	High	Medium	Low	Medium	High
Under 40	Low	Low	Low	Medium	Low	Medium	Medium
Comfort	Medium	Medium	Medium	Medium	Low	Low	Low
Organization							
Denominational Constraints	High	Medium	Low	Low	Medium	Low	Low
Resources	Low	Medium	Medium	Medium	Low	High	High
Political Culture	Low	Low	Medium	Medium	Medium	Medium	High
Environment							
Black Empowerment	Low	High	High	Low	High	High	Low
Community	Medium	Low	Low	Medium	Medium	Medium	High

environment direct the salience of political identity for each church over time. In this section, I tie the similarities among the churches together to illustrate how the four factors affect church engagement as well as each other.

Pastor

Pastors are not the sole reason for the creation and maintenance of political churches, but they nevertheless play an integral role. Much of the variation in church activism stems from pastors' interests. Pastors readily viewed themselves as primary figures in the direction of their churches and see churches as reflecting their pastors' interests. These responses lend support to the idea of charismatic pastors who can use their rhetorical skills and personality to sway the congregation to their will.

While several churches directly reflected their pastors, this phenomenon was strongest in churches whose pastors had long tenures. The pastors of Green Memorial, Orange Chapel, and Black Memorial had held their positions for at least a decade, allowing pastors and members to develop a relationship and to work together to implement successful plans for the church.

While each of these pastors was charismatic, their qualities as administrators were just as important. Their success in shaping their congregations reflected both personality and administrative skill. The length of pastors' tenures reflects their effectiveness in persuasion and leadership.

With lengthy tenures came higher levels of influence in churches. Pastors' social and political outlooks were more readily manifested in the church activities when clergy had served their congregations for several years. For example, Rev. Black, Rev. Green, and Rev. Orange expressed high levels of focus on social issues, and this perspective was apparent in the activities of their churches, which operated social assistance centers and were highly involved in humanitarian efforts. Rev. Green and Rev. Orange also strongly emphasized political engagement, although Rev. Black did not. As a result, Green Memorial and Orange Chapel actively engaged in the political process, while Black Memorial remained on the sidelines. Revs. Brown and Blue had significant tenures at their churches and expressed an interest in political engagement but saw more pressing issues to be resolved at their churches. Revs. Red and White were conscious of political events but remained cautious about involving their churches because of their short tenures.

Members

Along with the variations in leadership, variations in church membership are also a vital aspect in explaining church activism. The pastors were quick to note congregants' decision-making power. Members stated that as individuals they lacked a great deal of influence but that as a group they strongly influenced church activities. One member of Orange Chapel noted that the voluntary nature of churches constrains pastors, who consequently must work hard to secure members' acceptance of plans or adjust plans to meet the congregation's desires.

Because members can direct church action, the demographic composition of the congregation was important to understanding church action. Churches with lower numbers of members under the age of forty were less likely to report being politically engaged. As the respondents from Blue Temple pointed out, older members are less active than their younger counterparts, as was also the case at White Chapel, Red Memorial, and Brown Chapel. According to Rev. White,

> I've not been turned down for anything we tried to do here, so that means they're very cooperative, I guess it is. But I have weighed very carefully. And you're dealing with some things that are new to people with an older congregation, I guess, and some things have come along in their lives too late.

Beyond age, congregations with larger numbers of white-collar members were more politically conscious. Individuals with white-collar occupations have higher levels of education, a characteristic that is linked to greater levels of political interest (Verba, Schlozman, and Brady 1995). Those in white-collar professions are also more likely to possess the skills churches need to implement their programs. Rev. Red and Rev. Green noted that the lack of proper training on the part of their members played a strong role in shaping their activities. In contrast, a church such as Orange Chapel, with a large white-collar population, had members with the skills and training necessary to accomplish the goals of the organization.

Finally, members who perceive issues as threats to their interests factored into churches' activities. For example, several members in Black Memorial saw no need for the church to become involved in the police brutality issue because they saw such incidents as a mistake not on the part of the police but on the part of the people being apprehended. In this view, individuals who behave properly do not encounter the issue of police brutality. In contrast, the members of Orange Chapel saw instances of police brutality as infringing on their rights and wanted to make sure that something was done. Hence, this congregation was much more active on this issue. Likewise, the members of White Chapel were agitated by the school voucher proposition and wanted to see the church respond because many of them were educators who saw the voucher system as a threat to their interests. Detroit churches with fewer members working in the public school system had less interest in this issue and thus did not face pressure to respond.

Negotiation between the Pastor and Members

In general, the results reveal little conflict between pastors and church members over the political engagement of the church, even when they fail to agree completely with each other about the church's proper role in political activity. As chapter 1 points out, these conflicts can threaten a church's survival. In contrast to the civil rights movement era, the present negotiation process does not appear to stress the organization. Similar to Wood's (1981) examination of White Protestant churches in the late 1960s and early 1970s, I found that most of the conflicts that occurred in these churches involved the management of the church and worship service and did not concern the church's political activity. As with the churches in Wood's study, these churches avoided conflict regarding church-based political activism as long as clergy and congregants agreed on ministerial duties and pastors sent their messages in a nonthreatening way.

Consensus between the pastor and congregants about the minister's responsibilities—for example, management, preaching, and assisting the sick and shut-ins—provides a strong basis for conflict management. If pastors engage their churches in social and political activities and handle their core duties, members are less critical, as Green Memorial demonstrates. Rev. Green noted occasional disagreements with his members regarding his support of various candidates and issues; however, these differences did not become conflicts because members were pleased with Rev. Green's performance of his core responsibilities. Likewise, Rev. Blue noted that while his past members were not supportive of his political engagement, as long as he fulfilled his core duties, no conflicts arose.

While none of these churches reported a conflict over political engagement, one Detroit respondent noted a disagreement in his former church. The issue became a conflict because the members already felt that the pastor was failing at some of his core responsibilities. The pastor and the congregation had been at odds for some time over church operations, leading to membership declines and overall dissatisfaction with the pastor. When the school voucher issue emerged, the members for the most part opposed it, but the pastor was a supporter. This difference further fueled their quarrel.

> RESPONDENT: Support of school vouchers confirmed in people's mind that there was a difference in care, upbringing, between the pastor and the people.
> INTERVIEWER: So his support of school vouchers really showed that he was out of touch with everybody? Would you say he was not in touch with the members?
> RESPONDENT: That's probably the best way to say it.

Another way to avoid conflict within the church is for pastors to present their messages in a nonthreatening fashion. Both Rev. Green and Rev. White, who were active on opposite sides of the voucher referendum, consciously worked to avoid propagandizing their personal views but rather provided information and let church members decide for themselves. Similarly, at Red Memorial, Rev. Red did not tell her members for whom to vote but urged them to vote "right." She recounted that her former church had included a large contingent of Republicans. Herself a Democrat, she had to be careful about how she phrased her arguments. She also pointed to the separation of church and state to explain the ambiguity of her calls for action:

> It is illegal for a pastor to stand in a pulpit and personally feed that position, endorse a particular person, or even endorse a particular party. Most pastors don't give a rip, and they feel like nobody's going to bother them. I worked for the federal government for a long time, so as a federal employee they were much stricter. So I learned to use language.

In summary, even when members are not particularly interested in public affairs, the pastor can engage the church in a low level of activism as long as the church's primary goals are met. The fact that these clergy have to be careful about how they present their opinions on issues brings into question the pervasiveness of charismatic ministers. Ministers must make sure that their congregations are satisfied with their work and must be careful about how they send messages to members. Pastors must prove that their actions will mesh with their congregations' standards and attitudes. Even if pastors are charismatic, if they stray too far from church norms, they will face serious conflicts.

Organization

The organizations' many facets influence the level of political activism in the churches examined. Specifically, each church's resources, process, and culture played a prominent role in shaping its activities.

Resources are vital to a church's survival. Without ample resources, a church cannot fulfill its primary function, let alone engage in secondary activities such as political and social activism. Both Brown Chapel and Red Memorial have pastors who are socially and politically conscious, but their churches are low on financial and physical resources. The need to ensure their churches' continued existence in the face of capital short-ages diminishes Rev. Brown's and Rev. Red's focus on social and political engagement. Instead, they concentrate on building and sustaining the church infrastructure. Conversely, Black Memorial, Green Memorial, and Orange Chapel do not face these resource constraints and identify this state of affairs as a major reason for their social and political engagement.

Beyond the resource structure, each church has its own distinctive culture. Regardless of denomination, each church has a specific mode of operation, as is evident in the mission or vision statements of several churches. Mission statements reflect how each church sees itself and provides a path for behavior. Orange Chapel envisions itself as an activist church and embraces all forms of community involvement. Its mission statement makes an outward appeal to working in the community. Black Memorial perceives itself as a "Bible-teaching" church; its statement focuses on evangelism. This difference in organizational missions helps explain why Orange Chapel engages in a much higher level of political activism than does Black Memorial.

Along with the mission statements, each church's distinctive history plays a strong role in defining its culture. Orange Chapel had a history of taking part in social activism before Rev. Orange's tenure, and congregants expected the church to continue doing so. In the past, Red Memorial was extremely active in the Detroit community. Members supported Rev. Red's work to restore the church's position in the community because they recollected the prestige garnered by social and political activity. Historically, Blue Temple and Black Memorial were not politically engaged. As a result, members did not see activities such as protest marches as appropriate for their churches, although several members of Black Memorial routinely take part in protests as individuals.

The final organizational aspect is process—the rules and regulations that guide the church's actions and decision making. Process had the strongest effect in the Methodist churches. Rev. Brown, Rev. Blue, and Rev. Red noted that higher denominational authorities constrained activism. Rev. Brown noted that his denomination has outlined its stance on a multitude of issues and that he cannot publicly deviate from this stance. The Baptist churches, conversely, are highly autonomous, so they can take part in activities as they please. The only exception was the reaction of some Baptist churches to Orange Chapel's acceptance of female clergy. While Rev. Orange did not mention any conflicts, several of the members noted that the church's relationship with other Baptist churches in the area had begun to deteriorate.

> We had a lot of [other Baptist churches] not openly dissociate themselves from us, but for whatever reason, they didn't maintain an open relationship with us that they had prior to us bringing in [the female minister].

While the Baptist association could not sanction the church for its actions, other churches appeared to exert considerable pressure to bar women from the pulpit.

Environment

Finally, examining the environment in which a church exists is critical to understanding whether the church will become politically active. For the churches examined in this case study, location factored heavily into the decision to engage in politics. The Detroit and Austin environments differ considerably. One of the most glaring differences is the size of the Black population in these cities. According to the 2000 census, Blacks constituted more than four-fifths of Detroit's population, while Blacks account for less than one-tenth of the Austin population. In addition, Austin's Black population is steadily decreasing. In 1980, Austin had eighteen neighborhoods with at least 80 percent black residents; in 2000, that number had decreased to one (Alford 2005). The differences in the size of the Black populations have also affected Black political empowerment. Detroit has historically served as an example of Black empowerment (Bobo and Gilliam 1990). Detroit has had a Black mayor for more than three decades, and its current city council has only one non-Black member. Further, Detroit has a history of combining faith with politics. Dillard's (2007) work on clergy in Detroit highlights the various activities and progressive campaigns of religious leaders. In contrast, Black social and political life in Austin is less vibrant. According to one Black Austin resident, "Ron Kirk is from Austin, but he became mayor of Dallas. It would have been harder for him to become mayor of Austin" (Alford 2005, A1). In spite of these differences, Austin has elected blacks to city government since 1971, but to a lesser degree than Detroit. The Austin City Council has consistently included Black members for several decades; however, members of the Black community continue to question whether they have adequate representation in the city (Alford 2005). A recent Black candidate for the mayor's office garnered only 15.2 percent of the vote. Moreover, many African Americans cannot afford Austin's rising housing costs and subsequent rising property taxes, so they move to surrounding areas (Coppola 2004).

The cities also differ in terms of their economies. Detroit is an aging industrial city with high levels of poverty; in contrast, Austin is a growing urban locale with an economy driven primarily by the technology industry. While it is not clear how much the Black community benefits from this industry, the addition of new business has provided a boost to the local economy. This lack of extreme impoverishment may strongly influence the urgency with which the respondents in Austin felt their churches should react. One Austin pastor, whose church was not included in the case study, commented on these differences:

> The realities of urban poverty are more pronounced, and so it's more in your face, too. You can't hide from it, and so it becomes a matter of ignoring the obvious. Whereas here, unless you are in one or two parts of town, you don't even see [poverty], so it's not as real to us.

In addition, a significant amount of antagonism exists between the predominantly Black city of Detroit and predominantly White state of Michigan. This clash has fueled racial tension, especially between residents of inner-city Detroit and of the surrounding suburbs. Austin's Black population has a much lower level of conflict. Austin is one of the most ideologically liberal cities in Texas. After confronting the prospect that development projects in East Austin might lead to gentrification, the city attempted to put in place programs to protect homeowners and businesses. Finally, church members in Austin noted some racial tension but believed that it was less severe than in other cities. One member of Brown Chapel cited a lack of strong racial tensions as a reason for the lack of church activity in Austin:

> Maybe if we were in places like when Dr. [Martin Luther] King [Jr.] went to Mississippi and Alabama, places like that where it was really bad. Maybe— there are still burning churches in their news today. Maybe that is the reason why we never had to be like that in order to make change. Maybe we had some folk who where educated and who knew some people that helped us do things without having to have our head split open or have us locked up in jail.

As these cases demonstrate, environment plays a strong role in explaining activism. The presence of Black empowerment as well as a racial threat triggered church activism in Detroit. All but one of the Detroit churches in this sample had some history of engaging the political system. In Austin, only one of the churches had such a history. Detroit's political context provided both opportunities and motivation to engage the system, while Austin's political system did not provide the same access or threat.

In addition to intercity differences, intracity differences in church-based political activism could be attributed to variance in geographic location. Members of Brown Chapel and Blue Temple reported that the church's lack of political engagement reflected the fact that many members did not live in the community surrounding the church. Because members were no longer embedded in the community, they were unaware or unconcerned with its issues and did not call for their churches to respond. This geographical distance from the church took members' focus away from the community surrounding the church. Orange Chapel overcame this problem and remained an integral part of the local community by participating in the neighborhood association. McRoberts (2003) demonstrates that churches that embed themselves in their local community are more active than those that do not. Churches that draw many of their members from the local community or attempt to actively engage the local community on a regular basis are more in tune with the happenings of the community and therefore are more likely to respond.

CONCLUSION

The various components of political churches lead them to political engagement. The pastor, members, organization, and environment affect church-based political activism. While each of these factors may have an independent effect on church-based political activism, they are also interactive and perhaps reinforcing. As figure 1 shows, changes in any of these factors can shape the other variables. As members are no longer centrally located around their churches, they are less likely to be informed about community issues and less likely to view political action as an option for the church. In addition, as churches become resource poor, they are less likely to want to take part in activities for which they bear the brunt of the costs. Churches that have a history of political involvement can work to socialize the members and the pastor. It is therefore important to understand the various mechanisms that drive church-based political activism. The following chapters will provide a more in-depth analysis of these components to better understand how each of these factors shapes church engagement in politics.

CHAPTER 3

When Will the Call Be Made?
A History of Black Church
Political Activism

To-day the two groups of Negroes, the one in the North, the other in
the South, represent these divergent ethical tendencies, the first tending
toward radicalism, the other toward hypocritical compromise.
(Du Bois [1903] 1990, 147)

The preceding chapters documented the importance of the Black church in Black politics and provided an explanation and examination of Black church-based political activism. Within this discussion and analysis, the issue of environment repeatedly played a role in shaping church activism. Shifts within the sociopolitical environment greatly influenced the activities of churches. As W. E. B. Du Bois argues, Blacks in the North faced different sociopolitical conditions than did Blacks in the South. According to Du Bois, southern Blacks chose silence as a survival strategy: if they spoke out, they faced harsh repercussions. Northern blacks, by contrast, gained education but faced unemployment and poverty, leading them to agitate intensely. Furthermore, Du Bois asserts, the churches established by these two groups reflect these conditions.

This chapter presents an in-depth analysis of how changes within the sociopolitical environment direct the political engagement of Black churches. By providing a historical account of Black churches' political activism, I show how variations in context have shaped clergy and member attitudes regarding political activity. Using arguments developed in the social movement literature, this chapter examines how varying pockets of opportunity shaped the teachings and activism of the Black church. This understanding of the variations in church-based activism explains why some churches choose to be politically active while others do not.

POLITICAL OPPORTUNITY AND CHURCH ACTION

Group political participation depends on the group's ability to gain access to the political process. Several scholars note the importance of political opportunities in explaining the rise and fall of collective action (Eisinger 1973; McAdam 1982; Charles Payne 1995). Even when some groups have the capacity and motivation to act, if they are restricted from political engagement or the costs of action are high, the probability of action drastically decreases. Blacks have historically faced strong barriers to entry into the political system. These constraints have included legal restrictions (such as literacy tests and poll taxes) and societal repression (such as the threat of racial violence). As Walton (1985) notes, "Black political behavior is a function of individual and systemic forces" (7). Walton criticizes past scholars' failure to account for sociopolitical conditions when discussing southern Blacks' political behavior, an omission that has led many scholars to conclude that these Blacks failed to vote because they were maladjusted (see, e.g., Bullock and Rodgers 1972; Milton Morris 1975). Ignoring roadblocks to political institutions leads to false conclusions about participation. Until recently, Blacks and their institutions, including the church, faced many significant impediments when attempting to engage the political system. As the political system has provided increased opportunities for Blacks to engage the political system, church activity should also be expected to increase.

In addition to the ability to act, political pressures should also influence the form of activism taken. Piven and Cloward (1977) argue that defiance is shaped by institutional access. This argument is vital in attempting to explain the Black church's presence in American politics. When and how organizations have the opportunity to engage the political system plays a strong role in the types of activities in which the organization engages (Jack Walker 1991). When Blacks were afforded a high level of access to institutions, the Black church used its resources to lobby officials; however, when blacks lacked access, the church took part in contentious politics. Taking into account political opportunities and access to institutions provides a better interpretation of how changes in the sociopolitical environment affect the political behavior of individuals and their institutions. The social movement literature provides a framework for discussing the variations in Black church behavior over time and location.

COLONIAL PERIOD AND REVOLUTIONARY WAR

During the nation's early years, the Black church did not have a strong presence in American politics, but much of the framework for the Black church and Black religion was laid during this period. While several problems arose in efforts to bring Africans into the Christian fold, legal and theological adjustments permitted Blacks to have a strong presence throughout the American religious landscape. The period before the Revolutionary War provided the basis from which Black religion took shape and the Black church gained its mission.

As Africans were brought to the Americas, they were also being brought to Christianity. Some of those captured were already Christians. Others converted during the voyage across the Atlantic, and others converted after entering the colonies (Jordan 1968; Lincoln 1984). As the enslavement of Africans began to move toward permanence, the treatment and rights of converted Africans became contentious. Many slave owners refused to allow slaves to convert, fearing the challenges posed by Christian teachings that stressed the equality of men under God. For example, the widely held belief that Englishmen could not enslave fellow Christians meant that thousands of slaves would have to be freed. In recognition of this problem, several colonies, beginning with Maryland in 1664, passed laws stating that conversion did not mean the manumission of African slaves (Jordan 1968; Lincoln 1984).

In addition to earthly concerns, many Whites did not want to share heaven with their slaves. The idea of equality under God presented major problems for the ideals of White supremacy. As one woman stated, "Is it possible that any of my slaves could go to Heaven and must I see them there?" (Jordan 1968, 183). In addition, equality in the eyes of God might lead Africans to begin to see themselves as White equals in the here and now, and Whites feared that Christianized Blacks would begin to see themselves in a different light and become "saucy" and begin to rebel (Jordan 1968; Lincoln 1984). Because of this fear, the southern colonies banned Black churches.

In addition to such philosophical reasons for opposing slave conversions, slaveholders objected because it was not profitable. The process by which converts became familiar with various scriptures and rituals required a great deal of commitment on the part of the slave, slave owner, and clergy, and many slave owners found this time-consuming effort impractical and even more importantly not cost-effective. As one planter stated,

> Talk to a planter about the soul of a Negro and he'll be apt to tell you that the body of one Negro may be worth 20 pounds, but the souls of a hundred of them would not yield him one farthing. (Lincoln 1984, 42)

The time-consuming nature of conversion would be overcome with the emergence of the Great Awakening, a set of evangelical camps and revivals that spread throughout the colonies between the 1730s and 1740s. The Great Awakening focused on instant conversion, thereby permitting Blacks to convert en masse. The revivals of the Great Awakening treated Blacks as equals, with evangelists stressing egalitarianism and in some cases speaking out against slavery and some slaveholders responding by freeing their slaves. Another by-product of the Great Awakening was the emergence of Black preachers, who soon began to preach to both White and Black congregations (Lincoln 1984; Pinn and Pinn 2002).

The legacy of the Great Awakening also influenced the ideals of the American Revolution, as the revolutionists advanced the ideas of natural rights and egalitarianism. The Revolutionary War brought about advancements for Blacks, whose assistance the emerging nation needed to win the war. Of the American force of three hundred thousand soldiers, five to eight thousand were Black (Klinkler and Smith 1999), and many of them enlisted in the revolutionary cause after being promised their freedom in exchange for doing so (Lincoln 1984). American leaders also feared that Blacks would side with the British, who promised indentured servants and Black slaves freedom in return for fighting on the British side. In addition, many British-controlled areas did not enforce slavery (Klinkler and Smith 1999). For example, led by George Liele and David George, the members of South Carolina's Silver Bluff Baptist Church crossed the Savannah River to live in British-controlled Savannah, Georgia.

With a call for egalitarianism and recognition of Black support during the war, the new nation attempted to accommodate Black interests. Northern states began calling for an end to slavery and the extension of suffrage to Blacks. In 1777, Vermont became the first state to ban slavery; Massachusetts and New Hampshire followed in 1783. Nineteen years later, New Jersey became the last northern state to ban slavery, although it had been the first to extend suffrage rights to Blacks when it did so in

1776. Other states soon followed. These views of egalitarianism crept through the Upper South as Maryland, Delaware, and Virginia debated whether to end slavery (Klinkler and Smith 1999).

During this period of openness to the idea of Black citizenship, many Blacks took the opportunity to develop their own organizations. Tens of thousands of Blacks used the Revolutionary War as an opportunity to gain their freedom either through service in the revolutionary army or by escaping from plantations (Klinkler and Smith 1999). This increase in the number of freedmen and -women, along with the abolition of slavery in northern states, created a large free Black community in the North. Black institutions—most notably, the Black church—followed. During the early years of the nation, Blacks formed two separate Methodist denominations, the African Methodist Episcopal (AME) Church and the African Methodist Episcopal Zion Church (Pinn and Pinn 2002).

ANTEBELLUM PERIOD

The colonial and revolutionary periods provided the framework and the ability to develop the Black church. The antebellum period demonstrated the two realities that Blacks and the Black church existed. In the North, Blacks received fluctuating access to political institutions, as some northern states extended suffrage and legal protection to Blacks, thereby allowing Black religious associations, clergy, and members to lobby for an end to slavery and for equal rights. The South's slave system, however, prevented Blacks, free or slave, from speaking out or gaining any access to government officials, a situation that led the southern Black church to endorse accommodation or revolt.

Shortly after the Revolutionary War, Blacks in the North began to face challenges to the freedoms and rights they had gained. Northern states began to retrench because of White fears about how to handle the growing free Black population. Poor Whites and immigrants in particular held a great deal of animosity toward Blacks. Because of this perceived problem, many states began to move away from the ideals of racial egalitarianism. In 1807, New Jersey passed a law limiting the vote to Whites, and other northern states followed. In the developing western territories, Blacks were not allowed to vote, and in some cases, free Blacks were banned from entering. Colonization societies were also set up to try to move free Blacks to Africa. By 1820, most northern states had banned

Black children from attending school with Whites or from attending school at all. Nevertheless, Blacks were also expected to pay full taxes (Klinkler and Smith 1999).

In the North, Black churches used their resources to combat these problems, pushing not only for an end to slavery but also for education as well as economic development. The earliest Black Baptist conventions sought to provide assistance to individual churches as well as to provide members with a political voice. The Providence Baptist Association, founded in Ohio in 1834, and the Union Anti-Slavery Baptist Association, formed in 1843, used their resources to support the work of abolitionists (Pinn and Pinn 2002). Through the AME Church, Richard Allen fought a plan to send free Blacks to colonize Africa, and he formed the Free African Society, which worked with the abolitionist movement. Allen directed his calls for an end to slavery toward the government, not toward the slaves. Despite his deep animus toward slavery, he did not believe in a violent revolt, and he told slaves to love and obey rather than hate their masters (Hamilton 1972). Like Martin Luther King Jr., Allen abhorred the treatment of Blacks in America but did not support the use of violence to achieve better treatment (Hamilton 1972).

While Allen and his followers hoped that the government would take an active role in dismantling slavery, other Black clergy became disillusioned with the government and called for slaves to rise up, an effort in which Blacks apparently would have little support. The abolitionist movement began to wane, and government actions did not portend an end to slavery any time soon. The Constitution's Three-fifths Clause, as well as the gag rule on discussing slavery, legitimized human bondage and further suggested that Black rights would come second to the nation's desires (Walton and Smith 2003). Congress also passed numerous fugitive slave laws that became increasingly threatening to those who had escaped slavery as well as those who had never been enslaved (Klinkler and Smith 1999). Even religious denominations retrenched: the Methodist Episcopal Church and several White Baptist associations condemned slavery and threatened to remove slaveholding members, only to rescind these proclamations a few years later (Klinkler and Smith 1999; Lincoln 1984).

Many Black clergy responded by taking a more forceful stance against slavery and for improved treatment of Blacks. Many ministers moved away from working with Whites, and others advocated violence. In 1841, Henry Highland Garnet, a Presbyterian minister who worked primarily in northern New York, formed the Liberty Party, whose main goal was to end slavery and secure voting rights for Blacks in New York. Speaking to the National Black Convention in 1843, Garnett argued that God would not take kindly to those who accepted slavery. Although he did not endorse violence, he argued that Blacks needed to wage a more intense struggle to end the tyranny of slavery (Hamilton 1972). Garnett's speech received varying reactions, as many people still hoped that moral appeals would be the best way to end slavery.

Garnett was not alone in taking a more militant stance toward abolition. Jermain W. Loguen, a former slave who had escaped to freedom, became an AME Zion minister in Syracuse, New York. Shortly after the passage of the 1850 Fugitive Slave Law, he rallied the city of Syracuse to oppose the law and make it an "open city" for those seeking freedom. The 1850 measure created such a panic that numerous Blacks fled the North for Canada. According to one report, Boston lost 40 percent of its Black population within twenty-four hours of the bill's passage, while in Rochester, New York, 102 of one Black church's 114 members crossed the border (Klinkler and Smith 1999, 44). In an October 4, 1850, speech, "I Will Not Live a Slave," Loguen argued that he had escaped slavery through the grace of God and would not willingly go back:

> I don't respect this law—I don't fear it—I won't obey it! It outlaws me, and I outlaw it, and the men who attempt to enforce it on me. I place the government officials on the ground that they place me. I will not live a slave, and if force is employed to re-enslave me, I shall make preparations to meet the crisis as becomes a man. (Loguen 1999, 230)

Northern society's relative openness enabled Blacks to speak out against slavery and to develop a discourse about the best way to end it. In the South, however, the Black discourse regarding slavery was hidden. Blacks in the South, whether free or slave, lacked any true representation. Because Whites viewed free Blacks as a threat, states circumscribed their movements, and many states refused to allow them to enter. Slaves endured even worse conditions, as slave codes banned them from owning property or having any legal standing. Southern states worked hard to control Black churches. Some states banned Black churches entirely, while other states attempted to control the influence of these churches. In Delaware, all AME Church pastors had to come from slaveholding states; most other states banned the denomination outright (Pinn and

Pinn 2002). Throughout the South, states required Blacks to attend White churches or to attend churches with White supervision (Lincoln 1984). The Black church in the South consequently was highly constrained and could not provide a voice in the way that churches in the North did. The Black church, like its members, could push only for either acceptance or revolt.

Many scholars describe slave churches as places of otherworldliness that focused on rewards in heaven and worked to pacify the slaves, thereby winning the approbation of slave owners. For example, Whites praised George Liele, a Baptist minister who eventually worked to form Silver Bluff Baptist Church, because of his ability to use Christianity to make slaves more obedient (Hamilton 1972; Pinn and Pinn 2002). Nevertheless, the Black religious experience in the antebellum South encompassed considerably more than pacification and acceptance.

Many slaves openly rejected the religion of the slave master for what they believed was the true Christianity. Peter Randolph, a former slave who became a Baptist minister, discussed slaves' rejection of sermons that focused on obeying the master and included statements such as "It is the devil that wants you to be free." Randolph and other slaves met in swamps late at night to hear the sermons that they preferred (Randolph 1999, 66). Other slaves outright rejected the moral lessons taught by slave owners and the clergy, believing that stealing from their owners, for example, was acceptable because the slaves themselves had been stolen. In other instances, slaves openly disagreed with the lessons imparted by White clergy preaching to Blacks. On one occasion, when a White clergyman popular with the slaves began telling his Black congregants about slaves' duties and commanding them not to run away, half of his audience left while the rest began telling him that what he was preaching was not true (Raboteau 1978, 294).

Many slaves clearly rejected preaching that endorsed slavery, preferring "real preaching" that discussed not only their heavenly rewards but also their earthly condition—specifically, the means to gain freedom. This quest for freedom led to a strong attachment to the story of Exodus, since many slaves believed that the story of God delivering the Jews from Egypt paralleled their plight in the South (Raboteau 2001, 44). Former slave John Atkinson compared his escape to freedom to a religious conversion—one freed the body, while the other freed the soul (Raboteau 1978, 304–5). This type of thinking encouraged slave rebellions in many forms, from passively reading the Bible or attending prayer meetings to violent uprisings such as those planned by Denmark Vesey and Nat Turner (Raboteau 1978, 163–64).

Although Vesey's revolt was aborted, its potential terrified White southerners, as rumors held that he had gained the allegiance of close to nine thousand slaves as well as the support of the nation of Haiti. After Vesey, a slave, acquired his freedom, he settled in Charleston, South Carolina, and he eventually joined the AME Church there, one of very few in the Deep South. Vesey used his position as a leader of Bible study to recruit supporters for his planned insurrection, arguing that as in the story of Exodus, God intended for Blacks to overthrow their oppressors. Authorities learned of the plot, however, and Vesey and his collaborators were tried and hanged in 1822 (Harding 1969; Robertson 1999).

Nat Turner's revolt had even greater repercussions. From his birth, Turner had been seen as unique; he repeatedly received visions and was viewed as an excellent exhorter of the Gospel. During a February 1831 solar eclipse, Turner had a vision in which he saw White and Black figures fighting in the sky, and he interpreted the vision as a call to revolt. He initially planned the insurrection for the Fourth of July but fell ill. On August 13, 1831, he received another sign, an atmospheric phenomenon that turned the sun blue-green. On August 22, he gathered his followers and began the revolt, killing any White person they came across, including women and children (Turner 1999). In the end, the rebellion resulted in the deaths of fifty-five Whites and two hundred Blacks (Greenberg 2003).

The Vesey and Turner revolts were linked by the belief that God had willed Blacks to be free and by their basis in the teachings of the Black church, which posited Blacks and Whites as equals and focused not only on the freedom of the soul in the hereafter but also on the freedom of the body in this world. Black churches faced repercussions for their connection to these slave revolts. Shortly after Denmark Vesey and his compatriots were hanged, the First African AME Church was torn down and its pastor, Morris Brown, was forced to leave Charleston (Harding 1969; Clarence Walker 1982). The Turner rebellion provoked short-lived discussions about ending slavery in Virginia but instead resulted in the passage of a slew of laws intended to control the Black church. Virginia banned Black preachers in 1832, and Mississippi barred slaves, free Blacks, and mulattos from preaching. Other states passed laws that required special licenses for Black clergy or required that slave owners be present at any meetings of Blacks (Harding 1969; Raboteau 2001).

CIVIL WAR AND RECONSTRUCTION

The Black church in the North had divided feelings regarding the Civil War. AME Church leaders urged Blacks not to join the Union forces because the war was not about Black people but rather about territory—specifically, about who would control the western territories. Officials pointed out that supporters of the Revolutionary War had expressed the same egalitarian principles, but the conflict had not brought about improved conditions for Blacks (Clarence Walker 1982). Viewed in this light, church leaders argued, the current activities of the federal government did not indicate any true concern for Black rights: the president and Congress appeared to be willing to sacrifice Black interests to preserve the Union, as in a proposed constitutional amendment that would have prevented Congress from interfering with slavery (Franklin and Moss 1988; Klinkler and Smith 1999). After President Abraham Lincoln issued the Emancipation Proclamation and he and Congress took other steps to reassure Blacks that the war was in their interests, the AME Church declared its support for the war, and on September 10, 1863, Henry McNeal Turner was inducted as the Union Army's first Black chaplain (Clarence Walker 1982).

Throughout the war, Black clergymen followed the Union Army and reached out to newly freed men and women, gaining members for both the AME and AME Zion churches. The Black churches (and many White churches) believed that they had a duty to help educate and socialize the former slaves, telling them, among other things, that God was not White (Clarence Walker 1982). As a result of such efforts, membership in both the AME and AME Zion churches became predominantly southern. The AME Church rebuilt Charleston's First African Church, which had been destroyed in the wake of the Vesey revolt (Clarence Walker 1982, 121). The number of independent Black Baptist churches also began to explode as Blacks broke away from mixed Baptist churches (Fitts 1985; Harvey 1997; Raboteau 2001). In many ways, Reconstruction was a blessing for the Black church, but many battles still lay ahead.

Churches throughout the South facilitated both preaching and teaching. Black Baptists and Methodists opened a number of universities, including the Baptist Church's Shaw University in Raleigh, North Carolina, and the AME Church's Morris Brown in Atlanta (Fitts 1985; Raboteau 2001). Church leaders also recognized a need to involve themselves in politics, justifying their role as a responsibility to their members. During

Reconstruction, 237 Black clergymen held local, state, and nationally elected positions (Harvey 1997, 55). Black Baptists lobbied state constitutional conventions to protect the interest of Blacks, most effectively in Georgia, which had the largest Black Baptist population. Blacks served in many elected posts in Savannah, Augusta, and Atlanta (Harvey 1997, 55).

The quest for political power was also evident in the activities of Methodist clergy. Hiram Rhodes Revels, an AME minister, was elected to the U.S. Senate from Mississippi, taking the seat formerly occupied by Jefferson Davis. Another AME clergyman, Richard H. Cain from South Carolina, was elected to the House of Representatives (Montgomery 1993, 183–84; Clarence Walker 1982, 121–22). Several other clergy won election as officials or gained prominence in the Republican Party, the party of Lincoln. In one Baptist church, the commitment to the Republicans was so strong that any member rumored to have voted for a Democrat faced removal (Montgomery 1993, 162–63). Along with the mobilization of Blacks, the clergy also attempted to build a bridge between Blacks and Whites. Many officeholding Blacks tried their best to alleviate White fears and build some form of coalition. These attempts failed, and the relationship between Black churches and the Republican Party began to deteriorate (Montgomery 1993, 188–90).

While Reconstruction had begun with great hopes, Blacks soon realized that any prospect of equality would be sacrificed in the name of national unity and White supremacy. Although Radical Republicans in Congress pushed through the civil rights amendments and several civil rights bills, the executive and judicial branches soon curbed any thoughts of Black equal rights. Lincoln's successor, Tennessean Andrew Johnson, allowed states to institute Black codes, slight variations on the slave codes, in keeping with his view that "this is a country for White men, and by God, as long as I am President, it shall be a government for White men" (O'Reilly 1995, 50).

When Ulysses S. Grant became president in 1869, he remained silent on the issue of racial equality. The end of Reconstruction came with the election of Rutherford B. Hayes and the Compromise of 1877, which finalized the removal of all federal troops from the South and fully returned the South to southern White control. During his tenure in office, Hayes focused on reconciliation between Republicans and Democrats, and although he had previously worked as an attorney for fugitive slaves, he made symbolic gestures on behalf of Blacks but never followed through with substantive acts (O'Reilly 1995, 53–55).

The Supreme Court also did not embrace the idea of racial equality. In *Blyew v. United States* (1871), the Court dismissed the eyewitness testimonies of two Blacks, allowing murderers to go free (Howard 1999; Klinkler and Smith 1999, 83). In the *Slaughterhouse* cases, the Supreme Court granted states greater freedom to control citizens' activities, undercutting racial reform policies (Howard 1999, 88–93; Klinkler and Smith 1999, 83–85). Finally, in a case involving the 1873 Grant Parish Massacre, the court ruled that violent attacks on Blacks by Whites did not fall under federal jurisdiction because private individuals, not the state, had committed the actions and the state therefore should handle the matter. Racial terrorism could continue throughout the South (Howard 1999).

Congress also ceased to defend Black rights as southern Whites regained voting privileges and the Democratic Party began to exert more power, forcing the Republicans to move away from race issues to stay in office. With Whites again voting and racial terrorism keeping Blacks from the polls, Blacks no longer won election. Many Blacks became disillusioned with the Republican Party and abandoned the dream of equality in the United States, looking for it elsewhere (Harvey 1997; Montgomery 1993; Clarence Walker 1982).

Baptist minister Harry Johnson suggested that the state of Texas be reserved as a place for Blacks to live and achieve their freedom (Fitts 1985, 246–49). This plan did not gain widespread support, but the idea of immigrating to Africa received a great deal of attention. Early in the nineteenth century, AME minister Daniel Coker and other Blacks had settled in Sierra Leone as an attempt to escape their treatment in America and bring Christianity to Africa (Pinn and Pinn 2002; Clarence Walker 1982). After becoming disillusioned regarding the prospects for Blacks in the United States, AME Bishop Henry McNeal Turner revived Coker's vision, seeing the federal government's failure to protect the rights of Blacks in the South as a sign that their freedoms would be better protected in Africa. Turner gained the support of many churches in the South but received a great deal of criticism from the North. Frederick Douglass and other northern Blacks, for example, did not believe that migration was necessary. Henry Highland Garnet believed that Black freedom would not come from a migration to Africa. Turner ultimately led a mission to Liberia, but the mass exodus for which he had hoped did not occur. Many Blacks saw the action as too extreme, and many of those who made the trip failed (Montgomery 1993; Clarence Walker 1982).

JIM CROW AND THE GREAT MIGRATION

As the dream of Reconstruction ended, Jim Crow began to take hold in the South. With the removal of Union troops, the plan to redeem the South was now running at full speed. The North was no longer concerned with the South's actions, so White southerners closed ranks by making Blacks the scapegoats for the region's problems. Blacks again saw themselves left all alone. The congressional powers that had previously worked to protect Blacks became focused on imperialism, such as the acquisition of the Philippines, thereby undermining any northern criticism of the South's treatment of Blacks (Woodward 2002). And as during Reconstruction, the executive branch was unresponsive or worked to enforce racial subordination in the South (O'Reilly 1995). As president, Woodrow Wilson, who had sympathized with the plight of southern Blacks during Reconstruction, turned a deaf ear to their cause and worked to minimize their presence in the federal government (Klinkler and Smith 1999). The courts, too, continued to provide no support for Blacks; in the Civil Rights Cases of 1883, the Supreme Court issued what Henry McNeal Turner called a "cruel decision" (Howard 1999, 132) that paved the way for racial discrimination throughout the nation. *Plessy v. Ferguson* (1896) only secured Jim Crow's hold. Blacks and the Black church faced a worsening situation that kept them out of the political arena (Howard 1999).

Racial violence spread through the South. Many Black churches took a more timid approach to the "race problem." In 1908, Black Methodist bishops begged White America for assistance:

> We appeal to the friends of humanity to use their influence to rid this glorious country of mob violence which is sending so many to an untimely grave. We appeal to all who believe in fair play to assist us in banishing from our land the peonage and convict labor system, which are degrading and destroying the very vestige of manhood and regulating many to the most galling serfdom. (Franklin and Moss 1988, 285)

As difficulties began to mount, church leaders began to adopt a philosophy of hard work and thrift as the focus of the race. These clergy began to align themselves with the ideals of Booker T. Washington and his approach to racial uplift, which stressed that Blacks should focus on education as well as living a moral life. Such attempts, these leaders hoped, would eventually lead Whites to accept Blacks. Washington's approach took the focus away from political activism and postponed that fight for another day (Woodward 1971). In addition to preaching the rhetoric of hard work, Black clergy asked both their White counterparts and southern governors to help improve race relations (Harvey 1997; Montgomery 1993; Raboteau 2001). However, these calls for better race relations went unheeded.

Some ministers took a more direct approach to combating Jim Crow. Sutton E. Griggs of Nashville's East First Baptist Church used his pulpit to organize activities designed to help improve Blacks' position. Griggs organized a streetcar boycott, publicized incidents of police brutality, and participated in the Niagara Conference, the precursor to the formation of the NAACP. Griggs outspokenly opposed Washington's approach for a time, although when Griggs took a position at a church in Memphis, he moderated his stance (Harvey 1997). Nannie H. Burroughs worked through the Baptist church to bring about change for Blacks as well as women. She not only urged Blacks and Black clergy to assist organizations like the National Association for the Advancement of Colored People (NAACP) and urged Black schools to teach history that would uplift racial pride but also argued for the need to reevaluate gender roles in the church. Richard Henry Boyd, one of the founders of the National Baptist Convention of America, used his publishing house to attack Jim Crow and used his Sunday school books to uplift the race (Harvey 1997, 243–46). While southern Blacks appreciated these efforts, the failed promise of Reconstruction, the harshness of Jim Crow, and perceived opportunities in the North led to a massive movement of Blacks from the rural South to northern and urban areas.

Many Blacks saw leaving the South as their chance to gain true freedom. They quickly learned, however, that discrimination and racial hatred were not limited solely to the areas of the former Confederacy. Blacks who moved north were forced to settle in poorer areas of cities and constantly faced competition from immigrant groups. Riots broke out across the North. Blacks also found survival more difficult in the new environment (Franklin and Moss 1988).

Church leaders responded to the needs of the newly transplanted Blacks. The bishops of the AME Church met at Wilberforce University in 1917 to discuss the situation and released a statement:

> We would call to attention the unsettled condition of our people, on account of which thousands are leaving the homes of their childhood, and the child-

hood of the generations of the past, to seek a new home under new and un-tried conditions. Whatever may be the cause or causes of the exodus to cli-matic and customs, will be accompanied by problems varied and serious.

Our church work is situated in the very heart and center of the portions deserted, and those to which many thousands come. The greatest wisdom and patience will be required by both pastors and people to meet the press-ing combination of circumstances, consequent upon the movement. (Sernett 1999, 361)

The Great Migration brought a drastic increase in the membership of many northern and urban churches, which worked to expand not only their buildings but also the services they offered. Churches increasingly began to focus on earthly issues as well as otherworldly issues (Frazier 1974). Abyssinian Baptist in Harlem, Olivet Baptist in Chicago, and First Congregational in Atlanta, among other churches, began to provide day care, educational, and unemployment services as well as social activities (Raboteau 2001, 85).

Many Black pastors used the growing size of their congregations to exercise greater political influence. Most notably, Adam Clayton Powell Jr. used the Abyssinian Baptist Church to launch several campaigns to ease the conditions of Blacks in Harlem and the rest of the nation. He fo-cused strongly on the need for the Black church to take a leadership role in addressing the needs of Blacks (Franklin 1995). In 1940, Powell orga-nized a bus boycott; in 1941, he led massive relief programs and used his Coordination Committee for the Unemployed to help overcome Black unemployment in the city. Using the slogan, "Don't Buy Where You Can't Work," Powell and his organization improved Black workers' dire position in New York (Hamilton 2002, 83–108).

In 1944, Powell was elected to the U.S. House of Representatives from a newly created Harlem district. Using his church as a base for his campaigns, Powell overcame the city's machine politics. Powell re-mained in Congress until 1970, and during his tenure he pushed strongly for civil rights legislation. In 1952, he used his influence to force Demo-cratic presidential candidate Adlai Stevenson to strengthen his platform in relation to civil rights (Hamilton 2002; Paris 1991). After many states ignored the 1954 *Brown* decision, Powell began to attach civil rights amendments to all bills dealing with education.

The massive influx of Blacks into northern urban areas provided them with new experiences and allowed them to extend beyond the Black church. Marcus Garvey's Universal Negro Improvement Association

(UNIA) argued that Blacks should use group uplift to economically improve the race and create a Black nation and influenced Powell's political
activities (Franklin 1995). Garvey also felt that Blacks should leave America and immigrate to Africa to form a sovereign nation. Garvey's speeches
and recruitment activities featured numerous symbols, and the UNIA's
Negro Catechism cites the Bible as a source of inspiration. The UNIA's
success brought about FBI scrutiny, and Garvey was deported from the
United States in 1927 (Raboteau 2001, 86–89).

Blacks' historical identification with the biblical Israelites led many
Blacks to convert to Judaism. One of the first documented examples of
this phenomenon took place in Lawrence, Kansas, where William S.
Crowdy formed the Church of God in Saints in 1896, and the Com-
mandment Keepers followed in Harlem during the 1920s. The Father
Divine movement used religion to create a multiracial coalition to stand
up against the pressures of discrimination and racial hatred. Originally
based in Brooklyn, New York, Father Divine taught his followers that
negative thinking brought about their ailments and that he was a per-
sonification of God. Father Divine appealed to both Blacks and Whites,
who began to campaign against segregation and racial hatred (Raboteau
2001, 97–99).

Another alternative to the Black church was the Black Muslims. One
of the first such groups, the Moorish Science Temple, was founded in
1913 in Newark, New Jersey. The group taught that Blacks were originally from Morocco and their true religion was Islam. It also argued that
just as John the Baptist was a forerunner of Jesus Christ, Marcus Garvey
was a forerunner of the Moorish Science Temple's leader, Drew Ali. A
similar group, the Nation of Islam, founded in Detroit, eventually over-
shadowed the Black Muslims (Raboteau 2001, 90–91). Nation of Islam
leader Wallace D. Fard taught members of his movement that Islam was
the key to the uplift of the race and espoused a pro-Black philosophy of
self-help. Fard eventually ceded control of his organization to Elijah
Poole (later Elijah Mohammed), and the Nation of Islam expanded from
small congregations in Detroit and Chicago throughout the country, becoming one of the major alternatives to the Black church (Lincoln 1994,
94–129; Raboteau 2001, 91).

BLACK FREEDOM STRUGGLE

Southern Blacks reemerged into the political system as a consequence of
changes in the American social, economic, and political landscape. As in-

dustrialization spread, the South became more urban, allowing Blacks to build stronger networks and gain greater access to education. In addition, U.S. leaders' characterization of the country's involvement in World War II as a fight to keep democracy strong renewed Blacks' determination to fight Jim Crow. The Supreme Court also reversed its earlier hostility toward Black advancements, outlawing White primaries and restrictive covenants as the Court slowly chipped away at Jim Crow. The legal assault on segregation reached its apex with the 1954 *Brown* decision, which overturned *Plessy* (Howard 1999; Charles Payne 1995). Blacks also gained support from the executive branch, as the increased Black presence in the North transferred electoral votes to northern states where Blacks had voting power (Charles Payne 1995). The increased northern Black population also created a stronger Black presence in Congress. Despite its small size, this group exerted some influence (Berg 1994). The Black church played a key role in facilitating black engagement with the political system, and these two factors combined to give a new impetus to the Black freedom struggle.

Clergy were important leaders in the transformation of the South (Aldon Morris 1984). The Reverend T. J. Jemison, who led the 1953 Baton Rouge, Louisiana, bus boycott, used the collective resources of local churches to sustain the effort, a strategy also followed by similar boycotts in Tallahassee, Florida, and Montgomery and Birmingham, Alabama. The organizations created to protect Black rights in these cities were structured through local churches and led by clergy, enabling such groups to obtain funding without fear of outside influence.

The most notable of these groups was the Southern Christian Leadership Conference (SCLC). Churches throughout the South provided a network to carry the organization's message and mobilize the masses for an assault on Jim Crow. Unlike the NAACP, the SCLC developed indigenous leadership, and it was more flexible than the national organizations. The SCLC used preachers' charisma to help it gain resources and support throughout the South (Aldon Morris 1984). The most prominent of these ministers was Martin Luther King Jr., who used his oratorical skills to provide Blacks with a feeling of hope and with emotional fuel (Aldon Morris 1984; Raboteau 2001). Arguing that religious institutions were responsible for both spiritual and physical concerns, King and the SCLC mobilized Black and White clergy to fight Jim Crow. Unlike earlier southern Black clergymen, King told rather than asked White ministers to become involved in fighting racial hatred. While King was the hallmark of the movement, his plans were not fully accepted.

Joseph H. Jackson, the president of the National Baptist Convention, USA, was one of King's strongest critics. Jackson, originally from Mississippi and pastor of Olivet Baptist in Chicago, felt that King's and others' protest activities were premature (Paris 1991; Raboteau 2001). Like Booker T. Washington, Jackson believed that time and Black economic development would bring about an end to racial differences and that protest was not sufficient:

> Freed men are not free until they learn to exercise their new acquired opportunities to gain for themselves the economic, intellectual, political, moral and spiritual independence and self reliance. (Jackson 1999, 515)

The differences between followers of Jackson and of King eventually led to a split in the National Baptist Convention, USA, and to the formation of the Progressive National Baptist Convention (Raboteau 2001).

While Jackson criticized King for being too confrontational, others believed that he was not confrontational enough. One of King's key critics in the North was Malcolm X, a member of the Nation of Islam, who felt that King and other southern Black clergymen were too timid. Rather than seeking to integrate with Whites, Malcolm X believed that Blacks should work toward the separation and uplift of the race. His "by any means necessary" approach to obtaining equal rights for Blacks made him impatient with others who were less direct and confrontational (Lincoln 1994; Paris 1991; Raboteau 2001).

As the civil rights movement continued, younger Blacks became increasingly dissatisfied with the slow rate of progress by Congress and the presidency, which the new generation saw as signaling that Blacks needed to be more forceful in their demands for Black equality. The result was the Black Power movement, one of whose earliest supporters was Adam Clayton Powell Jr. (Hamilton 2002, 20–22). Along with Black Power came the development of Black theology, which is based on liberation theology and argues that Christians have a duty to help the oppressed. According to theologians including Cone and Wilmore (1993), anyone, Black or White, not working to defend the rights of the oppressed does not identify with the teachings of Christ. Black clergy began to accept this theology as their own and to offer strong criticisms of White clergy and Whites in general. According to a 1966 statement released by the National Conference of Black Churchmen, "So long as White churchmen continue to moralize and misinterpret Christian love, so long will justice continue to be subverted in this land" (Sernett 1999, 558). In 1969, the group called for all Christians to work for the liberation of oppressed groups:

> The demand that Christ the Liberator imposes on all men *requires* all blacks to affirm their full dignity as persons and all whites to surrender their presumptions of superiority and abuses of power. (Sernett 1999, 565)

The emergence of Black theology provided a justification for the church in the struggle to liberate Blacks and reaffirmed the teachings of Black Power.

The Black freedom struggle ultimately provided Blacks with permanent access to political institutions and thus changed Black politics. Blacks and their churches no longer needed to rely solely on outsider activities.

CONTEMPORARY POLITICAL INVOLVEMENT

The progress made during the civil rights and Black Power movements provided Blacks the opportunity to move from protest to politics. Passage of the 1964 Civil Rights Act and the 1965 Voting Rights Act gave Blacks stable access to the political process. Black political empowerment refocused Blacks and the Black church on methods of engaging the policymaking process from the inside. As in Reconstruction, Black churches became crucial in electoral politics at all levels of government, and they began to build cooperative relationships with government agencies.

Beyerlein and Chaves (2003) find that Black churches are significantly more likely to allow political candidates to speak to their congregations than are Catholic or White Protestant churches. During the 1984 and 1988 presidential campaigns, for example, Jesse Jackson recruited Black clergy throughout the nation to mobilize their congregations (Tate 1993). This strategy worked: Jackson gained 12 percent of the delegates at the 1984 Democratic National Convention and increased his share to 29 percent in 1988 (Walton and Smith 2008, 138). Al Sharpton followed a similar pattern in his 2004 quest for the White House, although he did not generate the same success. Carol Mosley Braun recruited Illinois's Black clergy to mobilize their members in her 1992 senatorial campaign (Harris 1999, 12) . Clergy such as Floyd Flake have also forged successful political careers. Like Powell, Flake has used his church, Allen AME in Queens, New York, as a political center for a congressional career (Stanton 1998).

In some instances, questions have arisen about Black churches' autonomy in political campaigns. After Christine Todd Whitman's successful run for the New Jersey governorship, consultant Ed Rollins boasted that the campaign had paid Black clergy to suppress the Black vote. His comments quickly created an uproar of protest from the Black religious community (White 1994). Rollins ultimately retracted the statement, and no one was charged with a crime, but the incident shook the Black church's foundations in politics.

Black churches are expanding their role as providers of services, forming coalitions with government agencies to assist in the administration of social services. As was the case during the Great Migration, Black churches now provide housing, job training, and recovery programs. Many churches now operate community development corporations, using funds from private and government agencies to implement such programs (Billingsley 1999; Owens 2006). Faith-based initiatives and other programs offer Black churches opportunities to strengthen their relationship with the government.

CONCLUSION

Activism by Black churches is shaped by multiple factors. While the members and pastor are key elements, the context within which they operate also plays a strong role. Blacks' political and social environments are also key factors in interpreting Black churches' political activism. As Blacks gained political prominence, the church became more active, but as Blacks lost access to political institutions, the church retreated. Black churches' activities reflect the cyclical treatment of Blacks in the United States. As Blacks became part of mainstream American politics, the church followed suit by adopting insider tactics such as campaign work and lobbying. However, when Blacks were barred from the political system, the people and the church engaged in contentious politics.

The Black church has always been highly concerned with protecting Blacks, and this concern has created variation in activities. Some church leaders believed that the best strategy was for Blacks to look inward and focus on their spirituality. Other church officials believed that they must confront the forces of discrimination and racial hatred to protect the Black community. These variations have led to different views of the church throughout its history. Recognizing these variations is important in understanding how the Black church has affected Black politics. Understanding the causes of these variations is the purpose of the remaining chapters of this volume, which empirically examine how the institutional, leadership, and membership components of the Black churches shape their political activism.

CHAPTER 4

Who Can Facilitate the Call?
The Role of Organizational
Dynamics in Shaping Church-
Based Political Activism

One of the key factors in explaining church-based activism is the church itself. Beyond the pastor and members, many questions about church organization must be asked. Does it have the ability to become politically involved? Is it constrained in terms of the types of activities in which it can take part? Finally, does the church foster an environment where political activism is a justifiable action? The various dynamics that make up a church, such as resources, process, and culture, play a vital role in shaping its activities. This chapter examines the organizational factors that lead churches to become involved in political matters. I first provide a theoretical framework based on organizational psychology, interest group, and congregational studies literature. Further discussion of the findings from the case studies discussed in chapter 2 follows. The third aspect of this examination applies this framework to the analysis of survey data quantitatively to assess the role of these factors in shaping political engagement by congregations.

ORGANIZATIONAL COMPONENTS OF CHURCH-BASED POLITICAL ACTIVISM

Chapter 2's examination of the causes of church-based political activism notes the importance of resources, process, and culture in shaping church activities. All these factors either directly or indirectly shape church activism, physically constraining church activities and psychologically constraining how the pastor and members feel the church should behave. Examining these dynamics provides further understanding of how the organization's makeup can shape its propensity to engage in political activism.

Resources

The assessment of any organization usually begins with its resources. Organizations, like individuals, are centrally concerned about survival. Resources allow the organization to endure and accomplish its goals. As a result, organizations always have concerns about maintaining or increasing resources (Scott 1998). While having resources allows organizations to accomplish their goals, the quest for resources may also shape those goals, most clearly for voluntary organizations. As the interest group literature has shown, the need to survive can place organizations in troubling situations (Berry 1977; Jack Walker 1991). The efforts to gain resources may sidetrack organizations from their original goals. In addition, some organizations may need to allocate a significant amount of their resources to the act of soliciting individuals for donations. In sum, voluntary organizations can face a great deal of difficulties in gaining resources.

Like any other voluntary organization, congregations are susceptible to the resource problem. Resources represent a key aspect in explaining church activism (Billingsley 1999; Frazier 1974; Lincoln and Mamiya 1990; Aldon Morris 1984; Charles Payne 1995). For example, Frazier (1974) points to resources as a major reason why churches in urban areas oriented their interests toward social issues. Churches rich in resources extended the number of activities in which they participated. Having a large number of members allowed churches to expand their programs and begin treating social and spiritual problems (Smith and Smidt 2003). Churches with more resources also enjoyed a greater level of independence (Myrdal 1962; Charles Payne 1995). Churches such as Abyssinian Baptist developed vast programs of social activities because of their resources. The church's large membership provided the resource base that allowed Adam Clayton Powell Jr. and his father to accomplish their goals (Paris 1991). In addition to financial capital, churches, like any voluntary organization, depend on human capital—that is, members must volunteer their time and skills to help maintain the church as well as accomplish its goals. As Hoge et al. (1998) point out, volunteer work by members supplements a church's financial capital.

The findings from the case studies highlight the importance of resources. The larger and more financially stable churches were more active than the financially constrained churches that had smaller congregations. For example, the pastor and members of Red Memorial wanted their church to become more involved in the community but lacked the resources necessary to do so. Rev. Brown wanted his church to become more involved, but the issue of bringing the congregation into financial stability was more important. In contrast, the financially stable Green Memorial and Orange Chapel engaged social and political issues in the community. Along with issues related to financial capital, several churches were struggling in regard to human capital, the importance of which several pastors noted. Having members who possessed the knowledge and the skills to undertake social action provided an immeasurable resource for the congregations. Black Memorial's social assistance center depended on the church having an adequate number of volunteers. In addition, when the Austin churches began holding community health fairs, they were initiated and led by members who were medical professionals. In terms of political activism, the human capital component is just as important as financial capital. Rev. Blue noted that although he was not actively involved in the debate about school vouchers, he had an attentive member who provided information. A lack of human capital can stall social action on the part of churches. Rev. Black noted his congregation's success in local humanitarian efforts but expressed dismay over the difficulty he faced trying to find members with the knowledge to apply for grants that would enable him to expand his social outreach. Brown Memorial, while not highly active, attempted to engage the congregation by establishing a position that focused on the church's role in regard to social issues. The person occupying this position was responsible for keeping the congregation informed of potentially relevant social and political issues. The position's effectiveness was determined by the skill level and commitment of the person assigned. The first occupant of the position was very active and skilled, but when another person took over, the level of activity dropped significantly.

Process

Resources provide the ability to act, but process guides the ways in which churches act and how they decide to act; process establishes the rules of operation. Process presents a leadership structure as well as limitations on behavior. By providing structure to the organization, process allows for a system of decision making and conflict resolution (Scott 1998). Organizational processes are not always limited to formal rules but can include informal practices and modes of behavior. Individuals who may not hold formal leadership roles may become de facto leaders because of experience or expertise.

Within churches, process works the same way. It provides a clear decision-making structure that allows the congregants to direct the church's actions. Each church has a set of rules for operation (Dudley 1998). Churches differ in terms of process: some churches provide their pastors with a great deal of decision-making power, while other churches place that power solely in the hands of the congregants. In addition, churches must take into account issues of denominational structure. Churches in hierarchical denominations, such as the Methodists, remain accountable to leaders outside of the local church. More autonomous churches, including the Baptists, are primarily free to act on their own. Lincoln and Mamiya (1990) argue that the more autonomous nature of Baptist churches provides them with greater flexibility regarding their involvement in political matters, a finding supported by the case studies. All of the Methodist clergy noted that they were responsible to their churches as well as the denomination. Both Rev. Blue and Rev. Brown explicitly noted that the denomination limited their activities, and denominational discipline governed many of Brown Memorial's social activities. The pastor and members repeatedly stated that because the denomination was incorporated, each church had to adhere to the denomination's guidelines, which dictated specific stances as well as political involvement. Rev. Blue noted that his Episcopal leader had banned churches from taking part in certain activities. The process structure for the Baptist churches differed substantially, however; each church developed its own bylaws that regulated activities and decision making. None of the Baptist churches had formal rules guiding political activity, but several had informal rules governing how to treat visiting candidates.

While the hierarchical structure of the Methodist denomination may constrain some activism, it may also provide resources for activism. For example, the Methodist denominations formally emphasize having well-educated clergy and pastors, an aspect of the process that may result in more skilled leaders and thus increased social and political action. The Methodist denominations also provide financial support for individual churches. Charles Payne (1995) notes that many Black Methodist churches were more independent from White churches than were their

Baptist counterparts because the Methodist congregations received financial assistance from the denomination. As a result of this independence, the Methodist churches became more involved in the civil rights movement than did the Baptist churches. Brown Memorial, for example, has survived because of support from the denomination. Process may constrain the activities of churches, but it may also serve as a safety net to ensure the survival of a church (Childs-Brown 1980).

Culture

The final and possibly most important dynamic of a church is its culture. As chapter 1 discusses, culture is closely linked to identity. Organizational culture should be understood as learned behaviors and worldviews within a particular organization. Organizational culture develops over a long period of time as members of the organization learn how to handle external and internal problems (Schein 2004). Organizational culture represents an amalgam of the organization's experiences. As organizations learn from past internal and external crises, they develop a mutual outlook on what types of behaviors are best for the organization. As they catalog their successes and failures, members of the organization develop assumptions about proper behavior that dictate their values and actions.

Congregations, like any other organization, develop their own culture. Over time, as an individual congregation confronts problems, it develops a shared outlook as to the proper behavior of the members and the church (Ammerman 1998; Becker 1999). One observable aspect of church culture is the worship service, which Schein (2004) refers to as an artifact of the organization—an observable phenomenon influenced by organizational culture. The rules or practices that direct the worship service provide an indication of the church's culture in many different ways. For example, Rev. Black noted that the "high worship" service at Black Temple reflected the church's attitude. The members sang hymns as part of a highly structured and traditional service. The church's culture was also indicated through its primary focus on maintaining itself without active involvement in the community. Rev. Black noted that changing the worship service so that is was more open was part of changing the culture of the church. By having a less structured and more open culture, the church could become more involved in the community.

While the worship service receives a great deal of attention, a church's history also strongly affects its culture (Ammerman 1998). All of the respondents discussed the institution's history as their way of understanding the church. Members of churches with histories of activism, such as Orange Chapel, noted that history served as a reason for supporting and expecting political activism by the church. The members of Blue Temple noted that the church had never been very politically active and did not see a need to change.

The individuals who make up the church also shape its culture (Ammerman 1998; Becker 1999; Tamney 1991). Variation among a church's members strongly affects the attitudes developed within the church (Huckfeldt, Plutzer, and Sprague 1993; Wald 1997; Wald, Owen, and Hill 1988). Members of several churches defined their institutions in terms of who attended. The members of White Chapel, for example, described it as a church with a strong education background; a significant portion of its members were teachers or administrators in Detroit's school system. Similarly, members of Brown Memorial described themselves as a blue-collar congregation and saw other Austin churches as wealthier.

In addition, residence was an issue in regard to church culture—specifically, social action as it pertains to church culture. As chapter 2 discusses, several pastors and members noted that their church's lack of community activism stemmed from the fact that the members did not reside in the community. Churches with members from the local community or with a culture strongly connected to the local community were more likely to be engaged.

As the literature notes and the case studies have found, each church develops a particular culture regardless of denomination or location. The experiences of the church as well as the combination of people who attend the church shape this culture. While each church developed its own way of doing things, all of the churches had cultures that acknowledged Black church culture, as almost all respondents noted. They openly acknowledged that because their churches were predominantly Black, they were unique religious institutions. Several interviewees evoked the history of Black churches. Members of Brown Memorial noted that even though their church was constrained by denominational processes, the fact that they were a Black church in a predominantly White denomination made them unique.

Church culture is also a response to the experiences of the church and thus is also a function of church resources and processes. As a church's resources change, its culture should also change. For example, Rev. Green commented that when he first entered his church, it was low on resources and possessed a culture that was mainly concerned with the church's survival. As the church's resources began to increase, the culture became more open to addressing the needs of the members and community. Red Memorial is the opposite; when the church had a great deal of resources, it developed a culture that promoted social action, but as the church began to lose those resources, social action lost its prominent place in the church's culture. In addition, process shapes culture by providing constraints on behavior and guiding decision making. Changes in the decision-making structure strongly affected activism. Several respondents noted that an increased openness in decision making coincided with a greater openness to social action.

BLACK RELIGIOUS TRADITIONS

Before examining how resources, process, and culture shape political activism in churches, it is important to understand the institutions being studied. When scholars discuss the Black church, they focus primarily on Baptists, Methodists, and Pentecostals, the three traditions that have historically attracted the vast majority of Blacks. These three traditions include seven major predominantly Black denominations, and each has a distinctive structure and history. Black Baptists and Methodists emerged as a result of the need to protect Black religious interests, while the Pentecostal denomination resulted from a theological shift. The Baptist and Methodist traditions enjoy a longer history, dating back to before the Revolutionary War, while Pentecostalism did not enter the American religious landscape until the early twentieth century.

Black Baptists

Africans were introduced to the Baptist faith soon after its arrival in the Americas. The Baptist message appealed to African slaves because it included religious equality. Baptists also spoke out against institutions that impeded the fulfillment of God's will. Slave owners interpreted these messages as a threat to their interests and resisted allowing Baptist ministers to preach to slaves. To spread their message, Baptist evangelists bowed to social norms and stopped preaching equality to slaves (Pinn and Pinn 2002). A massive influx of Africans into the Baptist faith nevertheless occurred, and Black Baptist churches were soon created. While the religious ceremonies of early Black Baptists were not autonomous,

Black Baptist congregations began to emerge. The first known Black Baptist church was founded in 1758, on William Byrd's plantation in Mecklenburg, Virginia. Several other Black Baptist churches were founded shortly thereafter, most notably the Silver Bluff Church in Silver Bluff, South Carolina, and the First Bryan Baptist Church and the First African Church, both of Savannah, Georgia. Although most Black Baptists lived in the South, they could not organize to form associations, which Whites saw as a sign of Black independence and a threat to the southern slave society. Such fears were not unwarranted: northern Black Baptist associations often took strong abolitionist stances (Fitts 1985; Pinn and Pinn 2002). These associations served not only as symbols but also as focal points for Black independence (Lincoln and Mamiya 1990).

The prominent Black Baptist associations today are the National Baptist Convention, USA (NBC), the National Baptist Convention of America (NBCA), and the Progressive National Baptist Convention (PNBC). The NBC was formed in 1895 as a collection of three smaller conventions, the Baptist Foreign Mission Convention of the United States of America, the American National Baptist Convention, and the National Baptist Educational Convention of the United States of America, and sought to provide spiritual and social development for freed slaves. The convention wanted to focus on providing the skills and attitudes needed for Black success, focusing on Black independence and self-sufficiency to help create a postslavery identity. The convention helped support numerous schools and universities, including Shaw University in Raleigh, North Carolina, and Morehouse College in Atlanta. Convention leaders believed that Black economic growth should begin in the church to facilitate independence. This agenda led to schisms over the issue of whether to work with Whites. Many convention members saw no need to do so, while other members argued that the convention needed to continue to work with White organizations as a sign of gratitude for early support (Lincoln and Mamiya 1990; Mead and Hill 1995; Pinn and Pinn 2002).

The Baptist associations maintain a strong focus on the individuality of the churches. Unlike the Methodist churches, which are connectional (that is, a hierarchy exists within the denomination), Baptist churches are relatively autonomous and can join multiple associations. As a result, the Black Baptist associations have historically suffered a proliferation of splinter groups. An internal dispute over the NBC's publishing board led to the formation of the NBCA at Chicago's Salem Baptist Church in 1915 (Lincoln and Mamiya 1990; Mead and Hill 1995; Pinn and Pinn 2002).

The PNBC was founded as a consequence of internal NBC disagreements regarding the leadership and direction of the civil rights movement. Many of the PNBC's founders, including Martin Luther King Sr., Martin Luther King Jr., and Ralph Abernathy, disagreed with NBC president Joseph H. Jackson's stance that these civil rights leaders were moving too fast. When they were unable to remove Jackson from office, they founded the PNBC in 1961, and the new association immediately took a very active role in the civil rights movement (Lincoln and Mamiya 1990; Mead and Hill 1995; Pinn and Pinn 2002).

Black Methodists

Like the Baptist Church, the Methodist Church concerned itself with saving African souls from soon after its arrival in America. Methodism appealed to Africans because of its style of services, baptism, and abolitionist stance, and by 1797 the denomination was almost 25 percent African. As with the Baptist faith, many slave owners saw Methodism as a threat, linking the teachings of Methodist ministers to slave revolts. The denomination's antislavery sentiment eventually faded as a consequence of the realization that opposing slavery would restrict Methodists' contact with Africans, thereby preventing missionaries from saving the souls not only of the slaves but also of their owners. The issue of slavery eventually led to a White denominational split and to the creation of the Methodist Episcopal Church, South (Lincoln and Mamiya 1990; Pinn and Pinn 2002).

Discrimination led Africans to create their own Methodist denominations soon after the Revolutionary War. The roots of the African Methodist Episcopal (AME) Church go back to 1787, when members of St. George Methodist Episcopal Church in Philadelphia withdrew to protest racial discrimination. Several of those involved in the protest built a separate chapel and obtained a Black pastor. They did not initially intend to create a separate denomination, styling themselves for the most part as African Methodists. By the mid-1810s, however, it had become clear that the African Methodists were to be a distinct body separated from the Methodist Episcopal Church, and in 1816, the AME was formally organized (Lincoln and Mamiya 1990; Mead and Hill 1995; Daniel Payne 1998; Pinn and Pinn 2002).

Since its inception, the AME has encouraged education and activism among its members. Richard Allen, a founder of the denomination, also created an abolitionist group called the Free African Society (Lincoln and Mamiya 1990). In addition, the AME created Wilberforce University, one of the first Black institutions of higher learning, in 1857.

Two other predominantly Black Methodist denominations exist. The African Methodist Episcopal Zion (AMEZ) Church was founded under conditions similar to those that led to the AME's creation. Black members of New York's John Street Methodist Episcopal Church were dissatisfied with their treatment and in 1796 petitioned the Methodist Episcopal Church for a separate place of worship. The request was approved, and in 1800 Zion Church was built and incorporated as the African Methodist Episcopal Church of the City of New York. Although the new church was controlled by Blacks, it remained under the official jurisdiction of the Methodist Episcopal Church until 1824, when the African Methodist Episcopal Church in America was formed. In 1848, the denomination changed its name to African Methodist Episcopal Zion Church to avoid confusion with the AME. Like the AME, the AMEZ identified strongly with education and activism. One of its most noted members was Frederick Douglass, who learned many of his ideals from AMEZ ministers. The AMEZ also played a strong role in the development of Alabama's Tuskegee University, and it was the first of the Black Methodist denominations to permit the ordination of women (Hamilton 1972; Lincoln and Mamiya 1990; Mead and Hill 1995; Pinn and Pinn 2002).

Unlike the AME and AMEZ, the Christian Methodist Episcopal (CME) Church was formed not out of protest but as the result of an agreement on the part of Black and White members of the Methodist Episcopal Church, South. During the Civil War and Reconstruction, the Methodist Episcopal Church, South lost more than half of its Black members to other churches. To stop the losses, church leaders allowed the creation of the Colored Methodist Episcopal Church, which was to be connected to the Methodist Episcopal Church, South. Such ties provided financial as well as organizational benefits for the new church, but the Methodist Episcopal Church, South retained some control, establishing rules for the new denomination that included a prohibition on political activity. Many Colored Methodist Episcopal clergy also resisted political activity because they did not want to offend their brethren in the Methodist Episcopal Church, South (Lincoln and Mamiya 1990). AME and AMEZ clergy argued that neither the new church nor its members were truly independent (Pinn and Pinn 2002). The denomination eventually shed its apolitical image and in 1956 changed its name to the Christian Methodist Episcopal Church. Like the AME and AMEZ, the CME supports several schools: one of the oldest is Tennessee's Lane College (Lincoln and Mamiya 1990; Mead and Hill 1995; Pinn and Pinn 2002).

Black Pentecostals

Pentecostalism, as it is known in the United States, began with the Holiness movement in the 1800s. The movement was based on John Wesley's writings on sanctification and the quest for perfection in Christianity and began in Methodist churches and spread through campfire revivals, resulting in the formation of the National Holiness Movement. Pentecostals focus on an actual sign of sanctification, speaking in tongues, which they believe to be a sign that a person has been baptized in the Holy Spirit. Speaking in tongues indicates a personal connection to the divine (Lincoln and Mamiya 1990; Pinn and Pinn 2002; Sanders 1996).

William Seymour, a Baptist minister, introduced Pentecostalism to Blacks after listening outside a lecture hall to talks by to one of the premier White Pentecostal ministers, Charles Fox Parham (Pinn and Pinn 2002). For three years, Seymour held the Azusa Street Revival in Los Angeles, attracting people from across the nation and creating a theological uproar as people assumed Pentecostal beliefs (Lincoln and Mamiya 1990; Mead and Hill 1995; Pinn and Pinn 2002; Sanders 1996). The revival played a role in the creation of the primary Black Pentecostal denomination, the Church of God in Christ (COGIC), the youngest but largest of the seven major Black denominations.

Elder C. H. Mason, who received his early training in the Missionary Baptist Church, founded COGIC in 1895 after finding that his beliefs did not mesh with those espoused by those of the church in which he had been ordained. Mason sought to establish a church with stronger appeal and greater encouragement for all Christian believers, emphasizing the doctrine of entire sanctification through the outpourings of the Holy Spirit (Lincoln and Mamiya 1990; Pinn and Pinn 2002; Sanders 1996). Twelve years after its founding, the denomination, headquartered in Memphis, Tennessee, consisted of only ten congregations, but in 1907, Mason attended the Azusa Street Revival, changing Mason's theology and giving COGIC a new direction. By the time of Mason's death in

1961, COGIC had become the second-largest Pentecostal group in America. Its success is particularly noteworthy because COGIC began as an interracial denomination in the South in the middle of Jim Crow. Because COGIC was one of the first denominations to ordain Pentecostal ministers in the South, Mason ordained White Pentecostals seeking to join the ministry. These White congregations eventually departed COGIC and joined White Pentecostal denominations (Lincoln and Mamiya 1990; Sanders 1996).

Consistent with its Pentecostal heritage, COGIC is Trinitarian in its doctrine, "stressing repentance, regeneration, justification, sanctification, speaking in tongues, and the gift of healing as evidence of the baptism of the Spirit" (Mead and Hill 1995, 114). Although some analysts contend that Pentecostalism focuses on otherworldliness, diminishing its adherents' interest in political engagement, other observers find that Pentecostalism need not be detrimental to political activity (Calhoun-Brown 1999; Harris 1999; McRoberts 1999). Mason, for example, was a strong pacifist and was arrested several times for protesting World War I. Moreover, the denomination took an active part in the civil rights movement and today has close ties to the Democratic Party (Lincoln and Mamiya 1990; Mead and Hill 1995; Sanders 1996). The denomination has a unique structure that mixes features of the Baptist and Methodist Churches. Although a denominational hierarchy exists, each church has a relatively high level of autonomy.

ORGANIZATIONAL DYNAMICS IN CHURCH ACTION

The quantitative analysis of the organizational dynamics begins with the urban subset of data used by Lincoln and Mamiya (1990). Lincoln and Mamiya surveyed 1,531 pastors within the seven major Black denominations as well as in minor Black denominations and in predominantly Black churches in predominantly White denominations. I analyze only churches that reported an affiliation with one of the seven major predominantly Black denominations, thereby reducing the sample size to 1,482.

The measures of activism are two indexes of social action. The first index captures church involvement in general social activities and is designed to measure the extent to which churches reach beyond their walls and engage others in their communities. This index is a four-point measure of (1) involvement in projects with churches outside of the denomination, (2) working with government agencies, (3) working with social agencies dealing with community problems, and (4) allowing nonchurch organizations to use the church as a meeting place. On average, the churches take part in 1.9 of these activities. A total of 34.5 percent of the churches report taking part in one or fewer of these activities, while 33.1 percent report taking part in three or more of the activities. These findings appear to show low levels of engagement, but as Chaves (2004) points out, involvement in general social activities is not the organization's sole purpose.

The second index resembles the first index but specifically targets political activities. This index is also a three-point measure that includes working with government programs, working with other churches and organizations, and facilitating these organizations. However, only political activities are counted. Churches that have cooperated with other churches in programs that address social problems are coded as 1, while all others are coded as 0. Churches that have cooperated with civil rights organizations, have cooperated with welfare rights organizations, have participated in police-community relations activities, or have reported assisting in a community crisis are coded as 1, while all other forms of cooperation are coded as 0. Finally, facilitating is limited to civil rights organizations, political organizations, and labor groups. On average, the churches take part in .87 of these activities. A total of 78.1 percent of the churches take part in one or fewer of these activities, while 3.9 percent take part in three or more.

Because this chapter focuses on organization, the explanatory variables in the model are limited to measures of resources, culture, and process. Resources are measured through the size of the membership, the church's yearly income, and the pastor's level of education. Both membership size and income denote financial resources for the church, while the pastor's level of education denotes resources in the form of skills. Following the logic of Verba, Schlozman, and Brady (1995), pastors with significant levels of education should posses certain skills necessary for social action, and church leaders' skills should serve as resource for their congregations (Smith and Smidt 2003).

Culture is measured using measures of Black religious consciousness, aspects of the worship service, church age, and region. Black religious consciousness denotes the degree to which churches emphasize the uniqueness of the Black church and promote positive images of Blacks. Because the Black church serves as a central institution in Black life, churches that more openly embrace this part of their culture are expected to be more socially active. Black religious consciousness is captured in two ways: whether the church teaches its children about the distinctiveness of the Black church, and whether the pastor of the church reports that his or her sermons reflect a change in Black consciousness since the civil rights movement. The worship service provides a vivid example of church culture. Churches that engage in "high worship," such as singing established hymns, are more traditional congregations that may not see social action as an important part of their culture. As the case studies suggest, churches that are more open to different forms of music might also be more open to social action. The model consequently includes a measure of church music approval, with respondents asked their opinions of three types of music: gospel, spirituals, and other Black music, such as jazz and blues. Because jazz and blues are not considered established forms of congregational music, opinions regarding those forms provide some idea of whether a church is traditional. Another important aspect of church culture is the degree to which the church is embedded in the community. Older churches are expected to have closer connections with their local communities, which may lead to higher levels of communication with other churches and organizations (Billingsley 1999; Chaves 2004). This level of communication can create a closer attachment to the local community and a need to respond to community needs. The final measure of church culture is region—specifically, whether the church is located in the South. The legacy of the civil rights movement and differing environmental pressures (Billingsley 1999; Lincoln and Mamiya 1990) lead to the expectation that Black churches in the South will behave differently than those outside the region.

The final aspect of the model is process, which is measured by the church's religious tradition. The Baptist churches are autonomous and because of their size have historically been engaged in Black political development. The Methodist churches have a hierarchical structure and a history of having highly educated and socially conscious members. The Holiness/Pentecostal churches have a hierarchical structure, but it is weaker than that of the Methodists. Moreover, these churches are most known for their theological conservatism. Baptists make up 45.8 percent of the sample, Methodists comprise 34.4 percent, and Pentecostals comprise 19.9 percent.

The differences in these traditions may provide support as well as constraints to social action. A comparison of the traditions shows significant differences. On the social action index, Methodists and Baptists (2.1 and 2.0, respectively) are significantly more active than the Pentecostals (1.5). Moving to political action, the Methodists and Baptists (.95 and .93, respectively) are again significantly more active than their Pentecostal counterparts (.56). This univariate analysis indicates differences between the traditions; however, the multivariate analysis will better explain the causes of these differences.

This study focuses on pastors and church members; however, the organization shapes their actions and attitudes. This chapter has focused on the various components of the organization, such as resources, culture, and process, to address how they direct church-based political engagement. Table 2 presents the results from the analysis of resources, culture, process, and organization, demonstrating that resources and culture explain church action. Resources, including membership and pastoral training, have dramatic effects: growth in size from one hundred to one thousand members increases social activism by 50 percent, while high pastoral training leads to a 41 percent increase in activism over low pastoral training. These two factors thus constitute vital aspects of understanding church-based social engagement.

Church culture also matters. Older churches as well as those that express Black pride are more active. Moving from the low end of the church age scale to the high end increases social activism by nearly 24 percent (see also Billingsley 1999; Chaves 2004). Older churches are more embedded in the community and are thus more prone to act; they are also significantly more likely to report sermons that express Black pride. Older churches also should be more financially stable than younger churches, and the data show that older churches have significantly larger memberships and better-educated pastors than do younger churches. Church age consequently provides resource and cultural explanations for church action.

In addition to age, aspects of the worship service, such as sermons and music, shape social activism. Churches with pastors who preach Black pride participate in 2.6 activities, while those that lack such pastors take part in 2.2 activities, a difference of 18 percent. Churches that allow a larger variety of musical forms take part in 2.9 activities, while those that are more musically restricted take part in 2.6, a difference of nearly 13 percent. While both of these aspects of the worship service may appear to have marginal effects on church action, churches that allow jazz are also more likely to possess pastors who express Black pride in their sermons. Churches that allow jazz and promote Black pride take part in 2.9 social activities, 33 percent more activities than churches that do neither. A final cultural aspect is region; churches in the South are less socially engaged than those in the North. This relationship is surprising, but the effect is marginal, as the movement of a church from the North to the South decreases social activism by less than 9 percent.

Resources play a strong role in explaining political activism, but culture also matters. Membership has the most dramatic effect on political activism, as small churches score at just over half the levels (.94) of large churches (1.8). In addition, pastoral training and church income factor into political activism. As in the case with social engagement, churches with better-educated pastors are more likely to participate. Moving from

TABLE 2. Predicted Values of Social and Political Action Given Variation in Organizational Determinants

	Social Activism			Political Activism		
	Low	High	Δ	Low	High	Δ
Resources						
Membership	2.16	3.24	50.14%	0.94	1.79	91.55%
Yearly Income	n.s.			1.08	1.36	25.25%
Pastor Education	1.93	2.73	41.25%	0.97	1.34	38.10%
Culture						
Black Church Distinctiveness	n.s.			1.13	1.27	12.30%
Black Pride Sermons	2.19	2.58	18.02%	0.98	1.27	30.33%
Church Age	2.41	2.99	23.78%	1.17	1.52	30.18%
Allows Jazz	2.58	2.91	12.91%	n.s.		
South	2.58	2.36	−8.52%	n.s.		
Process						
Methodist	n.s.			n.s.		
Baptist	n.s.			n.s.		
COGIC	n.s.			n.s.		

Source: Lincoln and Mamiya Urban sample.
Note: Both social activism and political activism are five-point indexes.
The predicted values are calculated from OLS regression analysis.
n.s. = not significant at .1 level (two-tailed test).

the low end of education to the high end increases political activism by 38 percent; moving from the low end of church income to the high end increases political activism by 25 percent.

The cultural aspects of the church also provide dramatic effects, as age and Black religious consciousness promote church political engagement. As in the case of social activism, older churches are more likely to engage in political activism. The most interesting effect is in churches that embrace Black religious consciousness, which participate in 30 percent more activities than churches that do not do so. In addition, churches that teach children about the distinctiveness of the Black church participate in 12 percent more activities than do churches that do not provide such teaching. Churches that take part in both activities increase their political engagement by 52 percent over churches that participate in neither activity.

While the findings indicate that resources have the most dramatic effect on social and political activism, culture is not far behind. Moreover, changes in resources such as membership and income are more difficult to achieve and sustain than are cultural changes. What children learn in Sunday school and what pastors incorporate into their sermons are easier to adjust than membership size and income. Resources are important for explaining church engagement, but culture should not be ignored.

Finally, these findings indicate that religious tradition does not matter. However, tradition may indirectly affect social and political activism. COGIC churches significantly trail their counterparts in terms of members, church income, and pastors' educational levels. Baptist churches have the most financial resources, while the Methodists have the most educated pastors. One of the most important cultural aspects is Black consciousness: COGIC churches are significantly less likely than Methodist churches to have Black pride sermons or teach children about the distinctiveness of the Black church. In this case, tradition's effect on social and political action appears through resources and church culture. Baptist activism stems from resources, such as members and income, while pastoral training and Black consciousness account for Methodist activism. Additional analysis of the relationship between resources and culture finds that churches with greater financial capital and pastors possessing higher levels of education are more likely to integrate Black consciousness into their culture. These findings support the argument that resources and process shape church culture.

2004 and 2005 Religion and Society Surveys

In addition to the data provided by Lincoln and Mamiya's study, the 2004 and 2005 Religion and Society surveys also illuminate the role of resources, culture, and process in shaping church activism. The 2004 version of the survey was conducted in July during the AME General Conference in Indianapolis. The survey yielded 315 respondents. The 2005 version of the survey was conducted in June during the NBC's Congress of Christian Education in Houston. The 2005 survey yielded 347 respondents. The surveys targeted clergy and highly active members. In the 2004 survey, 25.7 percent of respondents reported being members of the clergy, and 88.8 percent of the members reported holding some form of church position. In the 2005 survey, 25 percent of the respondents reported being members of the clergy, and 85 percent of the other respondents reported holding church positions. The survey examined clergy and members' attitudes toward religious experiences and toward church and political matters. Because of the timing of the surveys, the differences between the groups cannot be explained. The AME respondents were surveyed in the middle of the 2004 campaign season, while the NBC respondents were surveyed seven months after the 2004 election. While the survey findings do not permit generalization, they do provide a picture of church activities and some of the organizational dynamics that affect church activism.

This section of the quantitative analysis uses descriptive analysis to provide an updated picture of church-based political engagement and how organizational dynamics relate to it.[1] Table 3 shows the survey results using five measures of church-based political engagement. Contact with public officials is the most popular of these activities. Close to two-

TABLE 3. Comparison of AME and NBC Church Engagement

	AME	NBC
Public official spoke during the service	41.3	38.5
Invited public official to meeting	54.3	46.2
Allowed political organization to meet at the church	23.9	19.2
Church served as a polling place	19.6	7.7
Church held a political forum	28.3	3.8
Political Action Index	1.7	1.2

Source: 2004 and 2005 Religion and Society Surveys.

Note: To prevent overrepresentation of congregations, these results are limited to the responses of pastors.

fifths (AME, 41.3 percent; NBC, 38.5 percent) of both of the samples reported having public officials speak during services. More than half of the
AME respondents (54.3 percent) and nearly half of the NBC respondents (46.2 percent) report that their churches invite public officials to
meetings. The churches were less active in facilitating political action:
23.9 percent of the AME respondents and 19.2 percent of the NBC respondents report that their churches allow meetings by political organizations. Nearly one-fifth of the AME respondents (19.6 percent) and just
7.7 percent of the NBC respondents report that their churches serve as
polling places. The most common activity is hosting political forum,
which 28.3 percent of the AME respondents but only 3.8 percent of
NBC respondents reported took place at their churches.

A pattern of behavior among churches thus emerges. The next step in
the analysis is a bivariate examination of how resources and culture shape
church-based activism. An examination of correlations with measures of
resources and culture finds that these factors have a significant relationship with church-based political engagement.[2] Beginning with resources,
larger churches were more active overall for both samples. For the AME
sample, size significantly promoted all activities except for serving as a
polling place. For the NBC sample, respondents in larger churches were
more likely to report that their churches allowed political organizations
to meet, served as polling places, and held political forums. Moving to
culture, respondents in both samples who reported that their churches
displayed Black images of biblical figures were more likely to report
higher levels of church activism. For AME churches, having Black images significantly promoted all activities except having officials speak at
the church and holding political forums. For the NBC sample, the presence of Black images promoted all of the activities except having public
officials speak and serving as polling places. Additional cultural markers
such as region and community also had a significant relationship with engagement. Southern AME respondents were less likely to report having
public officials speak, while NBC respondents from the South were more
likely to report that their churches served as polling places. For both
samples, community shaped engagement. Both AME and NBC respondents who reported that their churches were located in the inner city reported higher overall levels of engagement on the part of their churches.

These findings coincide with those of Lincoln and Mamiya. Resources, culture, and process play a role in shaping church-based politi-

cal activism. Larger churches are more likely to be engaged, as are churches with a culture of Black consciousness.

CONCLUSION

Attempts to explain church political activism must pay attention to the churches themselves. Issues of resources, process, and culture shape churches, which in turn shape members' and pastors' capabilities and decisions. The literature and the case studies show that these three factors are important in understanding church-based activism. A lack of either financial or physical resources constrains church activism. Second, the guidelines that govern decision making and activism can also constrain activism by churches. Finally, churches' understandings of themselves shape their propensity for political activism.

Resources had the most dramatic effects on activism, but culture did not trail far behind. In addition, creating a church culture that embraces a Black religious consciousness is easier than increasing membership or income. Finally, process had no direct effect but influenced resources and culture. The differences between the traditions in terms of activism stemmed from differences in regard to resources and culture.

Chapters 3 and 4 provide a detailed discussion of the moderating factors in the negotiation between pastors and members. Chapters 5 and 6 offer an in-depth examination of pastors and members to better understand the types of clergy who call for church-based political engagement and the members who respond to that call.

CHAPTER 5

Who Will Make the Call? Pastoral Support for Church-Based Political Action

It is the firm conviction of the writers that the Negro pastor is one of the freest as well as most influential men on the American platform today. (Mays and Nicholson 1969, 289)

Black pastors are viewed as community leaders, championing community causes and playing a vital role in the defense and advancement of Black interests. As with the leaders of all organizations, church activities begin to reflect pastors' interests. Differences in leadership create differences in organizational outputs. Yet some Black clergy choose to take on the role of political elite, and others do not. This chapter examines the reasons behind these variations, addressing the forms of activism of which clergy approve as well as the determinants that lead clergy to convey the need for political action. I first discuss the factors that lead clergy to call for activism before moving on to a qualitative analysis of these determinants using the interviews of clergy from the Detroit and Austin case studies. The chapter then presents a quantitative examination of the determinants of clergy activism before concluding with a discussion of these various factors as well as the place of clergy in the creation and maintenance of political churches.

CONVEYANCE

Conveyance refers to a pastor's communication of a need for political engagement on the part of the church. Conveyance is expressed in the form of cues as well as direct action. Because the pastor "provides a face to the organization" (Scott and Lane 2000), conveyance is a primary prerequi-

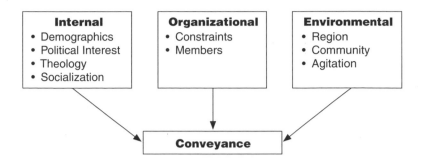

Fig. 2. Internal, organizational, and environmental determinants of conveyance

site for the formation and maintenance of a political church. For a church to become politicized, political identity must possess some level of salience with the pastor, who must convey this salience to members by attempting to take or encourage political action and to increase political awareness.

Implicitly built into the concept of conveyance is the notion that the pastor acts as the catalyst for raising a church's political identity. While both the pastor and the members ultimately must have aligning perceptions of the proper role of political activities in the organization's functioning, the leader must undertake mobilizing efforts to induce a change in the salience level (Olson 1965; Rosenstone and Hansen 1993; Verba, Schlozman, and Brady 1995).

But what determines whether a pastor will convey the importance of a political identity? The model of the propensity to convey in figure 2 highlights the internal, organizational, and environmental factors that affect pastoral decisions. Conveyance fluctuates over time as a function of these determinants. As they change, conveyance changes as well.

The internal determinants that explain the propensity to convey include factors such as basic demographics, political interest, theology, and socialization. Demographic characteristics such as sex and education can strongly affect the propensity to convey. As with political participation in general, education should have a positive relationship with the pastor's willingness to convey the salience of political participation (Guth et al. 1997). Sex should also matter—not necessarily in regard to the level of conveyance but rather in determining the types of issues on which clergy focus. The literature shows that gender roles and varying pressures lead female clergy to view their roles differently from male clergy (Crawford,

Deckman, and Braun 2001; Olson, Crawford, and Guth 2000). Chapter 2's discussion of Rev. Red supports this argument. The theology of a pastor—the way the pastor interprets religious doctrine—guides the decision to become active individually or to utilize the church as a vessel for social action (Guth et al. 1997). Pastors who have religious justifica-tions for engaging the political process are more likely to convey the importance of political activity by their churches. High levels of political interest can promote conveyance; the more interested pastors are in politics, the more likely they are to express its importance to their congregations. Finally, socialization plays a major role in shaping the propensity to convey. Clergy who have experienced church-based political action in the past should be more likely to support church involvement in political matters.

Organizational constraints act as boundaries to the types of activities in which the organization can participate (Simon 1964). Such constraints can arise from denominational factors and/or through attitudes toward religious figures and traditions (Childs-Brown 1980). Through rules and practices, organizational constraints shape behavior within the organization and perceptions of the organization in society. As chapter 4 shows, the differences between the three major Black Protestant traditions can shape political engagement. In addition, organizational constraints take the form of resources. As chapters 2 and 4 demonstrate, resources are positively correlated with church-based political action.

The pastor-member relationship is one of the most important determinants in understanding pastor action. All leadership theories stress that the leader's perception of members' wants plays a vital role in leader performance and decision making (Deluga 1998; Kirkpatrick and Locke 1995; Peters, Hartke, and Pohlmann 1985; Schriesheim, Neider, and Scandura 1998). Many pastors may want to keep their churches apolitical, but if members demand political mobilization, pastors are likely to respond by transforming the organizations (Chong 1991; Lee 2003; Charles Payne 1995). Pastors who perceive members as wanting to keep the church out of political matters are less likely to convey messages supporting church-based political activism (Guth et al. 1997; Jelen 1993).

As chapter 3 highlights, the church's environment is represented by the social and political context of the institution. The environment continually shapes the pastor's perceptions about issues and the need for activism. As economic, political, and social events occur, the propensity to convey the political identity should fluctuate. Crawford and Olson (2001) document that clergy serving churches in poor neighborhoods are more likely to address social needs than are clergy serving churches in more affluent neighborhoods. In addition, concerns arise about the level of comfort in the environment. Clergy who feel that members' interests are threatened should be more likely to call for action than those who feel comfortable in their environment. Clergy are expected to become political entrepreneurs when their surrounding environment has high levels of agitation.

ASSESSING THE DETERMINANTS OF CONVEYANCE

An analysis of face-to-face interviews with ten clergy from the Detroit and Austin case studies provides an in-depth examination of pastors' justifications for church-based political action as well as their various views regarding church activism. To complement these data, the second part of the analysis utilizes two surveys to further examine how these factors shape the attitudes and actions of clergy. I again employ the 2004 and 2005 Religion and Society surveys, focusing on clergy responses to examine support for church-based activism as well as levels of actual activism. The second survey, the 2002 Cooperative Clergy Survey, is a nationwide survey of clergy that allows for a higher level of analysis of conveyance and its determinants.

Qualitative Assessment of Conveyance

The Detroit and Austin case studies demonstrate that pastors are primary determinants in setting their churches' courses. This section provides an in-depth examination of pastors' attitudes. First, I analyze support and justifications for church-based political activism. A discussion of the boundaries clergy place on church-based political activism follows, highlighting areas pastors feel have been neglected. The section concludes with a discussion of members' role in helping clergy reach their goals.

All of the clergy expressed a need for church involvement in political matters and acknowledged their position as part of the political elite. However, they gave differing justifications for this status: many of the pastors cited theological reasons, while others based their support on socialization. Those using the theological justification gave biblical references and mentioned specific schools of thought such as liberation theology. For example, Rev. Green argued that churches could not ignore political issues:

I think that we cannot honestly embrace the things of Jesus Christ if we do not have a sense of political activism. When he walked this earth, he went against not only the religious system, but the political system also. He challenged people to be socially conscious to the point where he says, "When you've done it to the least of those, you've done it to me." I interpret that as Jesus saying he takes personally how we take [care of] those who seem powerless.

Rev. Brown based his position on his research on liberation theology:

That comes from how I was trained. I guess in seminary—my seminary allowed me to explore every dimension. And my dimension just happened to be Black liberation or liberation theology. I really appreciated that about my seminary. I really focused on African American liberation theology, and I was able to do a kind of specialty there. I was thoroughly convinced that that is part of who we are as a mission role, not only as a church but as Christians as individuals.

Those who saw their activism as based on socialization argued that political involvement was part of their understanding of the church. According to Rev. Maroon, the former pastor of Red Memorial, "That's all I've ever known. . . . I grew up in it. My father was [politically active]. Martin Luther King came to our house. So I grew up in it so I don't know pastoring any other way."

Rev. Red agreed:

As far as I'm concerned, we have no choice. Politics started in the church, and in order to be effective within the community, in order to meet the needs of the members of the church, we have to be involved in the political arena. We have to know certain individuals. We have to be able to cut through the bureaucracy. And if you're not involved, your hands are tied! You're helpless!

Rev. Orange noted that his commitment to political engagement came from his father, a minister who worked closely with Martin Luther King Jr. and others in the civil rights movement.

These two types of justification are not mutually exclusive. Several clergy who gave historical explanations for their support of church involvement in politics also gave biblical references that shaped their view of how the church should operate in the world.

Almost all of the pastors also justified their activism on the need to protect the Black community. Rev. Maroon, for example, based his support on the church's historical role as a central institution in African American life:

> The only way that the views and the needs and the objectives of the African American community could be heard was through the church. So whether we want to admit it or not, there is an explicit link between the life of the church and the social and political life of the community that it serves. This is steeped in history. All of the great political leaders that have had major impact both in centuries past and in the present time have all had their roots in their African American religious experience.

Rev. Maroon also argued that churches and clergy had a moral responsibility to become involved to make sure that their goals were achieved in a responsible manner:

> Who is going to lead if the religious community doesn't lead in the community? Then the riffraff leads. So therefore if the riffraff is leading, you are asking for chaos. In the case of Vernon Jordan being shot in Fort Wayne [in 1980], if preachers hadn't stood at the door, there would have been a total race riot in Fort Wayne. It never happened. And the reason why it didn't happen was because preachers took the leadership role.

Many of these clergy defined political involvement as electoral participation—voter registration, holding forums, or inviting candidates to services. Others saw political matters in terms of goals. Rev. Brown, for example, described political involvement as "advocacy," seeing the church as working to promote justice for the less privileged. Rev. Brown viewed the church as a place for healing and believed that defending people's rights formed part of the healing process. Similarly, Rev. Orange saw church involvement in politics as making sure that all people were treated with a certain level of dignity.

Clergy are very open to seeing churches involved in political matters, but they do not see all political activity as appropriate for the church. Pastors highlighted several activities as having the potential to violate the church's true purpose, with nearly all of those interviewed citing having candidates address the congregation as an unnecessary intrusion on the worship service. Rev. White stated,

> I'm very reluctant to let politicians come into my service and disrupt my service. There are special occasions where I do allow politicians to come in on a Sunday morning—very limited. But I don't believe in turning the church into a political convention or anything like that.

Rev. Green argued that politicians exploit churches when they take part in these activities:

> Politicians take the church for granted when they do that. They slide in, they make a five-minute speech, they rah-rah, and then there's no accountability. But when I sit you down at the table and my members say to you, "What are you going to do about these issues?" you are looking people straight in the eye and you're answering questions and you're making commitments, and they're able to measure your integrity.

Several pastors wanted to make sure they were aware of how they used their influence in the church and the community. According to Rev. Green,

> What I feel is inappropriate is for me to use my influence as a preacher to incite an emotional response from vulnerable people in order that I personally or my ministry in particular might be benefited by that.
>
> Any form of exploitive tactics that are used for a self-serving agenda I think are totally inappropriate. I think it is altogether appropriate that the church bring to bear its numbers—I should use the numbers of my congregation or to make a statement to the political gatekeepers that we will show up at city council, three, four, five, six, seven hundred of us, and we will pack the place, just by visible presence to say, "Look, this is who we represent in the community."
>
> But I think that anything that exploits people, I think that anything that is done from their monetary gain without regard to helping the people which should be helped is totally inappropriate, and quite frankly just too much of that goes on each and every day.

A pastor's decision to run for public office can be a controversial issue, with many observers seeing such political involvement as presenting a large set of conflicts. All of the clergy I interviewed supported the idea of pastors running for office, and several reported holding appointed positions and being asked to run for office. However, only Rev. Ivory, the former pastor of White Chapel, had won an election—for a position on the state school board. He worked hard to separate his roles as an elected official and as a pastor—for example, by refraining from discussing board-related issues in front of the congregation. He also made sure to fulfill what the members saw as his core responsibilities as pastor.

Rev. Maroon emphatically supported the idea that a pastor could run for office:

> He's a citizen of the United States, isn't he? What's to stop him from not? I mean, just because you're a preacher, you shouldn't run for political office? That's ludicrous. I mean, you're a citizen and you pay your taxes like everybody else. You have the right to run like any other individual that wants to run.

Although he never sought elected office, Rev. Maroon was very active in partisan politics. He worked with the Republican Party from the mid-1960s until 1980, before he joined Red Memorial. He worked primarily in the state party, serving as a delegate in the state convention. His support for the party was sparked by its willingness to help his church:

> The time that I spent in the Republican Party was the time when any time I went to the Democrats for anything, they were not willing to help. [But] each time I had [gone to the Republicans] with the issues that were concerning me and issues concerning my church or whatever, they came to my rescue, so I got pretty involved in it.

His loyalties changed when he moved to another state and found that the Democratic Party was far more supportive than the Republican Party. He also dropped his involvement in partisan politics because it required too much energy and he needed to devote more time to his church.

The clergy whom I interviewed believed that churches should expand their issue involvement, criticizing the Black church's lack of response to several issues they felt were central to the status of the Black community. Rev. Blue, for example, expressed his dissatisfaction with his denomination's lack of attention to the issues of abortion and the pending war with Iraq, noting, "I think that our members ought to know where we stand on certain issues." Rev. Red, the lone female pastor in the sample, expressed her dissatisfaction with the fact that the Black church has remained focused solely on racial issues.

> I think we sat on the sideline on the abortion issue. It didn't mean anything to us. I think we didn't speak to environmental issues. I think we were singularly focused on race parity. And what happened is [that] marching didn't work anymore, and a lot of what we thought about no longer was salient, and I think we slept. And I think we thought that we've made it, we got it, and then we look up and the school system is worst. . . . Some of those issues now that are affecting the urban area are pollution issues and environmental issues, . . . and we didn't speak to them—and health issues, we didn't speak to them. We spoke to making sure that we could get into the hospital, but we didn't speak to the health issue, and I think Whites spoke to those from a White perspective, and there was nobody speaking to it from our perspective, and now we're trying to play catch-up.

Finally, Rev. Orange, Rev. Green, and Rev. Red called for Black churches to pay attention to gender issues. Rev. Green instituted sex-segregated groups to allow male and female congregants to address issues they felt were important. As chapter 2 notes, Rev. Orange has worked to confront domestic abuse and to increase the presence of female clergy in his church, although many Baptist churches do not permit female clergy. Rev. Red was attempting indirectly to address gender issues by working them into her sermons as well as by changing the language used in the service to promote a gender-neutral vision of God. She planned to address such issues more directly in the future.

Clergy see part of their job as being spokespersons for their congregations and communities, but they know that the activities in which they engage as well as the success of those activities depends on church members. Rev. Red, for example, cites members as the main reason she has not taken a more head-on approach to matters of gender. A segment of the congregation opposed the hiring of a female pastor, further complicating the congregation's stance regarding gender issues.

> Some of the men say I overaddress [the subject of gender], and some of the women say I underaddress it.

Conversely, church members have supported Rev. Orange's attempts to advanced his concerns regarding gender issues, as in the matter of the church's hiring of female clergy.

All of the clergy understand that they need members' support to accomplish goals. However, they also believe that at times they must act even without congregants' support, and in such instances, they express their dissatisfaction with church members. Said Rev. Maroon,

> Would I blame them if [an important] issue did not pass and then statistics show that most of us didn't go vote? Then I sure do raise it, because I think it needs to be raised. We have the right to complain. You have a right as a citizen to vote on issues that are set on the ballot or issues that are set in the community, to address the council in terms of need in the area. If you don't do those things, then you don't have the right to ream nobody.

After learning that Travis County was the only Texas county in which a majority of voters failed to support a constitutional amendment banning same-sex marriages, Rev. Black expressed his dissatisfaction with his congregation.

Other clergy found that church members responded to their pastors' calls and even spurred them on to increased activism. As Rev. Brown stated,

> Every year we do annual evaluations, and that's kind of where it began to rain through a little bit. One particular year, we asked questions about what they would like to see, and one of them was that they would like to see our pastor be more involved in the community. I was like, "All right! Be careful what you ask for now." I love it here, because that is what I needed. I wanted the affirmation from them about where they were before I went out there and took a position that I felt I wasn't informed enough about how to represent the church, before I got too involved.

Thus a great deal of support for clergy activism exists, as do some limitations on their activities. Some pastors feel they must be careful about the issues to which they attach themselves, while others feel that their churches need more attention than do social or political issues. Finally, members play an important role in setting social and political goals. Clergy describe members' support as key to effective social/political campaigns and high levels of activism. Clergy realize that they potentially wield great influence over their members and take that role quite seriously, paying great attention to maintaining their independence from outside forces. Pastors recognize their role as political elites and accept that role when they deem doing so to be appropriate.

Quantitative Assessment of Conveyance

This section examines survey data on clergy to better understand the patterns of Black clergy behavior. The first aspect of this quantitative analysis will come from the 2004 and 2005 Religion and Society Surveys, which are ideal for addressing the issues posed in this chapter. The survey is designed to capture conveyance as well as its determinants. The 2004 version of the survey, which was administered to the African Methodist Episcopal (AME) sample, yields seventy-nine clergy respondents—forty-six pastors and thirty-three members of the ministerial staff. The 2005 version, which was administered to the National Baptist Convention, USA (NBC) sample, yields seventy-four clergy, including twenty-six pastors. The survey's nature prevents higher-level statistical analysis; however, like the interviews, it allows for an in-depth descriptive analysis of conveyance and how it correlates with its determinants.

The analysis of the Religion and Society surveys begins with clergy attitudes toward church-based and clergy political activism. Table 4 shows clergy support for church action. Clergy are willing to open their church doors to engage the governmental process. Clergy most support having churches invite public officials to meetings (AME 65.4 percent, NBC 36.6 percent) and serve as polling places (AME 53.9 percent, NBC 32.9 percent). Engaging the political system in a partisan matter, such as allowing political organizations to meet in churches (AME 42.3 percent, NBC 20.7 percent), received very low support. Clergy support the idea of using their status to encourage members to vote (AME 85.3 percent, NBC 67.1 percent), to address political issues (AME 76.0 percent, NBC 53.7 percent), and to contact officials (AME 58.2 percent, NBC 39.0 percent). However, clergy offer the least support for activities that would be seen as abuses of power, such as instructing congregants about what candidates to support (AME 16.5 percent, NBC 11.0 percent), forming political action committees (AME 38.0 percent, NBC 17.1 percent), and criticizing public officials (AME 31.7 percent, NBC 18.3 percent).

The survey also asked clergy about the role of churches and clergy in political matters. The 2004 version of the survey included several questions about how churches and clergy should operate. The findings show that clergy strongly support their role as political elite. Only 29.6 percent supported the belief that clergy should not express political views that differ from those of church members. Only 28 percent of the clergy believed that they should never bring political matters into the worship service; in contrast, 84.0 percent supported the idea that Black places of worship should be involved in political matters.

Whereas these questions tapped attitudes toward churches and clergy in general, the 2005 version of the survey sought to ascertain how clergy believed their churches should react to certain changes in the sociopolitical environment. Respondents were asked to rank on a sevenpoint scale, with 7 indicating very involved and 1 indicating not involved,

TABLE 4. Support for Church and Clergy Political Participation

	AME	NBC
Support for Church Actions		
Allow officials to speak during worship	29.9	32.9
Invite public officials to meetings	65.4	36.6
Allow political organizations to meet in church	42.3	20.7
Serve as a polling place	53.9	32.9
Hold political forums	52.6	29.3
Support for Clergy Actions		
Criticize public officials	31.7	18.3
Speak out on a political issue	76.0	53.7
Take part in a protest	55.7	32.9
Work with a political party	40.5	19.5
Tell the congregation for whom to vote	16.5	11.0
Form a political action committee	38.0	17.1
Hand out voter guides	45.6	30.5
Comment on political issues during sermon	46.8	36.6
Run for office	48.1	19.5
Contact a public official	58.2	39.0
Encourage congregation to vote	85.3	67.1
Place of Clergy and Churches in Politics		
Clergy who have different political views than their members should not express their views.	29.6	
Black churches or places of worship should be involved in political matters.	84.0	
Clergy should never bring political matters into the worship service.	28.0	
Response to Environmental Shocks		
How involved would you want your church to be in this situation?		
Social problem in your community		5.6
Reports of police brutality in your community		5.8
Reports of racial discrimination in your community		6.3
Plan to open an abortion clinic in your community		4.4
Plan to guarantee homosexuals the same rights as others		4.5

Source: 2004 and 2005 Religion and Society Surveys.

the degree to which they would want their churches to become involved in five different scenarios in their immediate communities: a social problem, reports of police brutality, reports of racial discrimination, a plan to open an abortion clinic, and a plan to guarantee homosexuals the same rights as others. As table 4 shows, clergy wanted the highest level of involvement on the part of their churches when there were reports of racial discrimination (6.3), followed by police brutality (5.8), a social problem (5.6), giving homosexuals the same rights as others (4.5), and the opening of an abortion clinic (4.4). A comparison of the means finds that the degree to which clergy wanted their churches to be involved in the racial discrimination situation was significantly higher than all of the other situations. In addition, the level of involvement for a social problem and reports of police brutality were significantly higher than for the final two scenarios. These results speak to some of the same concerns addressed in the interviews. A strong desire for involvement existed for explicitly racial issues, but nonracial issues did not spark action to the same degree.

How do various internal and external factors lead to conveyance? The following analysis uses pairwise correlations to examine the extent to which the various internal, organizational, and environmental factors shape support for conveyance.

An examination of internal factors shows that in both the AME and NBC samples, pastors are far more supportive of church-based political action than clergy who do not head churches. The AME pastors are more likely to support church and clergy action in general as well as the involvement of Black places of worship in political matters. In the NBC sample, pastors are more likely to support overall church action as well as call for higher levels of church involvement when there are social problems or reports of police brutality. Age, gender, and education also shape support for conveyance. For the AME sample, younger clergy are more likely to support all forms of clergy action, while older clergy are more likely to agree with church involvement in political matters. Older NBC clergy call for more church involvement when a social problem occurs. In both the AME and NBC samples, female clergy are less likely to support church action. The female NBC clergy call for lower levels of church involvement when their communities face social problems or reports of police brutality. For the AME clergy, female clergy are less likely to agree with church involvement in political matters but are also less likely to agree with the statement that clergy should not express views that conflict with those of their congregants. This finding further highlights the difficulties that female clergy face. Their lower level of support may stem from their need to legitimize their position as leaders within their church before they can engage the community. Education correlated with aspects of conveyance only for the AME sample, as clergy with higher levels of education were more supportive of church and clergy action and less likely to agree that politics should never enter the worship service.

Pastors' levels of political interest also shaped support for the various forms of church and clergy action. For the NBC sample, political interest is both positively and significantly correlated with all of the forms of action except overall church action. For the AME sample, political interest significantly reduces agreement with the belief that conflicting views should not be expressed. An additional measure of political outlook, political ideology, did not significantly correlate with any of the forms of activism for both samples. An examination of the correlations with the theological perspective finds that religious orthodoxy promotes support for activism among both AME and NBC clergy. Orthodoxy is positively correlated with AME clergy's support of church and clergy action. For the NBC clergy, orthodoxy promotes support for clergy action to encourage higher levels of church involvement in social problems and respond to police brutality. In addition to orthodoxy, those who subscribe to Black theology—that is, those who believe that Christ is Black, that God is on the side of Blacks, and that churches should display Black images of religious figures—are more likely to support clergy action in both samples. Moreover, support for Black theology increases the NBC clergy's support for church involvement in social problems and issues of police brutality. For the AME clergy, belief in Black theology promotes support for overall church activism and reduces support for the belief that conflicting views should not be expressed.

An assessment of the measures of socialization shows that generational differences and exposure to Black institutions shape conveyance. The generational differences are captured through the analysis of three age cohorts—those socialized before the civil rights movement (born before 1944), those socialized during the movement (born between 1944 and 1963), and those socialized after the movement (born after 1964).[1] All of the cohort effects are found in the AME sample. The AME clergy socialized before the movement are less likely to support church and clergy action and are more likely to support the idea that politics should never be brought into the worship service. No significant correlations exist for those socialized during the movement, but those socialized after the movement are more supportive of clergy action. Access to Black institutions correlates positively with support for conveyance. AME clergy who experience high levels of exposure to Black media are more likely to support church and clergy action as well as church involvement in political matters. NBC clergy in Black fraternal organizations are more likely to support church and clergy action. Finally, among AME clergy, membership in Black organizations promotes support for church action and involvement in political matters, while among NBC, such membership promotes church involvement when racial discrimination is present in the community.

With the relationship between the internal determinants and conveyance established, the analysis shifts to the organizational determinants. Among AME clergy, a higher level of weekly church attendance is significantly and positively correlated with support for church action. NBC clergy who have experienced major conflicts regarding political matters are less likely to want their churches to become involved if social problems arise in their community. Finally, overall member influence does not significantly correlate with the various measures of conveyance. The only case in which such a correlation exists is church involvement in politics. AME clergy who feel that their members influence their political decisions are more likely to feel that the church should be involved in political matters. In addition to the issue of member influence, it is also important to consider the degree to which clergy feel they and their members are in ideological agreement. For AME clergy, having members perceived as more conservative is positively related to support for church and clergy action. A more conservative congregation leads to less support for not expressing conflicting views and not allowing politics in the worship service. Having more liberal members reduces both the AME clergy's support for clergy action and the level of church involvement for which NBC clergy call when a social problem arises. AME clergy who feel that they and their members are in rough ideological agreement are more likely to support not bringing politics into the worship service. For the NBC clergy, having members with approximately the same ideology calls for church involvement when social, brutality, and racial problems arose in the community.

Environment has a significant correlation with action only for AME clergy in the South, who are less supportive of clergy action. NBC clergy, whose churches are located in the inner city, are more likely to support clergy action but call for less church involvement when confronted with racial discrimination. AME clergy with churches located in inner cities or suburbs are also more likely to support church action. Those in smaller urban areas, small towns, or rural areas are less supportive of clergy action and church involvement in politics. These findings may indicate differences in education, as NBC clergy in urban areas have significantly higher levels of education than those in small towns and rural areas. Finally, strong beliefs in the persistence of racial discrimination do not significantly shape conveyance, perhaps because of the lack of variance; more than 80 percent of both the AME and NBC clergy rate 10 or higher on the twelve-point discrimination scale.

These correlations show that these internal, organizational, and environmental factors strongly shape clergy support for taking on the role of political elite. Positions as pastors or members of a ministerial staff, along with demographics, political interest, theological outlook, and socialization, correlate well with the various measures of support for church and clergy action. Beyond the individual, the organization and environment also shape support. More liberal congregations exhibited less support for clerical activism than did more conservative congregations, perhaps because more liberal clergy historically have been politically involved. While the correlations do not indicate that ideology has a significant impact on conveyance, the effect of ideology relative to the congregation does. Clergy who perceive their congregants as more conservative may see a greater need for political involvement by churches to broaden members' views, whereas clergy who view their members as more liberal may want to prevent their churches from becoming too involved. Age differences between clergy and church members may also play a role. Clergy in the pre–civil rights movement generation are more likely to feel that they align ideologically with their members, while those in the post–civil rights generation are more likely to believe that their members are more conservative. Because churches are filled primarily with older individuals, clergy in the earlier generation may have more in common with their congregations because they share similar experiences, while younger clergy face difficulties because of generational gaps.

The analysis now moves on to examine pastors' activities in relation to conveyance, with the sample size reduced only to pastors to allow for a better understanding of how conveyance comes about. This analysis begins with the examination of the frequency of pastors' political actions, as table 5 illustrates. Encouraging congregants to vote (AME 62.5 percent,

NBC 53.9 percent) and speaking out on political issues (AME 67.4 percent, NBC 57.7 percent) represent the two most popular activities, while the pastors were reluctant to instruct church members about how to vote (AME 17.4 percent, NBC 19.2 percent). Activities that took pastors out of the pulpit were less common; of these activities, the pastors were most likely to contact public officials (AME 43.5 percent, NBC 38.5 percent) and least likely to run for public office (AME 8.7 percent, NBC 7.7 percent).

Clergy may also use their position informally to influence members, a phenomenon the survey addresses by asking questions about the frequency with which pastors have conversations with their members about politics. Among AME clergy, 51.3 percent talk to their members about political issues at least once a month, as do 34.7 percent of the NBC clergy. This difference likely results from the fact that the AME respondents were surveyed during a presidential election year. Further analysis finds that politics was a less prominent conversation topic for NBC pastors and their congregants than for the AME sample, which was more likely to discuss community and social issues.

As in the analysis of support for conveyance, I performed a set of pairwise correlations to examine how internal and external factors shape actual conveyance. Younger AME pastors are more likely to take part in

TABLE 5. Actual Reported Activities of Pastors

Actual Pastor Actions	AME	NBC
Criticized public officials	23.9	30.8
Spoke out on a political issue	67.4	57.7
Took part in a protest	30.4	19.2
Worked with a political party	26.1	26.9
Told the congregation for whom to vote	17.4	19.2
Formed a political action committee	28.3	11.5
Handed out voter guides	37.0	30.8
Commented on political issues during sermon	52.2	42.3
Ran for office	8.7	7.7
Contacted a public official	43.5	38.5
Encouraged congregation to vote	65.2	53.9
Monthly conversations with members		
Talks to members about political issues	51.3	34.7
Talks to members about social issues		57.1
Talks to members about community issues		70.5

Source: 2004 and 2005 Religion and Society Surveys.

overall political activism. For the NBC sample, younger pastors more frequently talk to their members about politics. Black theology boosts overall action for both NBC and AME pastors and is positively correlated with political statements for NBC pastors and direct action for AME pastors. AME pastors from the pre–civil rights movement cohort are less likely to take part in political activities overall, while those socialized during the movement are more likely to take part in direct action. NBC pastors socialized before the movement are less likely to talk to their members about politics than are pastors socialized after the movement. AME pastors with high levels of exposure to Black media are more likely to make political statements, while membership in Black fraternal organizations boosts overall activism for NBC pastors.

Shifting to the external determinants, the church's weekly attendance positively correlates with talking to members about politics. Pastoral tenure has a negative relationship with speaking about politics for AME pastors and with talking to members for NBC clergy: the longer pastors have been at their churches, the less likely they are to take part in these activities. This finding is counterintuitive, given the belief that pastors with longer tenures should feel more open to talking to members about political issues. However, longer tenures also mean that pastors and congregants may know more about each other's stances on issues and thus may have less need to discuss such matters. AME pastors who report having conflicts with members about political beliefs are more likely to report taking part in direct political action. AME pastors who perceive their members as being more liberal talk less frequently to them about politics than do such pastors who view their members as more conservative.

AME clergy in inner cities are more likely to make political statements, while those in small towns are less likely to take part in political activism. NBC clergy in inner cities are more active overall, while those in small towns are less likely to make political statements.

This examination of clergy confirms the discussion of the determinants of conveyance. The internal, organizational, and environmental determinants do not correlate with actual activism as well as with support for activism. This finding results in part from the fact that support for these activities does not necessarily translate into taking part in them. On average, these clergy participated in a considerable number of activities. Of the 11 political activities listed, AME pastors averaged 4.0, while NBC pastors averaged 3.4. Although this number may not appear large, political activism is not pastors' primary duty. This analysis demonstrates that individual traits as well organizational and environmental exposure play important roles in shaping conveyance.

This analysis allows only for a descriptive discussion of conveyance and its determinants. The next set of analyses allows for multivariate analysis to better isolate the internal and external factors that shape conveyance. To assess the role of Black churches in contemporary American politics, I have employed the 2002 Cooperative Clergy Survey, a nationwide mail survey of 7,829 clergy representing eighteen denominations, including 282 Black clergy, to whom this analysis will be limited. The survey specifically targets clergy in two predominantly Black denominations, the AME and the Church of God in Christ (COGIC), with 83 respondents from each denomination. This survey includes a large number of questions related to conveyance and its determinants.

To account for the multidimensionality of conveyance, I have created three scales to denote support for the various types of political participation: electoral activism, collective action, and political statements. I am also concerned with how clergy use the power of the pulpit—specifically, the degree to which clergy preach sermons on social justice and morality. Because social justice emphasizes community affairs, it historically has been linked to promoting political participation. Morality sermons, conversely, have been attributed to lower rates of activism because they emphasize individual behavior. I have also created individual indexes for these types of sermons.

With the measurement of conveyance established I now turn to its determinants. The internal factors include issues such as demographics, political interest, theological orientation, and socialization. This analysis accounts for demographics using education and gender. Political interest is accounted for by the degree to which respondents report being interested in political matters. Theological orientation is determined using individual measures of religious orthodoxy and liberation theology, since some scholars have blamed orthodoxy for Black churches' lack of activism. However, recent work such as Calhoun-Brown (1999) has shown that orthodoxy may indirectly increase Black political participation by increasing feelings of Black empowerment. In addition, the Religion and Society surveys have shown a positive and significant correlation between orthodoxy and support for clergy activism. Liberation theology, conversely, has been heralded as a way to bring religious institutions into politics (Rowland 1999). In Rev. Brown's case, training in liberation theology fuels support for church-based political activism. The Religion and

Society surveys also find a positive correlation between Black theology, a variant of liberation theology, and church and clergy activism. The final internal measure is socialization, which is captured through age cohort.

Organizational factors are captured through denomination, resources, and member attitudes. In this case, the denominational measure accounts for membership in the AME, COGIC, or a predominantly White denomination. AME and COGIC clergy differ from Black clergy in predominantly White denominations, as AME and COGIC clergy are more likely to report higher levels of religious orthodoxy and support for liberation theology. Moreover, AME clergy are more likely to report higher levels of political interest. Resources are captured using weekly church attendance. Member attitudes relate to members' levels of support for clergy activism. Finally, the physical environment is captured by the level of urbanicity.[2]

This section of the chapter provides multivariate analyses of the determinants of conveyance. Using ordinary least squares regression, I analyze how these internal, organizational, and environmental factors influence clergy support for political activism as well as actual activities. The section concludes with an analysis of sermon topics.

The results for internal determinants demonstrate that an interest in politics and theological focus play a strong role in shaping conveyance. Table 6 shows that political interest powerfully affects support for clergy action, nearly doubling the intensity of support for electoral activism: a minister with a low level of political interest scores .304, while a pastor at the high end of the scale scores .604. With regard to political statements and collective action, movement from high to low increases intensity of support by 49.19 percent and 58.96 percent, respectively. In addition, liberation theology boosts approval of all of these forms of activism: moving from low to high on the liberation theology scale boosts support for electoral activism by 28.49 percent. For political statements and collective action, the same shift produces increases of 16.73 percent and 23.10 percent, respectively. Along with liberation theology, orthodoxy also significantly affects political statements and collective action: increasing orthodoxy decreases support for political statements by 18.03 percent and decreases support for collective action by 19.33 percent. Cohort differences emerge in regard to political statements and collective action. Those socialized during and after the civil rights movement are more supportive of collective action than those socialized before the movement. Clergy socialized after the civil rights era are 16.83 percent more supportive of political rhetoric than those socialized before. Finally, gender and education also influence the level of support. Female clergy are 14.71 percent more supportive of electoral activism than are male clergy, while movement from low to high levels of education increases support for collective action by 51.54 percent.

Shifting to organizational and environmental determinants, the results show that congregational support has the most dramatic effect on

TABLE 6. Predicted Values of Support for Clergy Action Given Variation in Internal, Organizational, and Environmental Determinants

	Electoral			Political Rhetoric			Collective Action		
	Low	High	Δ	Low	High	Δ	Low	High	Δ
Demographics									
Female	0.527	0.604	14.71%	n.s.			n.s.		
Education	n.s.			n.s.			0.467	0.708	51.54%
Political Orientation									
Political Interest	0.304	0.604	98.88%	0.532	0.794	49.19%	0.459	0.729	58.96%
Theology									
Orthodoxy	n.s.			0.864	0.709	−18.03%	0.794	0.641	−19.33%
Liberation Theology	0.448	0.576	28.49%	0.658	0.768	16.73%	0.576	0.708	23.10%
Socialization									
Pre–Civil Rights Movement	n.s.				0.677			0.582	
Civil Rights Movement Generation	n.s.				0.726			0.658	
Post–Civil Rights Movement	n.s.				0.791			0.725	
Organizational									
Other		0.527		n.s.			n.s.		
AME		0.636		n.s.			n.s.		
COGIC		0.609		n.s.			n.s.		
Weekly Attendance	0.566	0.433	−23.49%	n.s.			n.s.		
Congregation Support	0.449	0.573	27.53%	0.551	0.828	50.22%	0.568	0.711	25.26%
Environment									
Urban	n.s.			n.s.			n.s.		

Source: 2002 Cooperative Clergy Survey.

Note: n.s. = not significant at .1 level (two-tailed test).

approval of all forms of activism. Moving from low congregational support to high increases approval of political statements by 50.22 percent. For electoral and collective action, this shift produces 27.53 percent and 25.26 percent increases in approval, respectively. In addition, denomination and congregational size influence support for electoral activism. AME and COGIC clergy are more supportive of electoral activism than their counterparts in predominantly White denominations, AME clergy by 20.67 percent and COGIC clergy by 15.51 percent. Finally, clergy with smaller congregations are more likely to support this type of activity. The transition from low to high weekly attendance reduces support for electoral activism by 23.49 percent. The case studies provide an explanation for this phenomenon. Several of the clergy I interviewed said that larger congregations were more heterogeneous, and pastors responded by attempting to avoid offending members through such activities as openly campaigning for candidates.

Political interest has the most dramatic effect on all forms of actual activism. As demonstrated in table 7, in two of the electoral and collective activism indexes, those at the lowest end of the political interest scale are expected to refrain from participating in any of these activities. Shifting from low to high interest nearly triples the intensity of political rhetoric. Education exercises its most powerful effect with regard to collective action, as a movement from low to high educational levels increases activism by 260.40 percent. For electoral activism and political statements, this shift in education produces changes of 73.00 percent and 31.78 percent, respectively. Theology also matters: moving from low to high on the orthodoxy scale reduces collective action by 45.17 percent, while moving from low to high on the liberation theology scale increases collective action by 147.21 percent. Finally, the socialization measures have a negative relationship: pastors socialized during the civil rights movement are 21.94 percent less intensive, while those socialized later are 42.14 percent less engaged. This finding is surprising because younger clergy were expected to be more supportive of this type of action. Clergy from the pre–civil rights era may be more established within their communities and thus may more often be recruited for electoral work.

Moving to the organizational and environmental determinants, congregational support and denomination stand out in shaping clergy activism. Shifting from low congregational support to high more than doubles the intensity of electoral activism. For making political statements, this same shift creates a 49.70 percent increase. AME and COGIC pastors are more engaged in electoral activities than are ministers in predominantly White denominations. AME clergy engage in 41.91 percent more electoral activism, while COGIC clergy engage in 33.49 percent more. The AME clergy lead all groups in collective action—43.32 percent more intensely mobilized than clergy in White denominations and 29.1 percent more engaged than the COGIC clergy. Finally, as in the case of approval, clergy in larger churches are less likely to engage in electoral activities. Transitioning from low to high church size decreases the intensity of electoral activism by 49.43 percent.

An examination of table 8 demonstrates that political interest and the-

TABLE 7. Predicted Values of Actual Clergy Action Given Variation in Internal, Organizational, and Environmental Determinants

	Campaigning			Political Talk			Group Work		
	Low	High	Δ	Low	High	Δ	Low	High	Δ
Demographics									
Female	n.s.			n.s.			n.s.		
Education	0.146	0.253	73.00%	0.418	0.551	31.78%	0.070	0.253	260.40%
Political Orientation									
Political Interest	0.00	0.316		0.219	0.630	188.17%	0.000	0.293	
Theology									
Orthodoxy	n.s.			n.s.			0.359	0.197	−45.17%
Liberation Theology	n.s.			n.s.			0.113	0.278	147.21%
Socialization									
Pre–Civil Rights Movement		0.293		n.s.			n.s.		
Civil Rights Movement Generation		0.229		n.s.			n.s.		
Post–Civil Rights Movement		0.170		n.s.			n.s.		
Organizational									
Other		0.229		n.s.				0.214	
AME		0.325		n.s.				0.307	
COGIC		0.306		n.s.				0.218	
Weekly Attendance	0.267	0.135	−49.43%	n.s.			n.s.		
Congregation Support	0.126	0.290	130.87%	0.397	0.595	49.70%	n.s.		
Environment									
Urban	n.s.			n.s.			n.s.		

Source: 2002 Cooperative Clergy Survey.
Note: n.s. = not significant at .1 level (two-tailed test).

ology shape the degree to which clergy deliver sermons based on social justice or morality. As with all previous analyses, political interest increases the frequency in which clergy deliver both types of sermons. In this case, progressing from low political interest to high increases the degree to which a sermon pertains to social justice issues by 55.37 percent and the degree to which a sermon pertains to morality issues by 24.64 percent. Theology operates as expected; liberation theology boosts the frequency for social justice sermons, while orthodoxy does the same for morality sermons. Moving from low to high in regard to liberation theology increases the frequency of social justice sermons by 15.73 percent, and the same movement on the orthodoxy scale increases the occurrence of morality sermons by 56.60 percent.

TABLE 8. Predicted Values of the Frequency of Giving Social Justice and Morality Sermons given Variation in Internal, Organizational, and Environmental Determinants

	Social Justice			Morality		
	Low	High	Δ	Low	High	Δ
Demographics						
Female	n.s.			n.s.		
Education	n.s.			n.s.		
Political Orientation						
Political Interest	0.483	0.750	55.37%	0.479	0.597	24.64%
Theology						
Orthodoxy	n.s.			0.378	0.592	56.60%
Liberation Theology	0.621	0.718	15.73%	n.s.		
Socialization						
Pre–Civil Rights Movement	n.s.			n.s.		
Civil Rights Movement						
Generation	n.s.			n.s.		
Post–Civil Rights Movement	n.s.			n.s.		
Organization						
Other	n.s.			0.567		
AME	n.s.			0.560		
COGIC	n.s.			0.675		
Weekly Attendance	n.s.			n.s.		
Congregation						
Support	0.574	0.743	29.30%	0.478	0.619	29.48%
Environment						
Urban	n.s.			n.s.		

Source: 2002 Cooperative Clergy Survey.
Note: n.s. = not significant at .1 level (two-tailed test).

Congregational support and denomination also influence the degree to which clergy give certain sermons. Moving from low to high congregational support boosts social justice sermons by 29.30 percent and morality sermons by 29.48 percent. COGIC clergy deliver morality sermons 19.0 percent more frequently than do clergy in White denominations and 20.5 percent more frequently than AME clergy.

Thus, these internal and organizational determinants indeed significantly affect conveyance. Internal factors influence clergy's willingness to support and engage themselves in various types of political activism. Political interest significantly promoted all forms of conveyance analyzed and exerted the most dramatic effect. But political interest does not tell the full story; theology also plays a major role. Orthodoxy and liberation theology help explain attitudes as well as engagement. However, these findings counteract each other: orthodoxy decreases support and engagement, while liberation theology increases them. This finding is contrary to the results of the analysis of the correlations in the Religion and Society Surveys: there, both orthodoxy and liberation theology encouraged support for church and clergy activism. A closer examination into the relationship between orthodoxy and liberation theology shows that they are negatively related to each other. Furthermore, orthodoxy significantly decreases political interest, while liberation theology exercises a positive but insignificant effect. Nevertheless, to conclude that orthodoxy is an opiate, as past scholars have, would ignore the complexity of the concept. In particular, the AME and COGIC clergy are significantly more supportive of liberation theology and more supportive and engaged in electoral activism, yet they also score significantly higher on the orthodoxy scale than their counterparts in predominantly White denominations. In addition, AME clergy outpace all other Black clergy in engaging in collective action, which orthodoxy reduces. These results reveal that orthodoxy is more complicated than many past studies have indicated. Orthodoxy may not promote activism, but it does not necessarily completely stop activism.

Organizational factors such as denomination and congregational support also weighed in heavily on support and engagement. As noted earlier, AME and COGIC clergy are more supportive and engaged than their counterparts in predominantly White denominations. The environment measure, urbanicity, was not significant in any part of the analysis, however, perhaps because the clergy in the sample came overwhelmingly from urban areas. Whereas 66.7 percent of the non-Black respondents in the sample were located in medium-sized cities or smaller communities, only 47.1 percent of the Black respondents were located in those types of communities. The most consistent of the external factors was congregational support. According to Mays and Nicholson (1969), Black clergy are politically elite because

> it is a part of the genius of the Negro church that is owned by a poor race, supported by its members. . . . [T]his fact alone gives the Negro minister an opportunity and freedom in his church life that ministers of some racial groups might well covet. (291)

My analysis confirms Mays and Nicholson's argument. The congregations of the clergy I studied strongly and consistently affected their support for and engagement in conveying a need for church-based political activism. Further analysis of the findings indicates that pastors who are highly interested in politics but have congregations that do not support engagement are 77 percent less active in electoral activities than politically interested pastors who enjoy the support of their congregations. Pastors with low interest in politics who serve congregations that support political activism are more than twice as likely to make political statements than pastors whose congregations are not supportive. This finding further reiterates church members' power to shape church-based activism.

CONCLUSION

Black clergy are very open to seeing themselves as political elite. Interviews and surveys of clergy demonstrate a great deal of support for their position among the political leadership. While some limitations on how they will engage themselves in politics may exist, they see their engagement as a salient part of their position. The presence of conveyance represents the culmination of the internal, organizational, and environmental factors I have identified. Both the qualitative and quantitative analyses find that clergy regularly contend with these factors, which shape pastors' propensity to convey messages of political activism. Who will respond to the message is the focus of chapter 6.

CHAPTER 6

Who Will Respond? Understanding Member Approval of Church-Based Political Activism

The ongoing function of a voluntary association depends on a basic consen-
sus among the membership as to the goals or purposes of the organization.
That is to say, if an organization is completely voluntary, its membership
must, in a broad sense, accept the organization's goals.
(Hadden 1967, 27)

As the earlier chapters discuss, a politicized church is a church that holds political awareness and activity as salient pieces of its identity. The organization's identity comprises those characteristics that members feel are central, enduring, and distinctive about the organization (Albert and Whetten 1985). Chapter 5 examines the characteristics that predict whether a church's leadership will support church-based political activism. This chapter examines the predictors of members' attitudes toward a church's political identity. Much of the literature on church-based activism has focused on the pastor as the catalyst (e.g., Billingsley 1999; Frazier 1974; Lincoln and Mamiya 1990; Aldon Morris 1984), ignoring or at best minimizing the role of parishioners. This omission proves problematic because members still play a strong role in determining whether political activism will be sustained. Earlier chapters identify the pastor, who conveys the message of political activism on behalf of the church, as the originator of church-based activism. However, the members serve as the fuel for the church's activism and often initiate church-based political activity. As the interviews in chapters 2 and 5 demonstrate, a pastor may call for activism, but if the members do not respond, the goals will be difficult to attain. Likewise, conflict will arise when congregations believe that their churches should be politically active but their pastors disagree. Thus, this chapter explains why members choose to constrain or support their churches' political activities.

THE IMPORTANCE OF MEMBER ATTITUDES

Voluntary organizations such as churches must pay considerable attention to members' wants and needs. The interest group literature includes extensive discussion of how organizations gain and maintain members to enable the organizations to accomplish their goals (e.g., Berry 1977; Hansen 1985; Olson 1965; Wilson 1973). Jack Walker (1991) assesses members' concerns as the basis of organizational survival, finding that leaders must focus their activities on issues that are pertinent to the members (105). Leaders and organizations that fail to do so face the danger of removal of leaders or organizational collapse.

This finding holds true for congregations. Leaders who stray from the wishes of their congregations jeopardize their positions as well as their churches' well-being, raising the possibility of conflict within the church involving a large exodus of members or punishment of the pastor. Quinley (1974) and Hadden (1967) highlight the problems that exist when pastors engage their churches in political activities not supported by the members. At the other end of the spectrum, pastors who refuse to allow any political elements in their churches have also faced opposition from church members. Gregory A. Boyd, the pastor of Woodland Hills Church, a conservative Protestant church in suburban St. Paul, Minnesota, recently refused to endorse policy stances or candidates or even to hang an American flag in support of the Iraq war effort. He explained that these actions did not reflect the purpose of the church. People who disagreed with his stance left the church, reducing the congregation from five thousand to four thousand members (Goodstein 2006).

Members of Black churches retain this level of importance in determining the appropriateness of church-based political activism. As Myrdal (1962) states,

> When discussing the Negro church as it is and as it might come to be, it must never be forgotten that *the Negro church fundamentally is an expression of the Negro community itself.*
>
> If the church has been otherworldly in outlook and indulged in emotional ecstasy, it is primarily because the downtrodden common Negroes have craved religious escape from poverty and other tribulations. If the preachers

have been timid and pussyfooting, it is because Negroes in general have con-
doned such a policy and would have feared radical leaders.

When the Negro community changes, the church will also change. (877)

This statement places responsibility for a great deal of the Black church's
success and failure on the shoulders of its members. Black churches
reflect their members' interests. Violating or ignoring these interests can
place the organization at risk.

Members not only can retard political activism by their churches but
also can accelerate church-based political activism. Just as conflicts arise
when members oppose activism by ministers, conflict also occurs when
pastors hesitate to support their congregants' activism. In these cases, the
literature points to the members, not the pastor, as the catalyst. As Chong
(1991) argues, solidarity incentives provided by members and the local
community triggered clergy involvement in the civil rights movement.
Charles Payne (1995) finds that members frequently served as catalysts
for church involvement in the civil rights movement; in some cases,
church women dragged their pastors and churches into the movement.

If political churches are to become environments that allow for political communication and mobilization, then the entire organization must
allow this environment to exist. The members play a crucial role in
defining and sustaining the church's political identity. What, then, pre-
dicts whether members of a church will be willing to use the organization
as a vehicle for political activity? The answer to this question lies in congregants' levels of receptivity.

RECEPTIVITY

The concept of receptivity resembles the idea of support. At the very
least, receptive members tolerate political actions taken by the church or
the pastor on behalf of the church. While receptivity does not mean that
congregants allow pastors to do anything they please, it does mean that
members provide some leeway for pastors to lead their churches into certain activities. Levels of receptivity range from uncommunicated opposition to taking a leadership role in church-based activism.

As figure 3 shows, the determinants of receptivity resemble those of
conveyance. Like conveyance, receptivity is driven by several internal,
organizational, and environmental factors. The internal determinants
that predict receptivity are demographics, political interest, theology,

and socialization. As with political participation in the general electorate, gender, education, and income should be correlated with the approval of church-based activism (Tate 1993; Verba, Schlozman, and Brady 1995). The gender gap in political participation is not as pronounced as was previously believed to be the case; however, a gender gap exists in terms of church members because women are more likely to attend than men. In addition, men and women have differing roles in churches. While men represent a clear minority, historically they have assumed the majority of leadership roles. As a result, men and women may see the church's role differently. The extent to which men and women will differ is not clear; men have historically taken the leadership roles when churches became politically engaged, but women have performed most of the behind-the-scenes work (Calhoun-Brown 2003; Charles Payne 1995). Income and education should also promote receptivity. As the case studies in chapter 3 demonstrate, churches with larger numbers of members with higher levels of education and income proved more likely to be socially active. Lee's (2003) examination of a Black Baptist church in Evanston, Illinois, supports this finding. Members with significant levels of education and income possess a greater awareness of political issues and expect their church to respond to these matters. An interest in politics should also have a positive impact on receptivity. Individuals interested in politics should prove more likely to support their churches' engagement in political matters. As Verba, Schlozman, and Brady (1995) note, an interest in politics is important to understanding participation. A church member engaged in politics would be expected to have clear ideas and expectations about how the church will involve itself in politics. In chapter 5, political interest on the part of clergy was the most consistent predictor of conveyance.

Moreover, church members' theology should factor into their support for church-based political activism. Internal religious beliefs have a strong effect on individuals' receptiveness to church-based activism. As discussed previously, orthodox beliefs have been seen as impediments to political action, but the results from the clergy analysis do not necessarily support this view. Historically, scholars argued that orthodox beliefs led Blacks to an otherworldly focus that distanced them from social issues (Du Bois 1990; Frazier 1974; Myrdal 1962). While this argument categorizing the Black church was initiated before the civil rights movement, subsequent work adheres to the same contention. For example, Marx (1967) argues that the Black church's high level of religiosity prevented

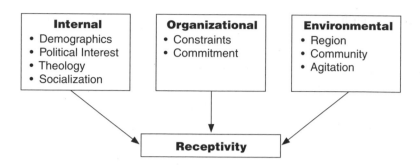

Fig. 3. Determinants of receptivity

Blacks from being active, referring to an otherworldly focus as an "opiate" because it turns attention away from social issues.

Nelsen, Madron, and Yokley (1975) began the defense of the Black church, arguing that after controlling for other variables, religiosity did not have a significant impact on participation. More recently, Harris (1999) finds that highly religious Blacks participate in conventional political activities such as voting but are less likely to participate or support more radical activities such as protests or violence. Calhoun-Brown (1999) finds that otherworldliness promotes feelings of racial empowerment and solidarity. These findings support the idea that orthodoxy does not hinder empowerment.

As an internal determinant, socialization should also factor into receptivity. People raised during times when Black churches were highly involved in political matters, such as during the civil rights movement, should be more supportive of church-based political engagement. Socialization factored heavily into clergy support for church-based political activism, and the same should be expected of members.

Institutional and environmental factors also will affect how members interpret the proper actions of an organization. As chapters 3 and 5 demonstrate, the institution itself can shape church engagement in politics. The institution factors heavily into receptivity because it places constraints on behavior. Denominational differences can constrain an individual's outlook on church actions. Chapter 5 found that differences among churches stemmed from resources and culture. Church of God in Christ churches had fewer resources and were less likely to adopt a Black-conscious culture. These differences represent the main reasons for the behavioral differences between the traditions.

Organizational constraints are connected to organizational commitment. Membership in an organization plays a strong role in how individuals perceive themselves, define their roles in the world, and decide how to solve problems (Pratt 2000; Weick 1995). This finding applies to church membership as well (Wald 1997). Members who invest substantial time and resources in an organization may be less receptive to new ideas and roles for it. Brown and Starkey (2000) argue that longtime members of an organization may be very resistant to an additional identity because they have close connections to an older identity. Stark and Glock (1968), who examined predominantly White denominations in the 1960s, find that members who attended, gave, and participated the most were least likely to support church-based activism. Their investment in the church may have led them to be socialized into a specific understanding of the proper role of the church and its leadership. In contrast, other work has shown that member commitment leads to heavy church involvement in political activism. Aldon Morris (1984), who focuses on Black churches in urban areas during the civil rights movement, finds that high levels of commitment by church members allowed pastors to be active. Charles Payne's (1995) work shows that female commitment to the church led to church involvement in rural Mississippi. These two examples demonstrate how commitment can sustain church-based activities. However, several of the pastors I interviewed explained that when they attempted to make changes in their churches, the most invested members proved most resistant. I thus believe that those who are strongly committed to churches are less likely to be receptive.

Finally, the environment continually directs actions by organizations and their members. The environment can pressure an organization to assume certain roles that would not normally be perceived as appropriate for that organization (Dutton and Dukerich 1991; Dutton, Dukerich, and Harquail 1994). A member may be more receptive to such activities if the church is in an environment that necessitates action. For example, Frazier (1974) argues that the changing needs of Blacks in urban areas during the Great Migration led to increased social outreach by churches. Therefore, differences in terms of region and population density should shape attitudes toward activism. Specifically, the legacy of the civil rights movement should lead members of southern churches to be more supportive of church engagement. The same should hold true in urban areas, where political entrepreneurs and parties have historically worked to mobilize individuals through their churches.

Along with the physical environment, interpretations of the conditions surrounding an individual can further shape receptivity. Truman (1960) and Wilson (1973) speak of how disturbances in the equilibrium of group interests lead to group mobilization for the defense of their interests. People who are comfortable in their current situations have less desire to act. Those who feel agitated are more likely to mobilize, as the civil rights movement demonstrated. Southern Blacks were more likely than northern Blacks to experience and recognize threats to their interests. Consequently, southern Black churches during this period were more likely to mobilize to protect and advance their interests than were northern churches (McAdam 1982; Aldon Morris 1984; Charles Payne 1995). Following this logic, members of Black churches who perceive threats to the group's interests will be more likely to support church-based engagement.

ASSESSING THE DETERMINANTS OF RECEPTIVITY

To test the validity of these hypothesized relationships, I utilize qualitative and quantitative data. The qualitative analysis of receptivity stems from sixty-six interviews of church members in Detroit and Austin, focusing on their reasons for supporting church-based political engagement as well as the limits they place on church action. The quantitative analysis utilizes three surveys: the 2004 and 2005 Religion and Society Surveys, which provide data regarding the attitudes of a large number of church elites regarding the church's proper role in political matters, and the 1993 National Black Politics Study, which allows for an assessment of the magnitude of the effect that various internal and external determinants have on receptivity.

Qualitative Assessment of Receptivity

A discussion of receptivity and its components necessitates a better understanding of how receptivity is practiced. Almost all of the church members I interviewed were receptive to church-based activism: only five of the sixty-six respondents disagreed with church involvement in politics.

Much like the clergy, the members gave historical and theological bases for their support of church-based political engagement. The historical explanations placed the church in the center of Black social development. One Detroit respondent argued that the church represents part of Black society:

I believe that churches should be politically active. Because the social fabric that most Afro-Americans enjoy is very, very closely aligned with the church. And I've always believed that most black people do go to church at some point in their life. Because when I was growing up, which was a long time ago, the only place that black people had to go was church. Church was the center of all of the social activity.

Another Detroit respondent argued that churches were required to become involved in political matters so that their members could achieve salvation:

It is part of the responsibility of the church to direct society to salvation. In order to direct society to salvation, you have to have a voice. In order to have a voice, you have to get involved with the activities—the socioeconomic political activities surrounding the community—so that the people will understand the voice that you carry. Your voice has a specific mention, and it is to direct people toward Christ and a Christlike life. If society is not moving in the direction that is indicative of Christian living or Christ living, then it's the responsibility of the church to help you understand the differences so that given the options and the choice, society can move in that direction.

In addition to the historical and theological motivations for supporting church engagement, several others indicated that a need for church involvement simply existed:

I think to some extent it's necessary . . . because it can be used as an information base to give knowledge to the people that would otherwise not get the information. A lot of times, people ignore politics only because they don't understand it. Churches tend to have a way of communicating on a level that people understand differently.

In this case, environment factors into receptivity. In the absence of access to other institutions that provide information, congregants advocate the use of the church for these purposes.

Respondents communicated some dissatisfaction with political activity by churches. One Detroit respondent felt that involvement in politics did not support the church's true mission:

I don't agree with churches being involved in politics. That's not what our Lord Savior Jesus Christ told the church to do. And in commission to the church he told us to go and spread the Gospel, not get involved in politics. And for the most part, I think that politics is sort of corrupt, and I don't think that churches should be involved in that system of corruption. I mean, it's not the best and the brightest necessarily. It's usually somebody washing somebody else's hand, and it's who you know and how much money you have. So to me it's not a fair system. And we have to deal with it because we're citizens and we are told to pray for those in office and all that, but I don't think churches should be involved as far as outside of voting. I don't think that we should get into that.

Other respondents mentioned the separation of church and state. One Austin respondent noted that his opposition to church engagement stemmed from a previous negative experience in a politically active church. The pastor had been highly critical of corporations and those who worked for them, and his criticism alienated some members. This experience had caused the respondent to believe that churches should not be involved in political matters.

Respondents' disapproval of church-based engagement was based on their definition of politics. When most of the respondents thought of politics or political matters, they thought of elections and parties, images that evoked negative responses. One respondent used the word *corruption* to describe her vision of politics. Such negative views of politics and politicians led many people to oppose church involvement in politics and were evident in almost all respondents' explanations.

However, those who supported church-based political activism felt that politics' corrupt and dirty nature created an even greater need for church involvement. According to one Detroit respondent,

> Many older women . . . have been taught that politics is dirty, and therefore polite young ladies and churchgoing people have no play in this particular game because it is not a nice kind of organization to belong to like the NAACP, but I've never believed that. I'm an inveterate newspaper reader, of magazines, and political activity really turns me on.

Political interest thus sometimes overrides theological concerns regarding the relationship between church and state.

Those who generally opposed church engagement in politics did not object to all forms of such engagement. All of the respondents felt that churches should provide members with community information and make sure that they vote. These respondents saw the church as an alternative source of information, reiterating the importance of the Black church in Black social and political life.

> I think it's important to do research on candidates to see who is a legitimate person. Because of course you have a lot of people who lie, who scheme, who do a lot of things, but I think that it is the job of Christians to find out are these people morally acceptable. Are these people for the people? Are these people someone we can trust to be in Congress, or trust to be a mayor, or trust to be part of the Supreme Court? Whether or not they have the background? Whether or not they have been voting on our side? Whether or not they have supported us? I think that's one thing that we as a church should do collectively and individually.

Another member strongly favored having churches provide pamphlets with political information as well as having political action committees:

> I think all churches should have a political-action committee that their occupation or responsibility would be to go out and research certain candidates for certain offices and bring that information back to the church so we can be better informed. Because there's no way for one individual to get all the information about all the candidates, but if you have a committee set up with that obligation only, I think it would be easier to get the information back to us in layman's terms.

One Detroit respondent who opposed church engagement in politics nevertheless was strongly influenced by the political information she gained in church:

> Usually I would follow the pastor's recommendations. . . . I don't think he recommended anybody I didn't agree with. Because I'm not into politics, so I don't know a whole lot about their platforms, so the information that was given helped me determine who I was going to vote for because I don't follow politics outside of just the average citizen and wanting different things.

Those who supported church involvement did not do so unreservedly. Only one respondent placed no constraints on church activity.

One specific issue of concern was the use of the church to further personal goals. One Detroit respondent commented that churches should be wary when they choose to become politically active:

> There are probably things that the church ought not get involved in, for this reason. If a man knows that he's a kleptomaniac, he ought not work for a bank. If a man knows that he's a nymphomaniac, he ought not work in a brothel. There are weaknesses in the church by virtue of the fact that it is a microcosm of society. It takes on the same sin nature that the society takes on. . . . We still are subject to insult. When we as a church body and community inject ourselves in the areas that we are incapable of handling, then we take on the same badge, the same banners, that society takes on and we blend in. Instead of being a transforming agent, we're conforming. And so the things that the church ought not get involved in are the things that the church cannot handle.

Other respondents specifically cited having politicians speak during worship services as inappropriate. In the words of one Detroit respondent,

> I think it is very inappropriate for leaders to come in and disrupt worship services. Because I think worship services per se are mainly for worship purposes. If you want to have some type of outside activity or maybe after service or something like that, before service, where you invite politicians to come in and speak, that's fine. But for politicians themselves to come in during worship service—the worship service is dedicated primarily to God, and that's our way of worshiping and praising God, so that's the time for that. So when things like that happen, I don't think that should be allowed. I think that when politicians come in and try to do fund-raising activities, I don't believe in that. I think politicians should be able to go outside of the church if they want to raise money. They can gain the support of pastors. They can ask for churches to support them, but to actually do a fund-raising campaign in churches, I don't think that should be allowed.

One Austin respondent had been a longtime campaign worker and had used churches to recruit voters. On one occasion, she took a candidate to various churches, interrupting several Sunday services, and the experience caused her to refuse any further participation in this type of campaign activity. Several churches have set up systems under which they acknowledge candidates during services but do not allow them to speak.

After the service is over, these churches provide a space in which the candidate can speak to congregants.

Members also voiced some concern about having pastors participate in political activities—specifically, running for or holding office. Said one Detroit respondent bluntly, "I want a preacher, not a politician." Others simply saw no reason for pastors to hold public office. As one Austin respondent stated,

> If you are going to be politics, be a politician. If you are going to be a churcher or a minister leading people, then you should do it. It should be separate.

Others believed that pastors should decide whether to run for political office. In the words of another Austin respondent,

> He has to choose what he wants to do. If God put him in the position to do that, then go do that.

Several respondents explained that the ability to handle both duties effectively should determine whether pastors seek public office. One Detroit respondent argued that the matter involved focus:

> Can you handle [both being a pastor and holding office] and stay focused? If you can't stay focused, if you can't make those hard decisions when you have to put down your political hat, then clergy does not need to be in political office.

Some respondents also expressed displeasure with the idea of churches taking stands on certain issues. Several Austin respondents expressed support for a ban on gay marriages but felt that churches should not exclude or alienate homosexuals.

Thus, church members support church-based political activism, but only to a point. Almost all of the respondents placed clear constraints on their churches' political activity. While the respondents readily recognized the importance of the church in Black social and political life, they felt that activism represented a secondary purpose for the church. Overall, these interviews demonstrate that the church's goals of facilitating both salvation and political activity fail to represent opposing ends of a spectrum. They reflect a combined effort on the part of the church. The respondents felt that their churches should be active, but only if such activity did not conflict with the church's primary goal.

Do attitudes about church-based activism lead individuals to choose a church based on its level of political activity? If congregants select churches based on their level of political activism, then church members have only a minimal role in determining whether a church is politically active. Political churches continue to exist because they recruit members who support the churches' political activities. Likewise, inactive churches maintain a membership that supports the divide between church and state. From this standpoint, churches decide to engage in political activism before recruiting many of their members. The congregants' role is only to continue the level of political activism already determined by the church.

However, studies to date have not supported this hypothesis. For example, Roof and McKinney (1992) find that denomination, proximity, and familiarity are the three key factors in church selection. Baptists usually choose Baptist churches. If there are multiple Baptist churches, people most likely attend the one closest to them, and they are more likely to attend a church that is attended by someone they know. Others who have examined the effects of a congregation's political behavior on individual behavior find no support for the idea that activism plays a part in church-selection decisions (Calhoun-Brown 1996; Huckfeldt, Plutzer, and Sprague 1993; McDaniel and McClerking 2005; Wald, Owen, and Hill 1988).

I also find evidence contrary to the notion that people choose their churches based on the political activity of the church. Respondents cited issues of denomination, proximity, and familiarity as the dominant reasons for church selection. Almost all of those interviewed belonged to churches in the denominations in which they had been reared: only five of the sixty-six respondents reported switching denominations. When switching occurred, it was usually because of a spouse. Most respondents reported that at one time, they lived close to their churches. One Austin respondent noted that her family had switched from Methodist to Baptist because the church was across the street from their home.

The most dominant factor in church selection, however, was familiarity. Only one of the respondents reported not knowing someone at the church before joining. One Detroit respondent explained that she had chosen her church because of its location:

I decided I'd come back to church, and I chose that one because it was close. It was very near to my house that I lived in.

Others reported that they later joined churches that friends had invited them to visit. One member of Black Memorial joined because Rev. Black had been the pastor of the church she had attended in another city. When she moved to Austin, she followed him to his new church.

Most respondents did not know about their churches' social activities before joining. Members of some of the most active churches were unaware of the social opportunities they offered until several months after joining. One respondent from Orange Chapel noted that he and his wife had been attracted to it in part because it was one of the few Baptist churches that allowed female ministers, and his wife had received the call to join the ministry. Outside of that instance, however, respondents placed little or no emphasis on a church's political activities when choosing where to attend services.

Survey data provide further evidence that church selection is not determined by the level of church-based political activism. The 2004 and 2005 Religion and Society Surveys gave respondents a wide array of reasons for choosing a church and asked them to select all the reasons that applied. As table 9 demonstrates, less than a tenth of the respondents cited the political activities of the church or the political activism of the pastor as among the reasons they had chosen their churches. The most prominent explanations for church membership include proximity, denomination, and familiarity. In addition to these factors, style of worship and children's services also played prominent roles.

TABLE 9. Reasons for Church Selection

	AME	NBC
Closeness to Home	32.7	38.1
Denomination	61.9	40.4
Knew Someone	50.4	49.8
Political Activities of Church	7.5	5.4
Prestige	6.6	9.0
Style of Worship	35.8	47.5
Political Activities of Pastor	6.2	4.9
Children's Activities	20.8	26.9
Other	4.4	24.2

Source: 2004 and 2005 Religion and Society Surveys.

In summary, the qualitative analyses support the idea that church-based political activism is not a strictly top-down process. While pastors often initiate their churches' entry into the political arena, members also play an active role in this process. At a minimum, the congregation must agree that the church's proper roles include engagement in political activity. However, congregants often initiate the decision to involve a church in political activity. As the qualitative data illustrate, factors such as theology, environment, and political interest influence receptivity to church-based political activity. Nevertheless, these results also indicate that individuals generally do not select their churches for political reasons; rather, church-based political activism becomes an issue only after congregants have selected their churches. The idea that church-based political activism is not predetermined helps explain why political activity on the part of the church does not remain static and why, as discussed in the historical analyses of the Black church's political activism, churches repeatedly enter and exit politics.

Quantitative Assessment of Receptivity

The interview data explain the meaning of receptivity and offer clear examples of the circumstances under which members will tolerate political engagement by their churches. I build on these findings using the 2004 and 2005 Religion and Society Surveys as well as two national surveys.

The Religion and Society Surveys provide an in-depth examination of support for church-based action and its determinants. For this analysis, the sample is reduced to nonclergy who are members of African Methodist Episcopal (AME) or National Baptist Convention, USA (NBC) churches. The 2004 version of the survey, administered at the AME General Conference, yielded 226 respondents. The 2005 version, administered at the NBC Congress of Christian Education, yielded 224 respondents. As in the previous chapters, the analysis of this data will be limited to the descriptive statistics and bivariate analysis.

Receptivity to church-based political activism depends largely on what types of activities are included. Table 10 shows that respondents are most supportive of church actions that assist in facilitating the political process—having churches serve as polling places (AME 54.0 percent, NBC 35.3 percent) and inviting public officials to meetings (AME 52.7 percent, NBC 31.7 percent). However, activities that infringe on the worship service or engage the church in activities that may be overtly partisan are not well supported. Allowing officials to speak during worship services (AME 31.0 percent, NBC 26.8 percent) and allowing political organizations to meet in churches (AME 38.5 percent, NBC 15.2 percent) receive low levels of support. Respondents strongly support having clergy engage in the political system but resist being told how to engage the system. Members most support having clergy tell congregants to vote

TABLE 10. Support for Church and Clergy Actions

	AME	NBC
Support for Church Actions		
Allow officials to speak during worship	31.0	26.8
Invite public officials to meetings	52.7	31.7
Allow political organizations to meet in church	38.5	15.2
Serve as a polling place	54.0	35.3
Hold political forums	40.7	22.3
Would like their church to be more active	63.8	45.4
Support for Clergy Actions		
Criticize public officials	27.9	17.9
Speak out on a political issue	67.3	47.3
Take part in a protest	42.9	28.1
Work with a political party	35.4	15.6
Tell the congregation for whom to vote	8.4	8.5
Form a political action committee	30.1	8.9
Hand out voter guides	48.2	33.9
Comment on political issues during sermon	39.8	25.9
Run for office	34.5	22.3
Contact a public official	47.8	29.9
Encourage congregation to vote	90.3	77.2
Would like their pastor to be more active	48.8	36.4
Place of Clergy and Churches in Politics		
Clergy who have different political views than their members should not express their views.	23.7	
Black churches or places of worship should be involved in political matters.	81.6	
Clergy should never bring political matters into the worship service.	28.0	
Response to Environmental Shocks		
How involved would you want your church to be in this situation?		
Social problem in your community		5.6
Reports of police brutality in your community		5.8
Reports of racial discrimination in your community		6.1
Plan to open an abortion clinic in your community		4.2
Plan to guarantee homosexuals the same rights as others		3.9

Source: 2004 and 2005 Religion and Society Surveys.
Note: Environmental shock questions are scaled from 1 to 7.

(AME 90.3 percent, NBC 77.2 percent), speak out on political issues (AME 67.3 percent, NBC 47.3 percent), and hand out voter guides (AME 48.2 percent, NBC 33.9 percent). However, telling congregants for whom to vote (AME 8.4 percent, NBC 8.5 percent), forming political action committees (AME 30.1 percent, NBC 8.9 percent), and criticizing public officials (AME 27.9 percent, NBC 17.9 percent) do not have a great deal of member support. This pattern resembles the clergy attitudes discussed in chapter 5.

The survey also gauged respondents' reactions to certain statements about churches and clergy as well as to community events. For the most part, AME respondents appear to allow their pastors and churches a high degree of freedom with regard to political issues. Only 23.7 percent of the respondents believe that clergy should be censored if their political views differ from those of the congregation, while 28.0 percent believe that political matters should never be brought into the worship service. Among the AME respondents, 81.6 percent believe that Black churches should be involved in political matters.

To assess how changes in the environment might shape support for church-based political engagement, the NBC respondents were asked to rank on a seven-point scale, with 7 indicating very involved and 1 indicating not involved, the degree to which they would want their churches to become involved in five different scenarios in their immediate communities: social problems, reports of police brutality, reports of racial discrimination, a plan to open an abortion clinic, and a plan to guarantee homosexuals the same rights as others. The responses to the environmental shock questions, presented in table 10, show that implicit and explicit racial issues grabbed more attention than did moral issues. The strongest response was in reaction to reports of racial discrimination, which averaged 6.1. The lowest level of support for church involvement came from responses to plans to guarantee homosexuals the same rights as others, which averaged 3.9. Even more striking, fewer than 2 percent of the respondents ranked reports of racial discrimination 3 or lower, with the percentages increasing slightly for social problems (4.5 percent) and reports of police brutality (4.0 percent). In contrast, 35.7 percent of the respondents selected 3 or less for plans to open an abortion clinic, as did 44.3 percent of the respondents for plans to give homosexuals the same rights as others.

I next conduct a series of bivariate analyses of these measures of receptivity to determine how these factors shape support for church-based political engagement. The measures are similar to the ones used in the previous chapter. Support for church action corresponds to a five-point scale (AME α =.674, NBC α =.548) comprised of the church action questions. Support for clergy action is ranked on an eleven-point scale (AME α = .812, NBC α = .754) comprised of the clergy action questions. The AME respondents (members = 2.2, pastors = 4.7) report significantly higher scores on both scales than do the NBC respondents (members = 1.3, pastors = 3.2).

The bivariate analysis[1] begins with the internal determinants, including demographics, theology, political attitudes, and socialization. The results from the correlations confirm the hypothesized model of receptivity. The correlations from the examination of demographics suggest that female respondents are less supportive of church and clergy action and Black church involvement in political matters. Education, conversely, expands the boundaries of action: more highly educated respondents are more supportive of church and clergy action and are less likely to censor the pastor and support the removal of political issues from the worship service. This finding also holds true for those with higher levels of income. Likewise, the examination of political interest finds that individuals who are interested in politics are less likely to constrain clergy and want to see more engagement by both their churches and their pastors.

The results for theological stance show that while highly orthodox individuals are more supportive of pastoral engagement, they are also more likely to support banning political issues from entering the worship service. In addition, those who embrace Black theology are more likely to support all of the forms of action and are less likely to want to constrain clergy and issues within the worship service.

Finally, an examination of the relationship between socialization and support for church-based activism among AME respondents finds age cohort and institutional exposure differences. Those socialized during and after the civil rights movement are more likely than those socialized earlier to support church and clergy engagement in political activity. In addition, connections to Black institutions such as historically Black colleges and universities, membership in Black organizations, and exposure to Black media promote receptivity. A connection to Black socializing institutions promotes support for church engagement in political matters.

The analysis finds similar results for the NBC respondents. Men are more likely than women to want politically involved churches and pastors. Respondents with higher levels of education and income are also more open to church and clergy action. In addition, respondents with higher levels of biblical orthodoxy want more church involvement in addressing social problems, issues of police brutality, and racial problems but do not differentiate themselves from others with regard to the morality issues. Those who embrace Black theology are more supportive of church and clergy action and want stronger church reactions when social or racial problems occur in the community.

NBC respondents' political interest largely tracks that of the AME respondents. Those with high levels of political interest are more supportive of church and clergy action and would like both their pastors and their churches to be more politically active. Contrary to the AME findings, however, NBC respondents socialized before and during the civil rights movement are more open to church action, while those socialized subsequently want less church involvement in issues of brutality or a racial problems. This difference may stem from a lack of connection to other Black institutions as well as lower levels of political interest. NBC respondents socialized after the civil rights movement are significantly less likely to report membership in Black organizations and have lower levels of political interest. Finally, much like the AME respondents, NBC members exposed to Black institutions demonstrate higher levels of receptivity.

Among AME respondents, experiences and attitudes toward the organization affect receptivity. Those who report having had personal conflicts with their pastors about political issues are more likely to support church involvement in political matters and less likely to argue that politics should never be brought into the service. This finding proves contrary to the interview evidence, where one respondent rejected church engagement because of a past conflict. However, this respondent was a member of the most politically engaged church in the sample, Orange Chapel, suggesting that even individuals who have had conflicts still see a place for church involvement. Those who feel that pastors strongly influence their political decisions are less likely to want to censor clergy or remove political issues from the worship service and are more likely to agree that churches need to be involved in political matters. Finally, as hypothesized, those with higher levels of church attendance are more likely to feel that politics should never enter the worship service, are less likely to believe that their churches should be involved in political matters, and have lower scores on the church and clergy action scales.

Region does not differentiate the AME respondents except in the case of banning politics from the worship service. AME members from the South are more supportive of keeping political matters out of the worship service. While this finding runs contrary to earlier hypotheses that southern churches will be more active, 34.6 percent of the southern respondents agree that politics should be banned from the worship service, while 53.8 percent disagree. Moreover, respondents from the South are also more likely to live in rural areas. Those who attend churches in more densely populated areas are more supportive of church-based political engagement. Those who attend churches in the inner city more frequently support church and clergy action, while members of suburban churches are more likely to state that they want their churches to become more active. Respondents who attend churches in small towns and rural areas offer less support for church activism. Finally, those who feel that Blacks face a great deal of discrimination are more likely to state that they want their church and pastor to become more involved politically.

The organizational determinants of receptivity among NBC respondents were not as significant as for the AME respondents. Contrary to what was found in the AME sample, the NBC respondents who attend church more frequently support clergy action and want more involvement from their churches when social problems occur. No clear regional differences emerged; however, members of inner-city churches expect more church involvement when social problems occur. Those in rural areas are less supportive of church and clergy action overall. Finally, unlike the findings for AME respondents, feelings of discrimination do not significantly correlate with any of the measures of receptivity among NBC members, perhaps because of a lack of variation: 78.8 percent of the respondents fall on the top third of the scale.

These correlations provide some insight into how internal, organizational, and environmental factors shape individuals' support for church-based engagement. For the most part, the findings confirm the hypotheses. All of the internal, organizational, and environmental determinants shape receptivity in some way. This analysis shows that race is an important aspect in determining support for church-based political engagement, exposure to Black institutions, and the recognition of a threat to racial group interests increases the likelihood of members being receptive. In addition, religious beliefs play a role in receptivity. Orthodox religious beliefs, along with an attachment to a social gospel such as Black theology, increase support for church-based activism. While racial and religious attitudes are the most apparent factors in shaping receptivity, religious experiences also play a significant role. These results provide a foundation for understanding the range of political activities congregants will support or oppose and present a basic picture of how demographic characteristics, connection with Black institutions, political interest, theology, environment, and organizational commitment predict support or opposition for church-based political activism.

Because these data have only limited generalizability beyond those interviewed, I conducted a multivariate analysis of the determinants of receptivity using the 1993 National Black Politics Study, conducted by the Center for the Study of Race and Politics at the University of Chicago. The results of this study permit me to examine the factors that determine receptivity in a representative sample as well as the relative impact of each factor simultaneously. The survey used a national cross-sectional design that yielded a sample of 1,206 African American adult respondents. The survey was chosen for its in-depth examination of the influence of religion on African American social and political attitudes and activities.

The measure of receptivity was an individual's agreement with the statement that "Black churches or places of worship should be involved in political matters." While this measure does not examine the full range of activities in which churches could be involved, it provides a general sense of whether individuals feel that the church has a place in politics and whether they would tolerate church political involvement. The measure is a dichotomous measure, with 0 indicating disagreement with the statement and 1 indicating agreement. More than two-thirds of the respondents agreed with the statement.

The measurements of the internal and external determinants of receptivity capture the various factors discussed earlier.[2] The internal determinants of receptivity include factors such as demographics, political interest, theology, and socialization. For this analysis, demographics are measured using sex, education, and income. Political interest, reflecting an individual's general concern with politics, is measured using the respondent's level of electoral participation. The internal determinants of receptivity also include theology, or religious outlook. Similar to the analysis of clergy in the previous chapter, theology will be measured in two forms. The first measure intends to capture an orthodox view of religion, while the other captures support for liberation theology in the form of Black theology. Orthodoxy is captured through the belief that churches should focus on personal salvation, while Black theology is captured through the belief that Black churches should have Black images of

Christ. Socialization provides the final aspect of the internal determinants of receptivity and is measured by age cohort.

Using both situational and behavioral variables, the measures of the external determinants of receptivity are designed to capture institutional affiliation and attachment, community, and comfort. The first external determinant examined in this analysis is the organization—specifically, religious tradition. As in the previous chapters, differences exist between the traditions. This analysis used four categories: Baptist, Methodist, Holiness/Pentecostal, and other traditions (Catholic, nondenominational, and predominantly White Protestant groups). The Baptists comprise 67.9 percent, while the other category accounts for 15.1 percent, Methodists make up 10.1 percent, and the Holiness/Pentecostals comprise 6.9 percent. Coupled with organizational differences is organizational commitment. Unlike the pastors, members can have varying levels of commitment to their churches, and those who do not associate with the organization should be less inclined to adhere to its outlook. Church attendance provides a means for measuring commitment. Environmental issues involve contextual matters and interpretations of an individual's surroundings. Two measures analyze the physical environment: region and community. Region is measured in terms of South and non-South. Community is measured in regard to the level of urbanicity. Finally, I gauge respondents' attitudes about their environment with the use of a racial discrimination scale.[3] This scale captures the degree to which respondents feel that American society and institutions threaten respondents' interests—specifically, racial interests.

Figures 4 and 5 confirm many of the hypothesized relationships outlined earlier in this chapter.[4] The strongest impact on receptivity comes from political interest, religious outlook, and social standing. A focus on political engagement, salvation, and concerns about racial and economic justice also play a strong role in shaping receptivity.

Among the internal determinants, political interest exercises the strongest impact on receptivity. As in the case of clergy, those with a strong interest in politics are more likely to support church-based political action. Those who have not participated in any electoral activities have a 63.8 percent chance of agreeing, while those who have engaged in all of the activities have a 91.6 percent chance, a difference of 43.5 percent. This finding indicates that those who are politically engaged want to see their religious institutions engaged as well, as would be expected from the results in chapter 5.

However, people who believe that churches should focus more on

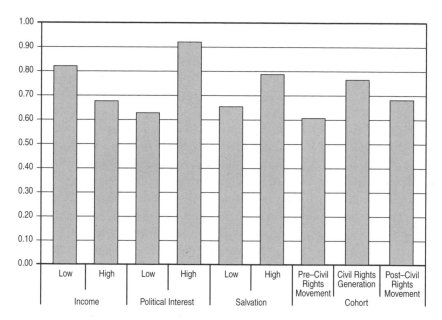

Fig. 4. Predicted probability of supporting church-based political activism given variation in internal determinants of receptivity

personal salvation are also more receptive to political activity by churches. Those who strongly oppose a focus on personal salvation have a 65.4 percent probability of being receptive, while those who strongly support such a focus have a predicted probability of 79.5, a 21.5 percent increase. This relationship may appear counterintuitive because focusing on salvation indicates an otherworldly perspective, but this is not the first set of analyses to find a positive and significant relationship between the salvation measure and support for church engagement. As Calhoun-Brown (1999) shows, the salvation variable promotes attitudes toward Black empowerment and racial solidarity. Furthermore, the bivariate analysis found that orthodox religious beliefs promoted church-based engagement in several forms. These findings demonstrate that spiritual salvation and physical freedom are not mutually exclusive.

In addition, social standing also strongly affects receptivity. People with lower incomes are more likely to be receptive, a finding that runs contrary to the relationship between income and receptivity in the earlier bivariate analysis. Those at the lowest income level have an 82.7 percent chance of agreeing with the statement, while those in the highest income

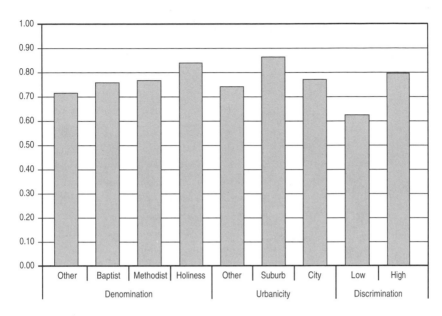

Fig. 5. Predicted probabilities of supporting church-based political activism given variation in external determinants of receptivity

group have a 67.7 percent probability of agreeing, an 18.1 percent decrease in the likelihood of support. Although members of both groups strongly support church political involvement, those at the lower rungs of the income ladder have a greater need for church-based political engagement. Because poorer Blacks lack access to other political institutions (Cohen and Dawson 1993; Harris, Sinclair-Chapman, and McKenzie 2005; Tate 1993), churches may serve as the only viable institutions for advancing their cause.

Finally, socialization matters. Among those socialized during the civil rights movement, 76.3 percent supported church involvement in politics, compared to only 61.0 percent of those socialized before the movement and 69.0 percent of those socialized afterward. A 25.2 percent difference existed in support for church-based activism between those socialized before and during the civil rights movement, indicating that Blacks raised when Black churches were highly engaged are more likely to support church-based action. People immersed in an era of strong political engagement by Black churches have come to expect this type of behavior.

The external determinants of receptivity follow a pattern similar to those demonstrated by the need for racial justice and exposure to Black denominations. The analysis confirms that individuals' comfort in their environments strongly affects their desire to mobilize themselves and their institutions. Those who feel that the aspects of American society have discriminated against them in the past and continue to do so prove more receptive to church-based political activism. Those at the low end of the discrimination scale have a 62.3 percent chance of being receptive, while those at the high end have a 79.7 percent chance, a 27.9 percent increase. Belief that group interests are being ignored or intruded on creates a need to use existing institutions to protect the group. When Blacks feel that the racial group's interests are under attack, they call on the Black church, their key institution, for protection.

Blacks in all four religious groupings strongly support church-based activism, but Black members of churches in denominations outside of the three major traditions are less supportive, with only a 70.9 percent chance of being receptive, less than those in the Baptist (76.3 percent), Methodist (76.4 percent), and Holiness/Pentecostal (84.0 percent) denominations. The difference in probability of support is significant only in the comparison between those in the Holiness/Pentecostal tradition and those outside of the Black traditions, where the probability increases by 18.5 percent. As chapter 4 points out, the Black Baptist and Methodist denominations arose from Blacks' need to revolt against the racism in White religious institutions; in contrast, the Holiness/Pentecostal churches resulted from a theological revolution. Because of their more orthodox nature and otherworldly focus, the Holiness/Pentecostal denominations are perceived as less receptive to political activism. However, empirical examinations find that members of those denominations are more supportive of Black empowerment (Calhoun-Brown 1999). This finding speaks to the need to further understand the nuances of Black religiosity. Several works have shown that a strong religious commitment boosts group attachment and Black empowerment (Allen, Dawson, and Brown 1989; Calhoun-Brown 1999; Ellison 1991).

Finally, the results also show that community matters. Those living in the suburbs have an 86.3 percent likelihood of being receptive, while those in large cities or less densely populated areas have 76.3 percent and 74.1 percent chances of being receptive, respectively. These findings contradict the results from the Detroit and Austin case studies, which indicated that suburban membership equated with low levels of activism. Several pastors and church members noted that members who did not live in the community where the church was located were unaware of relevant issues. This distance between certain members and the church's community either lowered calls for the church to respond or rendered these members unavailable to help their church. The qualitative findings examined behavior, while this analysis examines attitudes. Differences between these two analyses may help explain the variation in the findings. Similar discrepancies arose in chapter 5's examination of clergy support of activism and actual levels of activism. Moreover, Black suburbanites may see the Black church as a key institution keeping them in touch with the Black community and may thus be more supportive of its activism.

CONCLUSION

Qualitative interviews show that congregants exhibit a great deal of support for political action by their churches, although limitations exist and are rooted in the fear that the churches will be exploited for political gains. The qualitative study also reveals that congregants want their churches to provide information even when those congregants oppose having their churches take any formal political action. Finally, the interviews find that the support of church-based activism connects strongly to the belief that a church can be politically active yet still achieve its primary goal of facilitating salvation.

I explored more deeply the relative magnitude of the relationships between various internal and external factors and support for church-based activism. This quantitative analysis found that among the internal determinants, political interest, religious beliefs, and social standing strongly affect receptivity. Moreover, those who came into adulthood when the Black church was highly engaged are more supportive than those who came into adulthood in other periods. The environment also affects receptivity. As the interest group literature points out, feelings of threat factor strongly into receptivity. Finally, exposure to certain religious institutions shapes the likelihood of receptivity.

A few findings conflict with popular beliefs—most notably, the connection between religious conservatism and receptivity. Earlier works suggest that religious conservatism leads individuals to be less focused on political participation and more focused on otherworldly issues and salvation (Frazier 1974; Marx 1967). However, the tradition in the Black church and in Black religion holds that spiritual salvation and physical freedom are not mutually exclusive. As chapter 4 highlights, slaves' quest for physical freedom also constituted a religious experience, and this analysis confirms this finding. Black religious traditions are also significant in shaping Blacks' participation in politics as a group. The 1993 National Black Politics Study found that Blacks who were not part of the three major traditions offered less support for church-based political action.

Finally, not all issues have the same catalyzing effect on church-based political activism, and feelings of discrimination have a notable impact on receptivity. Although Blacks tend to be very socially conservative, I found that moral issues such as abortion and homosexuality do not carry great weight in Blacks' decisions to support church political activity. These findings lead to questions about the degree to which conservative White Christian groups, focusing solely on moral issues to the exclusion of race, can reach out to Blacks. Overall, Blacks strongly support church-based engagement, but how much this support extends itself beyond racialized issues remains unknown.

Although this chapter has painted a fairly detailed illustration of what determines members' support for church-based political activism, questions still remain. For example, what determines the prominence of political issues on a church's agenda? Cohen (1999) and others argue that the church and other Black institutions failed in the initial attempt to address the HIV/AIDS crisis in the Black community; however, these institutions have recently taken a more aggressive role. What explains the change? Did pastors or members force their churches to take a stronger position on the HIV/AIDS epidemic? Also, with the growth of megachurches, do members' attitudes have as much influence? Do members of a church have less of a say in determining the correct role of politics within the organization when the membership of that church exceeds a certain size? Although the current data do not provide answers to these questions, the concluding chapter offers some speculations.

CHAPTER 7

Conclusion

The Black church serves as the preeminent institution in Black social life. It receives praise for its ability to unite Blacks and defend their rights. But at the same time, the church also receives criticism for its lack of action. I do not intend to step into the argument over whether the Black church is a hero or a villain but rather to examine why people have such varying views. In particular, I explain what circumstances lead churches to choose to engage themselves in the political process. In so doing, I provide a more holistic view of the Black church that provides a better comprehension of the nature of its actions in the political realm. I argue that the political engagement of churches is a process that involves the members, pastor, organization, and environment. The pastor and members negotiate the proper role of the church, but this negotiation is moderated by the organization and the environment. A change in any of these four factors can lead to a change in church engagement.

To test this argument, I employed a multimethod approach that integrates quantitative and qualitative research. The findings from this analysis demonstrate that church-based political activism is more complicated than many observers have perceived. First, if churches are to engage the political system, the system must be willing to interact with them. When the hurdles to entry into the political system are high, churches are less likely to become politically involved. Second, the political engagement of organizations resembles that of individuals: organizations that lack the capability or motivation to engage the system will be less active. Third, pastors are necessary but not sufficient for church action. Although pastors are vital to church actions, other factors limit ministers' activities. Finally, members are central to church activities. The members provide an outlook for the church as well as the capacity to act. Members desires' cannot be ignored in attempts to explain the political engagement of the Black church. Members serve as both the retardant and accelerant for church-based political action.

The combination of these four factors shapes church activism. Moreover, churches' decisions to engage in political activities represent an ongoing process. Changes in any of the four factors can lead an apolitical church to engage the system or a politically active church to disengage. Organizations, like individuals, are not static. As organizations face internal and external changes, their actions should change as well. For example, the churches detailed in chapter 2 constantly reevaluate the decision to engage. If Orange Chapel, the most active church in the sample, faced a large resource deficit, it would likely retreat from the political realm. If Red Memorial lost Rev. Red, who pushed the organization into activism, its level of engagement would also be expected to decrease. Similarly, if the members of White Chapel called for more church action, the institution would be expected to become more prominent in Detroit politics. Finally, if Rev. Black and his members perceived Austin's political institutions as more accessible, Black Memorial would likely become more politically engaged. A Black church's silence or outspokenness is the combined product of these factors. As each of them changes, a change should occur within the church.

UNANSWERED QUESTIONS

This study has provided a holistic analysis of the determinants that shape black churches' political engagement. However, I have not accounted for all of the factors that influence church-based political engagement. A number of questions about what leads churches to engage the system remain unanswered. One of the first questions concerns the effect of a pastor's pursuit of public office. Running for office is a difficult decision for a pastor to make: members and clergy alike do not strongly support this type of activity, and few clergy whom I interviewed had run for office. But what happens to churches when pastors decide to seek public office? Ministers who had run for office worked hard to keep their political careers separate from their religious careers. However, members of churches that have pastors or congregants run for office may have increased levels of political interest. Pastors developing campaigns may recruit members as volunteers. In addition, campaign publicity may create an increased political discourse within the church. For example, Adam Clayton Powell Jr.'s political campaigns politically energized Harlem's Abyssinian Baptist Church. Although none of the pastors I interviewed held public office at the time I conducted the interviews, one member of Orange Chapel was running for the Austin City Council. Several casual discussions took place after services during which people reminded each other to vote as well as of the fact that one of their own was running for office. In this case, a member's candidacy increased political interest. Several church members I interviewed recalled past instances in which pastors had run for office, and their descriptions resembled what I observed at Orange Chapel. Members became actively involved in pastors' campaigns and paid increased attention to political issues, especially those related to the pastors' goals. Clergy who run for office can thus increase congregants' political interest and engage them in the political process. However, churches that had had pastors run for office noted higher levels of political involvement at that time as well, indicating a selection bias: pastors of active churches are more likely to run for office than those whose churches engage in little activism. As a result, pastors who run for office may not necessarily increase their congregants' level of political interest but instead may be a by-product of already high levels.

Questions also remain about how outside groups work to mobilize churches. Within a particular church's environment, certain organizations—parties, interest groups, or corporations, for example—may attempt to build relationships with the church based on shared interests. This study has focused on how churches reach out to the community and its organizations but has not examined how community organizations reach out to the church. Other entities within communities may attempt to influence and mobilize churches. How do corporations and interest groups interact with churches, and to what degree do these institutions shape the church's actions? Churches have increasingly partnered with the federal government, but churches also foster relationships with nongovernmental entities. As Walton (1988) and Smith (1996) demonstrate, although incorporation in to the political system is a primary goal of Blacks, it does have its pitfalls.

These questions provide a few areas for future research on the political engagement of the Black church, but some of the biggest questions stem from the changes in the social and political climate.

THE FUTURE OF THE BLACK CHURCH

As the American religious and political landscapes change, these developments may affect the Black church's presence in American politics. Specifically, how will these changes affect the ability of the Black church to aid individual participation as well as act in the defense of Blacks as a group?

Megachurches

Megachurches have an average attendance of three thousand or greater, and their numbers have grown exponentially since the early 1990s. In 1991, the United States had an estimated forty-five megachurches; today, that number exceeds four hundred. Fewer than one-tenth of these megachurches are predominantly Black (Pinn 2002). Because of their size, megachurches have the potential to provide a wide array of services to their members and communities; however, these institutions also have drawbacks, as many observers have pointed out. One of the most common complaints is that they lack the intimacy of smaller churches and that members consequently are less connected to each other and to their pastors (Stonebraker 1993). In addition, the size of these institutions leads them to be highly professionalized, and members are not needed as volunteers. The lack of input by members not only may reduce their ability to influence church actions but may also affect the civic skills that members develop through volunteering. Several megachurches have sought to overcome this problem by developing a vast array of services intended to keep members connected to the church and each other (Pinn 2002). However, these solutions do not address the issue of building civic skills and processes that incorporate member input within the church community.

Further, megachurches cast a wide net in recruiting members, which may water down their message. Anthony Pinn (2002) argues that the megachurch's attempts to recruit members "will shift its center from doctrine to corporate jargon" (138). In addition, many megachurches have adopted a prosperity theology, which argues that God wants Christians to have material possessions and personal salvation (Pinn 2002). A message that focuses on material possessions undercuts the social gospel message for which Black churches have received praise. A move by Black churches away from a focus on social consciousness to a focus on individualism and material goods may present major problems for the defense of Black interests.

On the other side of the ledger, no empirical evidence suggests that these megachurches are curtailing Black political participation. While the messages and structure of these churches have the potential to reduce members' motivation and capacity to act, no data empirically establish this possibility. Moreover, not all megachurches shy away from socially conscious messages. Fred Price, the pastor of the Crenshaw Christian Center, has repeatedly spoken out against racism and religion's role in perpetuating it (Pinn 2002). Although megachurches concern many scholars, the effect of these institutions on Black political participation remains unclear, as does their level of responsiveness to members' desires.

Gender

Some observers have championed the Black church as the defender of the Black race, shielding them from the harshness of racism in American society. However, other observers have chastised the same institution for its inability or unwillingness to confront other issues that Blacks face on a regular basis (Calhoun-Brown 2003; Higginbotham 1993). Perhaps most obviously, Black women face the challenges of race and gender on a daily basis (Crenshaw 1992; Dawson 2001; Harris-Lacewell 2004). Many scholars argue that if the Black church is the protector of all Blacks, it should be conscious of these challenges (Burroughs 1999; Higginbotham 1993). In addition, women have served as the backbone of the Black church but have not received the same credit and accolades as men. Churches are populated and maintained mainly by women, but the majority of leadership positions are occupied by men (Higginbotham 1993). This discrepancy has sparked a great deal of debate in churches. While the Methodist denominations ordain women and have elected women to high-standing denominational positions, debate is still being waged in Baptist and Church of God in Christ churches (Pinn and Pinn 2002). Baptist churches can decide autonomously whether to ordain and include women in leadership positions, as the examination of Orange Chapel in chapter 2 showed. Churches of God in Christ churches ordain women only in special circumstances. Even with the ordination of women, questions still arise in regard to the church's attentiveness to the issues that affect women. Both Rev. Red and Rev. Orange noted that addressing gender issues can be highly controversial.

To offer some insight into how those in the Black church feel about gender issues, the Religion and Society Surveys asked questions related to female clergy and gender issues. Table 11 shows that churches have faced a considerable level of conflict over gender issues. Close to a third of the African Methodist Episcopal (AME) respondents and more than two-fifths of the National Baptist Convention (NBC) respondents report clashes over gender in their churches. The fact that conflict is so common in AME churches is surprising given that more than four-fifths of respondents feel that churches should allow women to preach, compared to two-fifths for the NBC respondents. In addition, the divide between men and women on this issue is not as drastic for the AME respondents. Close to three-quarters of the male AME respondents agree with women preaching, as do more than four-fifths of female respondents. In the case of the NBC respondents, slightly more than a third of the men and slightly less than half of the women agree. In regard to actual clergy activities in the defense of women's rights, such as working with women's groups or speaking out on women's rights, there is a considerable level of support from the AME respondents. Close to half of the respondents agree with both types of activities. In contrast, less than a quarter of NBC respondents support these types of clergy activities. A comparison indicates no significant gender differences in support for these activities. Finally, feeling thermometers were used to gauge attitudes about male and female clergy. In both groups, male clergy received higher scores than female clergy. While the differences between the scores are significant for both groups, the difference is far greater for the NBC respondents.

To expand on this discussion of the church and women's rights, the AME respondents were asked a set of questions to understand their support of female clergy as well as how attentive Black leaders have been to the interests of Black women. More than three-quarters of respondents believe that churches should allow more women to enter the clergy, while only slightly more than a tenth of the respondents believe that women's participation in the clergy violates God's plan for women. The majority of respondents feel that Black male leaders have ignored Black women's issues. In all three of these cases, no significant differences existed between the male and female respondents. Among the AME respondents, a significant level of support exists for female leadership in the church as well as for the recognition that women's issues have taken a backseat to other issues in the Black community. It is important to remember that female leadership is not new to the AME church; the denomination began formally ordaining women in 1948 and since 2000 has elected three women to the office of bishop. However, the lack of a significant gender gap in regard to female clergy and the need to address women's issues may indicate that some churches within the denomination can address these issues more aggressively than others.

Sexuality

The issue of sexuality presents substantial problems for the Black church. First, the Black church has been soundly criticized for ignoring the issue of homosexuality. Cohen (1999) and other scholars argue that the growth of the AIDS/HIV epidemic stemmed from the reluctance of Black institutions, such as the Black church, to address sexuality. In addition, homosexual groups have framed their cause as an issue of civil rights, presenting an obvious contradiction for the Black church, the focal institution for defending civil rights. In response, several Black religious leaders, including Jesse Jackson, who referred to the comparison as a "stretch" (Clemetson 2004, A1), have argued that the two movements have little in common.

TABLE 11. Attitudes toward Women's and Gay Rights

	AME	NBC
Gender Roles		
Has your church had a conflict over gender issues?	30.98	42.57
Churches should allow women to preach.	80.41	44.33
Clergy can work with women's rights groups.	43.1	22.67
Clergy can speak out on women's rights.	47.81	22.33
Black churches should allow more women to become clergy.	79.65	
Women's participation in the clergy conflicts with God's plan for women.	12.04	
Black women have been ignored by Black male leaders.	55.32	
Feeling Thermometers		
Female Clergy	81.02	57.02
Male Clergy	83.81	75.54
Sexuality		
Churches can allow homosexuals to preach.	7.77	4
Clergy can work with gay rights groups.	6.73	6.33
The homosexual quest for equal rights is similar to that of Blacks.	15.55	16.04
Churches should take part in more outreach to the gay community.	40.24	
Churches should oppose any legislation that provides homosexuals the same rights as others.	48.85	
Feeling Thermometers		
Homosexuals	30.98	22.95
White Homosexuals		22.14
Black Homosexuals		25.14

Source: 2004 and 2005 Religion and Society Surveys.

The Black church was forced to confront sexuality when gay marriage entered the political discourse. Several Black clergy adamantly opposed the idea of gay marriage, with one clergyman stating, "If the K.K.K. opposes gay marriage, I would ride with them" (Clemetson 2004, A1). Many historically Black denominations, including the AME, the NBC, and the Church of God in Christ, passed resolutions or made statements that prohibited their clergy from officiating at same-sex marriage ceremonies. However, Black churches reached no consensus on this stance. Several Black ministers framed banning same-sex marriages as discrimination and argued that as such, the Black church could not support it. As one clergyman stated, "Oppression is oppression is oppression" (Banerjee 2005, 23).

While this issue presents the Black church with a multitude of difficulties, churches' reactions to the sexuality issue significantly affect their political behavior. Shaw and McDaniel (2007) find that homosexuals who report having pleasant church experiences are more likely to be politically engaged and that exposure to political churches and the adoption of Black theology promote acceptance of homosexuals. Even though sexuality is a volatile topic, some Black churches are willing to promote tolerance and acceptance of homosexuals. While churches that embrace homosexuals have a strong impact on behavior, it is not clear which churches will engage in this activity. Even in the most active churches, sexuality is a difficult issue to address. The members of Orange Chapel, the most active church I studied, readily stated that they did not want to address the topic of sexuality. Several people I interviewed commented on how divisive the subject was. So although the church confronted gender issues, it remained highly cautious about the divisions that might stem from a discussion of sexuality. As one member stated,

> We don't really discuss the issue because of the divisiveness it creates. We don't let it come up. We don't discuss it, and we don't let it come up to discuss it. Because we understand that it's—again, it's between that person and their savior. I am convinced in my heart that God is a God for anybody; he loves us all the same. So when we start saying that "God is going to expose you. You have just committed a sin," and maybe you will be the one that is exposed.

To offer some insight into how churches respond to the sexuality issue, the 2004 and 2005 Religion and Society Surveys asked questions designed to capture attitudes toward homosexuals' role in churches and how the church should react to homosexuals. The results, presented in table 11, demonstrate that a consensus exists regarding the role of homosexuals in churches. Less than a tenth of the respondents in both samples agree with homosexuals preaching or clergy working with gay rights groups. Only about one-sixth of the respondents in both surveys saw similarities between the homosexual and Black quests for equal rights. The AME respondents were asked two additional questions about how the church should react to homosexuals. Close to two-fifths of the respondents felt that the church should conduct more outreach to homosexuals, although the question did not indicate whether this outreach should attempt to support homosexuals or to change their habits. Respondents were also asked how the church should respond to policies that would give homosexuals the same rights as others: almost half believed that churches should oppose any legislation that would give homosexuals the same rights as others, while nearly one-third disagreed with that idea, perhaps because they did not want to support what may be perceived as discriminatory practices. An examination into the relationship between these two questions finds a significant and negative relationship. Those who support outreach for homosexuals are less likely to support church opposition to gay rights. This finding indicates that support for outreach constitutes an attempt not to change homosexuals but to work with them. Finally, the respondents were asked to report feeling thermometer scores for homosexuals. Both the AME and NBC respondents reported cool feelings toward homosexuals. However, the NBC sample also had a chance to provide separate scores for Black and White homosexuals. Although respondents still had cool feelings toward members of both groups, the score for Black homosexuals was significantly higher than the score for White homosexuals. This snapshot indicates that people do not want their churches working too closely with homosexuals, but supporters of interaction between Black churches and homosexuals hope to bridge the gap between the groups, not necessarily to change homosexuals. In addition, as members of Black churches begin to think of homosexuals as part of the racial group, congregations may become more open to bringing gays into the fold rather than ostracizing them.

White Evangelicals and the Republican Party

The rise of issues such as gay marriage has raised additional questions about where the Black church positions itself in comparison to other religious groups and the political parties. The growing body of work examining the relationship between the Black church and White evangelicals finds that although some similarities exist between the groups, the building of long-lasting coalitions is not expected in the near future. Calhoun-Brown (1998) and Robinson (2006) note that Black and White evangelicals share the same attitudes on moral issues but that these issues mobilize Whites but not Blacks. Wilcox (1990a) finds that although Blacks supported Pat Robertson early in his 1988 presidential campaign, that support began to wane as Blacks gained more information.

My interviews with clergy may provide an explanation for this phenomenon. Baptist clergy in particular expressed dismay with White evangelicals and suspicion regarding some White churches' involvement in politics. These misgivings stemmed from what the pastors perceived as an unwillingness to address the history of racism within and outside of their churches. The people I interviewed argued that the White church needs to hold itself and its members accountable for past and current discriminatory practices. As Rev. White stated,

> All of the church has to be honest, Black or White, and say government has not done what it should do for the people. . . . They've not done well for the people. And the church as a whole has to stop being about the business about giving warm fuzzies to politicians and, in the White church, hiding some of their predators under the guise of family values and high moral status.

Rev. Green felt that a significant divide existed between the Black and White churches:

> The Black church has always had to fight with the White church on this central thing. Why? How can you allow the grand wizard [of the Ku Klux Klan], who burned down my house and raped my sister and cut out the genitalia of my grandfather, to serve on your deacon board? How can you pray for these men who sat upon other human beings and they are allowed not only entrée into these White churches but when they take their hoods off, some of them are sitting up in the pulpit with you. And it might even be you.

Rev. Orange had previously worked with White evangelical groups but stopped doing so because of their unwillingness to address issues of racism within and outside of their congregations.

The Methodist clergy I interviewed did not have the same suspicions. They expressed a need for Black and White churches to be politically active and acknowledged that White churches have used their influence in areas, primarily concerning morality issues, that the Black church has for the most part ignored. Rev. Ivory harbored no uneasiness toward White churches and attributed this attitude to his positive working relationship with them. Many of his community projects received support from White churches, specifically the Congregationalist churches, before Black churches.

The Methodist clergy's less critical attitude toward the White church may well reflect strides toward reconciliation made by the major White Methodist denomination during the civil rights movement (Findlay 1993). In contrast, predominantly White Baptist denominations such as the Southern Baptist Convention have a long history of supporting racial conservatism and have only recently attempted to reconcile with Black Baptists.

The Religion and Society Surveys asked several questions about respondents' closeness to White Evangelicals and the Religious Right as well as about how these groups might affect Black churchgoers' lives. As table 12 shows, significant level of support exists for the idea that the Religious Right harms Blacks—more than one-third of the AME respondents and more than one-quarter of the NBC. AME respondents expressed somewhat warm feelings toward White Evangelicals and the Religious Right. The respondents in the NBC sample, which received additional measures of attitudes toward evangelicals, were warm to all types of evangelicals but were significantly warmer to Black evangelicals than to White evangelicals. Like the AME respondents, those in the NBC sample expressed tepid feelings regarding the Religious Right. Feelings about the Religious Right are negatively related to education. Highly educated respondents in both surveys held cooler feelings toward the Religious Right and were more likely to believe that they harmed Blacks.

The Republican Party has also attempted to make inroads with the Black church, which has been a haven for the Democrats since the New Deal. The Republican Party recently has attempted to recruit more Blacks through a variety of methods (for a detailed discussion, see Philpot 2007). In particular, George W. Bush has used faith as an avenue for opening a dialogue with the African American community. He has been very open about his religious beliefs and has actively sought to discuss faith-based initiatives with members of the Black clergy (Oppel and Niebuhr 2000). The Bush administration and Republican Party appear to have a burgeoning relationship with some Black church members based on shared values and the Black church's ability to create change in the community (McDaniel 2003; McDaniel 2007). However, this relationship has generated significant criticism. Other Black institutions, such as the National Association for the Advancement of Colored People, have harshly criticized Bush administration policies, including faith-based initiatives (Miller 2001). Evidence of the criticism is found in reports that few of the Black churches that support the faith-based policy have received funds (Fletcher 2006).

Several questions in the Religion and Society Surveys tapped into feelings about the parties and their perceived effectiveness at protecting Black interests. Both sets of respondents overwhelmingly felt that the Democratic Party was the better protector, although nearly one-fifth of the respondents in both groups argued that neither party was better. The majority of those in the NBC sample believed that the Black church should provide more support to politicians who express a strong commitment to Christianity, while one-eighth agreed that President Bush's ex-

TABLE 12. Attitudes toward White Evangelicals and the Political Parties

	AME	NBC
Attitudes toward White Evangelicals		
Religious Right is harmful to Blacks.	36.05	27.52
Feeling Thermometers		
Evangelicals		70.43
White Evangelicals	62.23	64.08
Black Evangelicals		71.32
Religious Right	66.17	69.92
Attitudes toward the Political Parties		
Which party best represents Blacks?		
Republican Party	0.35	2.9
Democratic Party	78.82	69.35
Neither	17.71	19.68
Both	3.13	8.06
Politicians who have shown a strong commitment to Christianity should receive more support from the Black church.		55.86
President Bush's expression of faith shows that he is a good ally for the Black church.		12.88
Feeling Thermometers		
George W. Bush	17.95	25.23
John Kerry	63.87	56.78
Republican Party	21.48	25.02
Democratic Party	75.11	72.46

Source: 2004 and 2005 Religion and Society Surveys.

pressions of faith indicate that he is a good ally for the Black church. In general, respondents wanted to support candidates who are committed to their faith. However, the case of Bush proves to be an exception. Members of both the AME and NBC groups had warm feelings toward the Democratic Party and John Kerry and cold feelings toward the Republican Party and Bush. While these results indicate that the Republican Party's current attempts to broaden its base among Blacks are falling on deaf ears, this strategy may ultimately benefit the GOP. As Philpot (2007) finds, continued GOP efforts to appeal to Blacks may lessen hostility toward the party and eventually lead to support.

Class Issues

The overarching issue of class cries for greater attention. Mays and Nicholson (1969) praise the Black church for its openness to all, regardless of class. Research has shown that Blacks with low levels of resources are less likely to be politically engaged (Cohen and Dawson 1993; Harris, Sinclair-Chapman, and McKenzie 2005). One of the reasons that political churches are praised is that they allow those with less income and education to be a part of the political process (Tate 1993). The multivariate analysis in chapter 6 demonstrates that those with lower incomes are more supportive of church involvement. Those at the lowest rungs of the social ladder have a greater need for the church to defend their interests. However, social class plays a role in church membership (Roof and Mc-Kinney 1992). The findings from chapter 2 suggest that churches with a large number of individuals who are not well educated or who are from lower income brackets are less likely to engage the political system. These results coincide with McDaniel and McClerking's (2005) finding that those with higher levels of income and education are more likely to report exposure to political churches. In this case, those who most need to learn skills and gain motivation are the least likely to do so. In addition, Smith (1996) and Cohen (1999) have strongly criticized Black institutions such as the church for catering primarily to the needs of white-collar Blacks and pushing aside the needs and concerns of lower-class Blacks. In many instances, these institutions have served as the scapegoats for Blacks' failure to advance in American society. The growing popularity of prosperity theology creates an even greater fear that poor Blacks' interests' will be further marginalized. In light of the growing economic divide within the Black community, churches must work to make sure that they protect those who are most vulnerable.

BEYOND THE BLACK CHURCH

This volume has provided an account of how groups use existing institutions to defend and advance their interests. At its heart, political science studies groups and how they compete for scarce resources, which requires an understanding of how groups use their existing resources. The framework of the argument for explaining the political engagement of Black churches can be applied to other institutions. Several scholars document how White evangelicals have left behind their apolitical outlook, becoming energized for political action (Wald and Calhoun-Brown 2007; Wilcox and Larson 2006). With methods similar to those used by the civil rights movement, including using churches as networks for recruitment, White evangelicals have created and sustained a social movement that has defended and advanced their interests. But how did this change in evangelical churches come about? Why do some churches openly accept the call, and why do others refuse to engage themselves? The framework established in this volume can assist in answering these questions.

This framework can explain how various groups, both religious and nonreligious, have adjusted their institutions to obtain more leverage in the struggle for resources. From time to time, clubs, associations, and other apolitical organizations have mobilized to engage the political process. The reasons behind such changes as well as the means by which they were sustained or discontinued remain important topics of study. Because politics is an ongoing process, social institutions will routinely enter and exit the political arena over time. Social institutions are important in facilitating political participation. As passive vehicles, they provide civic training and networks of recruitment, thereby making individuals more likely to engage the political system and maintain the basic tenets of democracy. As assertive vehicles, social institutions directly insert their members into the political realm and provide them with the tools to create political change and the motivation to fulfill their goals. Noting changes in leadership, membership, organizational structure, and the outlying political environment allows for a better explanation and prediction of organizational actions. A better understanding of social institutions' entrance into and removal from the political system provides better knowledge of the maintenance, expansion, and contraction of group interests.

APPENDIX A: CHAPTER 2

To directly test my hypothesis, I conducted interviews with pastors and members of four churches in Detroit, Michigan, and three in Austin, Texas. The Detroit interviews were conducted during the summer and fall of 2002, while the Austin interviews were conducted during the fall of 2005 and spring of 2006. Four of the churches are Baptist, while the other three are Methodist. I selected Detroit because of the city's large Black population and thus large sample of churches from which to choose. In addition, the city faced a school voucher vote in 2000, a mayoral election in 2001, and gubernatorial and congressional elections in 2002. Churches and clergy played prominent roles in all of these campaigns. Despite its much smaller Black population, Austin too offered several churches from which to choose, and the city is currently facing some race-related issues. From 1988 to 2005, Austin recorded fourteen police-related deaths, with thirteen minority victims (Troubling Questions 2005). In the spring of 2007, the U.S. Department of Justice announced that it would launch an investigation into the Austin Police Department's use of force (Plohetski and George 2007). The city is also wrestling with a combination of increasing growth and decreasing minority presence. Since 1980, minorities have steadily moved out of Austin and into its suburbs or into other cities (Alford 2005). While I was conducting the interviews, Austin held a city council election, and the city's 2006 mayoral election included a Black candidate. Finally, in 2005, Texas held a statewide referendum on adding a constitutional amendment to ban same-sex marriage. Black clergy have played prominent roles in the police brutality situation and the mayoral race but have been less prominent in the other events.

I selected two of the Detroit churches because their pastors spoke out in the debate over the school voucher vote and chose the other two because they did not publicly react to the issue. I selected one Austin church because it was highly active in the police brutality situation and the other two because they remained out of the discussion. In addition to pastors and members of these churches, I also spoke to other individuals. In Detroit, I interviewed the former pastors of two of the churches to learn more about the city and the churches. I also interviewed two members of other churches to gain a larger perspective on the city. In Austin, I interviewed the pastor of another church for the same purpose. I interviewed a total of seventy-six people—ten pastors and sixty-six church members.

The church members were selected by using theoretical sampling (Eisenhardt 1989). In the Baptist churches, I targeted members of the ministerial staff as well as deacons, trustees, and older members. In the Methodist churches, I targeted members of the steward and trustee boards and older members. The interviews were semistructured; all but six were one-on-one interviews. Two of the Detroit and two of the Austin interviews were conducted with two respondents at the same time, and I conducted one six-person focus group in Detroit and one in Austin. The member interviews focused on issues of church selection, history, activities, and decision making. The pastor interviews were similar but focused more on members' roles in decision making. In addition, both the pastor and member interviews included questions related to church-based political engagement.

DETROIT MEMBER INTERVIEW PROTOCOL

Background and Church Membership

1. Why don't you take a few moments to talk about yourself? What is your age? What is your occupation? Where do you live now, and where are you from originally?
2. How long have you been at this church? Have you held any positions in the church?
3. What were you looking for when you selected your church? Why did you become a member of this church?

Receptivity

1. How do you feel about churches being involved in politics and political activity? Please describe why you feel that way.
2. What types of activities do you believe this entails?
3. Are these feelings specific to the Black church, Christian churches more generally, or to all religious institutions?

4. Ideally, how active would you want your church to be politically? Could you describe some of the activities? What types of activities do you feel are inappropriate for the church?
5. How well do you feel your church fits your ideal vision of the church in politics?
6. Has there ever been a time when you felt the church acted inappropriately on a political issue? Why did you feel that way?
7. How did you express your dissatisfaction?

Negotiation Process (Probe any mention of conflict to establish who was involved and how it was resolved)

Now I want to ask you some questions about how the church reacted to a specific event.
1. How did you feel about the school voucher issue? (If they are not familiar with the voucher issue, explain it as a program that will supplement the costs of private schools. DO NOT PROVIDE A FRAME.)
2. How many others do you think agreed with your views? How many others disagreed with your views? Did you hold the same feelings on this issue as the pastor?
3. How did you and the other members express your concerns about the school voucher issue to each other?
4. How did you communicate your feelings about this issue to your pastor?
5. How did the pastor communicate the proper role of the church during this event?
6. How do you feel the congregation reacted to this? Was there any dissatisfaction with the pastor's stance on the issue?
7. Overall, how do you feel about the way the church handled the school voucher issue? What might you have done differently?

Thank you for participating in this study; your responses were very helpful, and I truly appreciate you providing your time and energy to support me and my work.

AUSTIN MEMBER INTERVIEW PROTOCOL

Background and Church Membership

1. Why don't you take a few moments to talk about yourself? What is your age? What is your occupation? Where do you live now, and where are you from originally?

2. How long have you been at this church? Have you held any positions in the church?

3. What were you looking for when you selected your church? Why did you become a member of this church?

Receptivity

1. How do you feel about churches being involved in politics and political activity? Please describe why you feel that way.

2. What types of activities do you believe this entails?

3. Are these feelings specific to the Black church, Christian churches more generally, or to all religious institutions?

4. Ideally, how active would you want your church to be politically? Could you describe some of the activities? What types of activities do you feel are inappropriate for the church?

5. How well do you feel your church fits your ideal vision of the church in politics?

6. Has there ever been a time when you felt the church acted inappropriately on a political issue? Why did you feel that way?

7. How did you express your dissatisfaction?

Reaction to Recent Events

Now I want to ask you some questions about how the church reacted to a specific event.

1. How did your church react to some of the recent events in Austin (police brutality, gay marriage, or gentrification)?

2. How many others do you think agreed with your views regarding this issue? How many others disagreed with your views? Did you hold the same feelings on this issue as the pastor?

3. How did you and the other members express your concerns about (gentrification, police brutality, or gay marriage) to each other?

4. How did you communicate your feelings about this issue to your pastor?

5. How did the pastor communicate the proper role of the church during this event?

6. How do you feel the congregation reacted to this? Was there any dissatisfaction with the pastor's stance on this issue?

7. Overall, how do you feel about the way the church handled these issues? What might you have done differently?

Thank you for participating in this study; your responses were very helpful, and I truly appreciate you providing your time and energy to support me and my work.

DETROIT PASTOR INTERVIEW PROTOCOL

Background

1. Why don't you take a few moments to describe yourself? What is your age? Where did you gain your training? Where are you from originally? How long have you been at this church?

Conveyance

1. How do you feel about churches being involved in politics and political activity? Please describe why you feel that way.
2. When you think of politics and political activity, what do you think of?
3. Are these feelings specific to churches in general?
4. What do you feel is the proper role of your church in politics? What types of activities do you feel are inappropriate for the church to take part in? Please describe why you feel that way.
5. How well do you feel your church fits your idea of the appropriate role of the church in politics?
6. Has there ever been a time when you felt the members of the church did not support a stance you have taken on a political issue on behalf of the church? Why do you feel that way?
7. Did you express your dissatisfaction? How did you express your dissatisfaction?

Negotiation Process

1. How did you feel about the school voucher issue?
2. How did your congregation feel about the school voucher issue? Were there members who disagreed with you?
3. How did you find out how others felt about this issue? How did your members communicate their feelings about this issue to you?
4. How did you tell your church to handle this event? How did you communicate this to your congregation?
5. Were there any conflicts as to the proper role of the church on this issue? What was the conflict based on? Who was involved in these conflicts?
6. How were these conflicts resolved?
7. Overall, how do you feel about the way the church handled the school voucher issue? What might you have done differently?

AUSTIN PASTOR INTERVIEW PROTOCOL

Background

1. Why don't you take a few moments to describe yourself? What is your age? Where did you gain your training? Where are you from originally? How long have you been at this church?

Conveyance

1. How do you feel about churches being involved in politics and political activity? Please describe why you feel that way.
2. When you think of politics and political activity, what do you think of?
3. Are these feelings specific to churches in general?
4. What do you feel is the proper role of your church in politics? What types of activities do you feel are inappropriate for the church to take part in? Please describe why you feel that way.
5. How well do you feel your church fits your idea of the appropriate role of the church in politics?
6. Has there ever been a time when you felt the members of the church did not support a stance you have taken on a political issue on behalf of the church? Why do you feel that way?
7. Did you express your dissatisfaction? How did you express your dissatisfaction?

Reaction to Recent Events

1. How do you feel about the recent events in Austin (police brutality, gay marriage, or gentrification)?
2. How did your congregation feel about these issues? Were there members who disagreed with you?
3. How did you find out how others felt about this issue? How did your members communicate their feelings about this issue to you?
4. How did you tell your church to handle this event (police brutality, gay marriage, or gentrification)? How did you communicate this to your congregation?
5. Were there any conflicts as to the proper role of the church on this issue? What was the conflict based on? Who was involved in these conflicts?
6. How were these conflicts resolved?
7. Overall, how do you feel about the way the church handled these issues (police brutality, gay marriage, or gentrification)? What might you have done differently?

APPENDIX B: CHAPTER 4

CODING FOR ANALYSIS OF LINCOLN AND MAMIYA SURVEY

Resources

Membership is a five-point variable ranging from 0 to 1, with 0 representing a membership of one hundred or less and 1 representing more than one thousand members: 31.9 percent of the churches have one hundred or fewer members, while 11.3 percent have more than a thousand members.

Church income is a six-point measure ranging from 0 to 1, with 0 indicating that the church's yearly income is less than five thousand dollars and 1 indicating a yearly income of fifty thousand dollars or more: 8.6 percent of the churches had incomes of less than five thousand dollars, while 39.4 percent reported incomes of fifty thousand dollars or more.

The pastoral education variable is a nine-point measure scaled from 0 to 1, with 0 indicating three years or less of formal education and 1 indicating five or more years of post–high school education: 55.7 percent of respondents had at least some college education.

Culture

The two Black religious consciousness measures are dichotomous: 63.4 percent of the churches reported changes in sermons, while 71.7 percent reported teaching children about the distinctiveness of the Black church.

The worship measure is a dichotomous measure: 28.2 percent of respondents approve of this type of music in church.

Church age is measured as the number of years since the church's founding. The variable is scaled from 0 to 1. The church ages ranged between one year and two hundred years; the average age was fifty-seven years.

The South measure is a dichotomous measure. Churches were coded as being in the South if they were located in Alabama, Georgia, Mississippi, Florida, Louisiana, Texas, Kentucky, Virginia, North Carolina, South Carolina, Tennessee, Arkansas, or Maryland. In the sample, 47.6 percent of the churches were located in the South.

Process

The coding of traditions was based on denominational affiliation. Churches belonging to the National Baptist Convention, USA (NBC); the Progressive National Baptist Convention; and the National Baptist Convention of America were coded as being part of the Baptist tradition. African Methodist Episcopal (AME), African Methodist Episcopal Zion, and Christian Methodist Episcopal churches were coded as being part of the Methodist tradition. Finally, the Church of God in Christ (COGIC) was coded as being part of the Pentecostal tradition.

TABLE B1. OLS Analysis of Determinants of Church Social and Political Action

	Social Activities Index	Political Activities Index
Membership	0.217°°°	0.172°°°
	(0.033)	(0.028)
Yearly Income	0.041	0.055°
	(0.032)	(0.027)
Pastor Education	0.159°°°	0.074°
	(0.040)	(0.034)
Distinctiveness of Black Church Taught	0.024	0.028°
	(0.017)	(0.015)
Black Pride Sermons	0.079°°°	0.059°°°
	(0.016)	(0.014)
Church Age	0.001°	0.000°
	(0.000)	(0.000)
Jazz Music Acceptable	0.067°°°	0.013
	(0.017)	(0.014)
South	−0.044°	−0.011
	(0.017)	(0.015)
Methodist	0.009	0.003
	(0.026)	(0.022)
Baptist	−0.015	−0.008
	(0.024)	(0.021)
Constant	0.152°°°	−0.011
	(0.035)	(0.030)
Adjusted R^2	.262	.207
N	965	927

Source: Lincoln and Mamiya Urban sample.
Note: COGIC used as the comparison category.
°.1   °°.05   °°°.01 (two-tailed test)

TABLE B2. Pairwise Correlations of Church-Based Political Engagement and Organizational Determinants for AME Respondents

	Political Action Index	Public Official Spoke	Invited Public Official	Host Political Organization	Served as Polling Place	Held Political Forum
Resources						
Average Attendance	0.274°°°	0.153°°°	0.115°	0.081	0.240°°°	0.209°°°
Culture						
Displayed Black Images	0.156°°°	0.016	0.111°	0.098°	0.109°	0.074
of Religious Figures	0.156°°°	0.016	0.111°	0.098°	0.109°	0.074
South	−0.095	−0.201°°°	−0.006	−0.040	−0.059	−0.014
Inner City	0.131°°	0.067	−0.007	0.009	0.201°°°	0.078
Suburb	0.058	0.010	0.111°	0.092	−0.057	0.049
Small Town	−0.129°°	−0.064	0.001	−0.097°	−0.173°°°	−0.076
Rural	−0.087	−0.029	−0.094	0.018	−0.028	−0.065

Source: 2004 Religion and Society Survey.
°.1   °°.05   °°°.01 (two-tailed test)

TABLE B3. Pairwise Correlations of Church-Based Political Engagement and Organizational Determinants for NBC Respondents

	Political Action Index	Public Official Spoke	Invited Public Official	Host Political Organization	Served as Polling Place	Held Political Forum
Resources						
Average Attendance	0.151°°	0.005	0.048	0.087	0.162°°°	0.094
Culture						
Displayed Black Images						
of Religious Figures	0.139°°	0.012	0.100°	0.036	0.035	0.124°°
South	−0.003	0.033	−0.045	0.013	0.140°°	−0.074
Inner City	0.154°°°	0.113°	0.056	0.033	−0.066	0.197°°°
Suburb	−0.094	−0.066	−0.048	0.078	0.004	−0.096°
Small Town	−0.011	−0.045	0.021	−0.121°°	0.138°°	−0.058
Rural	−0.123°°	−0.052	−0.061	0.027	−0.065	−0.128°°

Source: 2005 Religion and Society Survey.
°.1   °°.05   °°°.01 (two-tailed test)

CODING OF RELIGION AND SOCIETY SURVEYS FOR ORGANIZATIONAL-LEVEL ANALYSIS

Resources

Resources are measured using average weekly attendance. The attendance measure is a six-point measure ranging from 0 to 1, with 0 representing an average attendance of twenty or fewer and 1 representing an average attendance of three hundred or more. For the AME sample, 6.7 percent of the churches had twenty or fewer attendees, while 15.5 percent had more than three hundred attendees. For the NBC sample, 0.6 percent of the churches averaged fewer than twenty attendees, while 29.1 percent had attendance of three hundred or more.

Culture

Culture is measured through the use of Black religious images and physical environment. The Black religious images measure is based on whether the respondents indicated that their churches displayed Black images of religious figures. Among the AME respondents, 39.1 percent reported that their churches had Black images of biblical figures, while the corresponding figure for NBC respondents was 15.4 percent. Physical environment is measured using region and community: 54.8 percent of AME respondents and 69.7 percent of NBC respondents attended churches in the South. For community, 51.3 percent of AME respondents and 54.6 percent of NBC respondents attended churches located in inner cities; for small towns, those numbers were 22.7 percent for AME respondents and 20.3 percent for NBC respondents; for rural areas, those numbers were 14.3 percent for AME respondents and 15.6 percent for NBC respondents; and in suburbs, the numbers were 11.7 percent for the AME and 9.5 percent for the NBC.

APPENDIX C: CHAPTER 5

CODING OF RELIGION AND SOCIETY SURVEYS
FOR THE CLERGY ANALYSIS

Internal Determinants

The internal determinants are measured using demographics, political outlook, theology, and socialization. Demographics are measured through position, age, sex, and education. Among the AME clergy respondents, 58.2 percent were pastors of their churches, while 35.1 percent of the NBC clergy were church pastors. Age is based on the respondents' year of birth, scaled 0 to 1. The AME clergy averaged 56.9 years old, while the NBC clergy averaged 47.2. In regard to gender, 43.6 percent of the AME clergy were women, while 31 percent of the NBC clergy were women. Education is a six-point variable scaled 0 to 1, with 0 indicating less than a high school degree and 1 indicating a graduate or professional degree. The AME clergy averaged .85 on this scale, while the NBC clergy averaged .77.

Political outlook is measured through political interest, ideology, and beliefs about racial discrimination. Political interest is a seven-point measure scaled 0 to 1, with 0 indicating no interest in politics and 1 indicating high interest. The AME clergy averaged .79, while the NBC clergy averaged .77. Ideology is also a seven-point measure ranging from 0 to 1, with 0 indicating very liberal and 1 indicating very conservative. The AME clergy averaged .43 on this measure, while the NBC clergy averaged .50. The final political outlook measure captures the extent to which the respondents believe that racial discrimination still exists. The discrimination measure is a thirteen-point scale (AME α = .564, NBC α = .682) based on the degree to which respondents believe that discrimination leads Blacks to have worse jobs, lower income, and worse housing than White people. Both the AME and NBC clergy averaged .87 on this scale.

Theology is measured through orthodoxy and black theology. Orthodoxy is a five-point scale (AME α = .677, NBC α = .653) ranging from 0 to 1, based on respondents' level of agreement with the following statements: Jesus was born of a virgin; the devil actually exists; the Bible is the literal word of God; Jesus Christ is the only salvation; and Adam and Eve are historical figures. The AME clergy averaged .73 on the scale, while the NBC clergy averaged .77. Black theology is a three-point scale (AME α = .579, NBC α = .484) ranging from 0 to 1, based on respondents' level of agreement with the following statements: Jesus is Black; God is on the side of Blacks; and churches can display Black images of biblical figures. AME clergy averaged .37, while NBC clergy averaged .18.

The final measure of internal determinants is socialization, which is measured using age cohort and exposure to Black institutions. The age cohort measures indicate socialization during differing periods—specifically before (born before 1944), during (born between 1944 and 1963), and after the civil rights movement (born after 1963). Among the AME clergy, 35.2 percent are in the pre-movement cohort; 57.8 percent are in the movement cohort, and 7.0 percent are in the post-movement cohort. Among the NBC clergy, 13.2 percent are in the pre-movement cohort, 55.9 percent are in the movement cohort, and 30.9 percent are in the post-movement cohort. Exposure to Black institutions is measured through membership in Black organizations, such as the National Association for the Advancement of Colored People; membership in Black fraternities or sororities; and exposure to Black media. An overwhelming 90.4 percent of the AME clergy belonged to Black organizations, as did 54.8 percent of the NBC clergy. The Black fraternity and sorority membership question was asked only of the NBC, and 30.6 percent of respondents belonged to these types of organizations. Only AME respondents were asked about exposure to Black media. The measure is a six-point measure (α = .673) ranging from 0 to 1 and indicating exposure to a local Black radio show, national Black radio show, Black newspaper, Black magazine, local Black television show, or national Black television show. The AME clergy averaged .49 on this measure.

External Determinants

The external determinants of conveyance are captured using measures of the organization, members, and environment. The organization is measured using weekly attendance, pastor tenure, and conflicts within the church. Weekly attendance is measured in the same way as in chapter 4: AME clergy averaged .42, while NBC clergy averaged .68. Tenure is based on how long the respondent has been associated with this church and is scaled from 0 to 1. The average tenure for AME clergy was 5.9 years and for NBC clergy was 16.1 years. The final aspect of the measurement of organization is conflicts. Respondents were asked if serious conflicts over political matters had ever arisen in their churches. Among AME clergy, 10.3 percent reported such conflicts, as did 9.2 percent of NBC clergy. Respondents were also asked whether pastors and members had ever come into direct conflict over political issues. Among AME clergy, 18.4 percent reported such conflicts, as did 13.0 percent of NBC clergy.

The measurement of members is based on the degree to which clergy believe that their members influence their decisions and on differences in ideological attachments. The member influence variable is a seven-point measure scaled from 0 to 1, with 0 indicating very little influence and 1 indicating a great deal of influence. The AME clergy averaged .45, while the NBC clergy averaged .42. The ideological difference measures are based on ministers' rankings of themselves as more liberal, more conservative, or about the same as their members. Among the AME clergy, 25.7 percent believed that their members were more liberal, 30.0 percent believed that their members were more conservative, and 44.3 percent believed that they were about the same. Among the NBC clergy, 25.8 percent believed their members to be more liberal, 21.0 percent believed their members to be more conservative, and 53.2 believed that they and their members were about the same.

The final aspect of the external determinants is environment, which is measured in the same way as in chapter 4. Among AME clergy, 35.9 percent were located in churches in the inner city, 7.7 percent were located in the suburbs, 33.3 percent were in small towns, and 23.1 percent were in rural areas. Among NBC clergy, 52.8 percent were in inner-city churches, 11.1 percent were in suburban churches, 20.8 percent were in small-town churches, and 15.3 percent were in rural churches. The majority of both groups (AME 68.6 percent, NBC 61.2 percent) were in the South.

CODING FOR ANALYSIS OF 2002 COOPERATIVE CLERGY SURVEY

Approval of Activism Scales

The electoral activism scale (α =.806) is a twenty-five-point scale comprised of approval of clergy publicly supporting a candidate, working actively on a campaign, joining a national political organization, contributing to a PAC, and running for public office.

The collective action scale (α = .791) is a twenty-point scale comprised of approval of clergy taking part in a protest, committing civil disobedience, forming a study group within the church, and forming an action group within the church.

The political statements scale (α = .731), is a fifteen-point scale comprised of approval of clergy taking a stand on a political issue outside of the pulpit, taking a political stand within the pulpit, and delivering a sermon on a controversial issue.

TABLE C1. Pairwise Correlations of Internal Factors and Support of Church and Clergy Activism for AME Clergy

	Church Action	Clergy Action	Conflicting Views Should Not Be Expressed	Involved in Political Matters	No Politics in Worship Service
Pastor	0.2364°°	0.2726°°	−0.1792	0.2008°	0.0348
Demographics					
Age	−0.1613	−0.2287°	0.1514	0.22°	0.2076
Female	−0.168	−0.0838	−0.2313°	−0.3542°	−0.1276
Education	0.3421°°°	0.311°°°	−0.1895	0.0449	−0.2199°
Political Outlook					
Political Interest	0.0923	0.1509	−0.2141°	0.1472	−0.1187
Conservative	−0.1139	−0.1476	0.1407	0.0148	0.1244
Discrimination	−0.0618	−0.0076	0.1822	−0.0414	0.1115
Theology					
Orthodoxy	0.2671°°	0.2037°	−0.1204	−0.1353	−0.013
Black Theology	0.3241°°°	0.463°°°	−0.3882°°°	0.0684	−0.1831
Socialization					
Age Cohort					
Pre–Civil Rights Movement	−0.235°	−0.2736°°	0.0987	0.1403	0.2696°°
Civil Rights Movement	0.1921	0.1468	−0.0129	−0.0944	−0.1714
Post–Civil Rights Movement	0.0638	0.2234°	−0.1491	−0.0746	−0.1581
Black Institutions					
Black Organization	0.3241°°°	0.1824	−0.0519	0.2379°°	−0.1177
Black Media	0.389°°°	0.4166°°°	−0.101	0.2381°°	−0.1489

Source: 2004 Religion and Society Survey
°.1   °°.05   °°°.01 (two-tailed test)

Activism Indexes

The electoral activism index is a twenty-four-point index comprised of the frequency with which clergy have publicly supported candidates, joined national political organizations, run for office, displayed campaign support material, endorsed candidates while preaching, and attended political rallies.

The collective action index is a twelve-point index comprised of the frequency with which clergy have taken part in protest marches, participated in civil disobedience, formed study groups within the church, and formed action groups within the church. The political statement index is a sixteen-point index comprised of the frequency with which clergy have taken political stands outside the pulpit, taken stands within the pulpit, mentioned political issues during sermons, and preached entire sermons on controversial issues.

Social justice sermons are captured through the use of a social justice index. The social justice index is a twelve-point index comprised of the

TABLE C2. Pairwise Correlations of External Factors and Support of Church and Clergy Activism for AME Clergy

	Church Action	Clergy Action	Conflicting Views Should Not Be Expressed	Involved in Political Matters	No Politics in Worship Service
Organization					
Weekly Attendance	0.1969°	0.0472	−0.0466	0.1397	0.0178
Experience					
Pastor Tenure	0.1019	0.0375	0.0595	0.0731	0.1902
Political Conflict	−0.0577	−0.0675	0.1213	0.0556	0.0191
Conflict with Pastor	−0.014	0.0825	0.0674	−0.003	0.0527
Environment					
Inner City	0.2546°°	0.2749°°	−0.1546	0.1236	−0.0813
Suburb	0.2024°	0.1452	0.0611	0.1312	0.0224
Small Town	−0.288°°	−0.225°°	0.0713	0.0671	−0.0496
Rural	−0.0967	−0.1531	0.0578	−0.3024°°°	0.1314
South	−0.1521	−0.253°°	0.2068	−0.0835	0.0106
Members					
Member Influence	−0.0767	−0.0089	−0.0011	0.2219°	−0.1975
Member Ideology					
More Liberal	−0.1441	−0.2986°°	0.105	−0.0525	−0.048
About the Same	−0.0867	−0.0438	0.2005	0.0485	0.2464°°
More Conservative	0.234°	0.3322°°°	−0.309°°	−0.0029	−0.2179°

Source: 2004 Religion and Society Survey.
° .1   °° .05   °°° .01 (two-tailed test)

frequency with which clergy preached sermons on the following topics: poverty, gender equality, civil rights, and the environment.

Morality sermons are captured through the use of a morality index. The morality index is an eighteen-point index comprised of the frequency with which clergy preached sermons on the following topics: drinking, abortion, pornography, the nuclear family, gambling, and homosexuality.

All of the scales and indexes are scaled from 0 to 1 to indicate the intensity of support or activism. A 0 on a scale or index indicates complete disagreement or inactivity, while a 1 indicates complete agreement or extreme activism.

Internal Determinants

Demographics. Chapter 4 demonstrates the importance of pastoral education in church-based political engagement, as churches with highly educated pastors were significantly more active than those with less edu-

TABLE C3. Pairwise Correlations of Internal Factors and Reported Activities of AME Clergy

	Pastor Political Activity Index	Speaking about Politics	Direct Political Action	Frequency of Talking to Members
Demographics				
Age	−.2864°	−0.3033°°	−0.361°°	−0.0316
Female	0.0588	0.0447	0.1296	−0.1772
Education	0.088	0.1206	0.0505	−0.0060
Political Outlook				
Political Interest	−0.1373	−0.0174	−0.1005	0.1224
Conservative	0.0751	0.1006	0.029	−0.2287
Discrimination	0.171	0.0529	−0.0005	0.0987
Theology				
Orthodoxy	0.0339	0.1068	−0.0083	−0.0256
Black Theology	0.265°	0.1386	0.2858°	0.2295
Socialization				
Pre–Civil Rights Movement	−0.2837°	−0.2991°°	−0.3412°°	0.0920
Civil Rights Movement	0.173	0.1873	0.2601°	−0.1058
Post–Civil Rights Movement	0.2349	0.2364	0.1623	0.0486
Black Organization	0.0015	0.1613	−0.1171	0.1884
Black Media	0.1168	0.2885°	0.0324	0.2325

Source: 2004 Religion and Society Survey.
°.1   °°.05   °°°.01 (two-tailed test)

cated pastors. Among respondents, 72.2 percent were college graduates. The literature and interviews show that female clergy face different pressures and view their roles differently than their male counterparts. Many female clergy align themselves with women's issues (Olson, Crawford, and Guth 2000). In addition, female clergy face different pressures than do their male counterparts (Crawford, Deckman, and Braun 2001). While only one of the COGIC clergy was female, 23.2 percent of the AME clergy were women, as were 23.2 percent of the clergy from predominantly White denominations.

Political Interest. Political interest is measured using a question regarding general interest in politics. The measure is a seven-point scale from 0 to 1, with 0 indicating no interest in politics and 1 indicating a strong interest. Only two of the clergy indicated they had no interest in politics, while 32.0 percent expressed a strong interest in politics. As the

TABLE C4. Pairwise Correlations of External Factors and Reported Activities of AME Pastors

	Pastor Political Activity Index	Speaking about Politics	Direct Political Action	Frequency of Talking to Members
Organization				
Weekly Attendance	0.0523	–0.1351	0.1408	0.0974
Experience				
Pastor Tenure	–0.0217	–0.289°	0.0295	–0.0676
Political Conflict	0.1665	–0.0186	0.1118	0.0764
Conflict with Pastor	0.152	0.1143	0.1427	0.1940
Environment				
Inner City	0.1839	0.2935°°	0.0853	0.0679
Suburb	0.0653	0.1472	–0.068	–0.0084
Small Town	–0.2926°°	–0.2068	–0.2115	–0.0907
Rural	0.0757	–0.1901	0.1753	0.0269
South	–0.0891	–0.0588	–0.0991	–0.1373
Members				
Member Influence	0.1351	0.0682	0.0933	0.2311
Member Ideology				
More Liberal	–0.0862	0.0556	–0.0404	–0.2632°
About the Same	–0.161	–0.217	–0.1635	–0.0435
More Conservative	0.2415	0.1729	0.2034	0.2785°

Source: 2004 Religion and Society Survey.
°.1   °°.05   °°°.01 (two-tailed test)

interviews and the Religion and Society surveys show, clergy with a strong interest in politics are more supportive of church-based activism.

Religious Outlook.   The orthodoxy scale (α =.939) is a thirty-five-point scale ranging from 0 to 1 that measures the degree to which respondents agree with the following statements: Adam and Eve are historical figures; Jesus was born of a virgin; the devil actually exists; the Bible is the in-errant word of God; Jesus Christ is the only salvation; and Jesus will return someday. Among the respondents, 46.8 percent fall at the high end of the scale.

The liberation theology scale (α =.693) is a ten-point additive scale comprised of the degree to which clergy feel that liberation theology and social justice lie at the heart of the Gospel. Among the clergy, 11.4 percent rank at the high end of the scale.

TABLE C5. Pairwise Correlations of Internal Factors and Support of Church and Clergy Activism for NBC Clergy

	Church Action	Clergy Action	Social Problem	Police Brutality	Racial Discrimination
Pastor	0.1993°	0.1514	0.219°	0.0733	0.2376°°
Demographics					
Age	0.0481	–0.0328	0.2223°	–0.125	–0.0628
Female	0.0039	–0.1008	–0.2615°°	–0.2137°	–0.1679
Education	0.0882	0.129	0.1946	–0.0267	–0.0577
Political Outlook					
Political Interest	0.2003	0.2678°°	0.5234°°°	0.2208°	0.3392°°°
Conservative	–0.0116	–0.0597	–0.0139	–0.0581	–0.0938
Discrimination	–0.0316	–0.0231	0.0959	–0.0258	0.1098
Theology					
Orthodoxy	0.1195	0.2858°°	0.2367°	0.2839°°	0.0661
Black Theology	0.1159	0.4163°°°	0.2247°	0.15	0.018
Socialization					
Age Cohort					
Pre–Civil Rights Movement	0.0536	–0.1351	0.2062	–0.0973	0.0302
Civil Rights Movement	0.0021	0.1003	–0.0435	0.0772	0.0282
Post–Civil Rights Movement	–0.0415	–0.0087	–0.1106	–0.0098	–0.0535
Black Institutions					
Black Organizations	0.1297	–0.082	0.1764	0.1138	0.2043°
Black Fraternal Organizations	0.2234°	0.202°	0.0283	0.1227	0.0797

Source: 2005 Religion and Society Survey.
°.1   °°.05   °°°.01 (two-tailed test)

Socialization. Socialization is measured based on the age cohort of the respondent. As in the analysis of the Religion and Society surveys, I have created three dichotomous variables representing three age cohorts. Those born before 1944 are considered to have been socialized before the civil rights movement; those socialized between 1944 and 1963 are considered to have been socialized during the movement; and those born after 1963 are considered to have been socialized after the movement. The pre-movement cohort makes up 28.3 percent of the respondents, while those socialized during and after the movement make up 65.1 percent and 6.6 percent, respectively.

External Determinants

Denomination. Denomination is accounted for with dummy variables for AME and COGIC membership. Black clergy in predominantly White denominations serve as the baseline group. This approach enables me to determine the degree to which clergy in these two predominantly Black denominations differ from their counterparts in predominantly White

TABLE C6. Pairwise Correlations of External Factors and Support of Church and Clergy Activism for NBC Clergy

	Church Action	Clergy Action	Social Problem	Police Brutality	Racial Discrimination
Organization					
Weekly Attendance	0.0697	−0.0629	0.0419	0.0444	0.0019
Experience					
Pastor Tenure	−0.0689	−0.1244	0.1367	−0.0875	0.0803
Political Conflict	−0.0915	−0.0203	−0.3272°°	−0.0387	−0.0716
Conflict with Pastor	0.1971	0.1828	0.1022	0.0641	0.0121
Environment					
Inner City	0.0171	0.3012°°	0.0775	0.0588	−0.2135°
Suburb	−0.101	−0.1328	0.0769	0.0278	0.0058
Small Town	0.0766	−0.1277	0.0106	−0.0998	0.1242
Rural	−0.0221	−0.1579	−0.1802	0.0095	0.1516
South	−0.037	−0.1922	0.0724	−0.0801	0.0685
Members					
Member Influence	0.0112	−0.0291	0.055	0.0464	−0.0513
Member Ideology					
More Liberal	−0.091	−0.0364	−0.2768°°	−0.1831	−0.1437
About the Same	0.1132	0.0571	0.3249°°	0.2962°°	0.2925°°
More Conservative	−0.0409	−0.0309	−0.1049	−0.1728	−0.211

Source: 2005 Religion and Society Survey.
°.1   °°.05   °°°.01 (two-tailed test)

denominations. Also, having dummy variables for these denominations allows me to test the degree to which the coefficients of AME and COGIC clergy differ.

Church Resources. I capture resources with a measure of average weekly attendance. The weekly attendance measure is an eight-point ordinal measure scaled from 0 to 1, with 0 indicating twenty or fewer attendees and 1 indicating five hundred or more attendees. Among respondents, 14.4 percent reported twenty or fewer attendees each week, while 2.5 percent reported five hundred or more attendees.

Member Attitudes. The congregation support measure is a five-point measure scaled from 0 to 1, with 0 indicating that the congregation greatly discourages activism and 1 indicating that it greatly encourages

TABLE C7. Pairwise Correlations of Internal Factors and Reported Activities of NBC Pastors

	Pastor Political Activity Index	Speaking about Politics	Direct Political Action	Frequency of Talking to Members
Demographics				
Age	−0.1213	−0.1585	0.0323	−0.7189°°°
Female	.	.	.	.
Education	0.347°	0.3291	0.2478	0.3487°
Political Outlook				
Political Interest	0.0543	0.1485	−0.004	0.0524
Conservative	−0.0074	0.1541	−0.1562	−0.1102
Discrimination	−0.2058	−0.2639	−0.0478	−0.1577
Theology				
Orthodox	0.0915	0.0843	0.0511	−0.0185
Black Theology	0.3689°	0.3711°	0.302	0.1771
Socialization				
Age Cohort				
Pre–Civil Rights Movement	−0.2673	−0.3266	−0.1657	−0.5241°°
Civil Rights Movement	0.2385	0.2828	0.2871	0.0607
Post–Civil Rights Movement	−0.0081	0	−0.1657	0.4845°°
Black Institutions				
Black Organizations	−0.202	−0.2055	−0.1372	0.0852
Black Fraternal Organizations	0.408°°	0.2653	0.3454°	0.3082

Source: 2005 Religion and Society Survey.
°.1   °°.05   °°°.01 (two-tailed test)

activism. Among respondents, 47.4 percent reported that their congregations encouraged political involvement. AME and COGIC clergy were more likely than their counterparts in predominantly White denominations to report that their congregations' beliefs encouraged political activism. In fact, none of the AME clergy reported that their congregants' beliefs discouraged political involvement.

Environment.   The measure of urbanicity is based on the clergy's response to a question about the type of community in which their churches were located. The measure is an eight-point measure scaled from 0 to 1, with 0 representing a rural area and 1 representing a very large city. Rural areas accounted for only 8.0 percent of the clergy, while 22.5 percent lived in very large cities.

TABLE C8. Pairwise Correlations of External Factors and Reported Activities of NBC Pastors

	Pastor Political Activity Index	Speaking about Politics	Direct Political Action	Frequency of Talking to Members
Organization				
Weekly Attendance	0.2106	0.0374	0.2496	0.5111°°
Experience				
Pastor Tenure	–0.207	–0.1783	–0.0371	–0.4348°°
Political Conflict	0.1391	0.3226	0.0141	–0.227
Conflict with Pastor	0.2275	0.0388	0.389°	0.1659
Environment				
Inner City	0.4888°°	0.4681°°	0.3454°	0.1461
Suburb	–0.2305	–0.2237	–0.1616	–0.3331
Small Town	–0.288	–0.3989°°	–0.0847	–0.0568
Rural	–0.1339	0.012	–0.2294	0.0525
South	–0.0752	–0.2887	0.1172	–0.0776
Members				
Member Influence	0.2191	0.1629	0.1377	0.2061
Member Ideology				
More Liberal	0.2171	0.1681	0.1112	0.0179
About the Same	–0.1496	–0.3059	0.053	–0.2031
More Conservative	–0.0663	0.2241	–0.2218	0.2678

Source: 2005 Religion and Society Survey.
°.1   °°.05   °°°.01 (two-tailed test)

TABLE C9. OLS Analysis of Clergy Support for and Engagement in Political Activities

	Support for Electoral Activism	Support for Collective Activism	Frequency of Electoral Activism	Frequency of Collective Action
Female	0.078°°	0.028	−0.013	−0.013
	(0.038)	(0.036)	(0.041)	(0.041)
Education	0.077	0.241°°°	0.107°	0.183°°°
	(0.058)	(0.054)	(0.059)	(0.064)
Political Interest	0.300°°°	0.270°°°	0.328°°°	0.303°°°
	(0.060)	(0.056)	(0.064)	(0.065)
Orthodoxy	−0.025	−0.153°°	0.027	−0.162°
	(0.078)	(0.072)	(0.082)	(0.084)
Liberation Theology	0.128°°	0.133°°°	0.079	0.166°°°
	(0.054)	(0.050)	(0.056)	(0.057)
Civil Rights Movement Generation	0.063	0.143°°°	−0.124°°	0.021
	(0.052)	(0.047)	(0.052)	(0.053)
Post–Civil Rights Movement Generation	0.036	0.076°°°	−0.064°°	−0.015
	(0.030)	(0.028)	(0.031)	(0.032)
AME	0.109°°°	0.048	0.096°°°	0.093°°
	(0.034)	(0.032)	(0.037)	(0.036)
COGIC	0.082°°	−0.010	0.077°°	0.003
	(0.035)	(0.033)	(0.037)	(0.038)
Weekly Attendance	−0.133°°	−0.063	−0.132°	0.111
	(0.067)	(0.062)	(0.070)	(0.073)
Congregation Support	0.124°	0.143°°	0.164°°	0.074
	(0.072)	(0.067)	(0.078)	(0.078)
Urban	0.024	0.029	−0.019	0.015
	(0.042)	(0.039)	(0.044)	(0.044)
Constant	0.097	0.158	−0.157	−0.183
	(0.108)	(0.100)	(0.112)	(0.115)
Adjusted R^2	.272	.214	.284	.336
N	217	216	201	204

Source: 2002 Cooperative Clergy Survey.
°.1   °°.05   °°°.01 (two-tailed test)

TABLE C10. OLS Analysis of Clergy Support for and Frequency of
Political Statements and Sermon Topics

	Support for Political Statements	Frequency of Political Statements	Frequency of Social Justice Sermons	Frequency of Morality Sermons
Female	0.002	−0.027	0.025	−0.023
	(0.043)	(0.041)	(0.035)	(0.046)
Education	0.078	0.133°°	−0.012	−0.040
	(0.065)	(0.060)	(0.052)	(0.069)
Political Interest	0.262°°°	0.412°°°	0.267°°°	0.118°
	(0.066)	(0.064)	(0.053)	(0.069)
Orthodoxy	−0.156°	−0.053	−0.076	0.214°°
	(0.085)	(0.082)	(0.070)	(0.090)
Liberation Theology	0.110°	0.043	0.098°°	−0.038
	(0.059)	(0.057)	(0.048)	(0.063)
Civil Rights Movement Generation	0.114°°	−0.022	−0.063	0.018
	(0.056)	(0.052)	(0.045)	(0.058)
Post–Civil Rights Movement Generation	0.049	0.042	−0.016	0.018
	(0.033)	(0.031)	(0.027)	(0.034)
AME	−0.013	−0.003	−0.013	−0.007
	(0.038)	(0.036)	(0.031)	(0.040)
COGIC	0.057	0.054	−0.013	0.108°°°
	(0.039)	(0.037)	(0.032)	(0.041)
Weekly Attendance	0.082	0.087	0.049	0.103
	(0.073)	(0.072)	(0.060)	(0.078)
Congregation Support	0.277°°°	0.198°°	0.168°°	0.141°
	(0.080)	(0.079)	(0.065)	(0.085)
Urban	−0.002	0.059	0.058	0.015
	(0.046)	(0.044)	(0.038)	(0.049)
Constant	0.293°°	−0.088	0.362°°°	0.199
	(0.118)	(0.113)	(0.096)	(0.127)
Adjusted R^2	.407	.319	.203	.096
N	211	202	214	211

Source: 2002 Cooperative Clergy Survey.
 °.1   °°.05   °°°.01 (two-tailed test)

APPENDIX D: CHAPTER 6

CODING OF RELIGION AND SOCIETY SURVEYS FOR THE MEMBER ANALYSIS

Internal Determinants

The internal determinants for members resemble those for clergy. Demographics are measured using age, sex, education, and income. The average age of the AME respondents was 56.6, while the average for the NBC was 48.0. Women made up a clear majority (AME 82.7 percent, NBC 82.3 percent) of the respondents in both groups. The average education level for AME respondents was .76 and for NBC respondents was .73. Income is a ten-point scale ranging from 0 to 1, with 0 indicating an income of five thousand dollars or less and 1 indicating an income of one hundred thousand dollars or more. The AME respondents averaged .67, while the NBC respondents averaged .63. Political outlook is measured using political interest and ideology. The AME respondents averaged .78 on the political interest scale and .42 on the ideology scale; the NBC respondents averaged .71 on the political interest scale and .52 on the ideology scale. Theology is measured using orthodoxy (AME α = .555, NBC α = .672) and adherence to Black theology (AMEα = .351, NBC α = .462). AME respondents averaged .69 and .29 on these scales, respectively, while NBC respondents averaged .71 and .13. The final measures of internal determinants are measures of socialization, which is measured using age cohort and exposure to Black institutions. Among the AME respondents, 43.1 percent were in the pre-movement generation, 13.9 percent were in the post-movement generation, and 43.1 percent were socialized during the civil rights movement. Among the NBC respondents, 18.3 percent were socialized before the movement, 30.5 percent were socialized after the movement, and 51.3 percent were socialized during the movement. On the Black media exposure index (α = .545), the AME respondents averaged .59, and 41.7 percent attended historically Black colleges or universities. Among the NBC respondents, 47.5 percent reported membership in Black organizations, and 20.6 percent reported membership in Black fraternities or sororities.

External Determinants

The external determinants are measured using aspects of the organization and environment. The organization is measured in two ways. The first set of measurements examines experiences and evaluation of leadership. The second set measures commitment to the organization. Experiences are measured using reports of past church conflicts regarding political issues, and 8.2 percent of AME respondents and 9.9 percent of NBC respondents reported having such conflicts with the pastors of their churches. Only 9.3 percent of AME respondents and 6.6 percent of NBC respondents had had serious conflicts in the church regarding political matters. The evaluation of leadership is captured through a pastor performance scale and a pastoral influence scale. The NBC respondents were asked to respond to a seven-point pastor performance scale scaled 0 to 1, with 0 indicating that the pastor is doing a very poor job and 1 indicating a very good job. The NBC respondents averaged .84. Respondents were also asked about the degree to which their pastors influence their political decisions, with answers ranked on a seven-point measure, scaled 0 to 1, on which 0 indicates no influence at all and 1 indicates a great deal of influence. The AME respondents averaged .31, while the NBC respondents averaged .49. The final aspect of organization is commitment, which is measured by church attendance and by holding a position in the church. Church attendance is a five-point measure, scaled 0 to 1, with 0 indicating never attending church and 1 indicating attending church services more than once a week. The AME respondents averaged .91, while the NBC respondents averaged .92. Among AME respondents, 85.8 held positions in their churches, while for NBC respondents, that number was 85.3 percent.

Environment is measured using physical environment and comfort in the environment. The physical environment is measured using region and the community in which the church is located. The majority (AME 50.2 percent, NBC 71.8 percent) of both samples were in the South. Among AME respondents, 56.8 percent attended church in the inner city, 18.9 percent attended church in small towns, 13.1 percent attended church in suburban areas, and 11.2 percent attended church in rural areas. Among NBC respondents, 55.6 percent attended church in the inner city, 20.4 percent attended church in small towns, 15.3 percent attended church in rural areas, and 8.8 percent attended church in suburban areas. Comfort in the environment is measured using the same discrimination scale used in chapter 5 (AME α = .645, NBC α = .564). The AME respondents averaged .88, while the NBC respondents averaged .84.

CODING FOR 1993–1994 NATIONAL BLACK POLITICS STUDY

Internal Determinants

Demographics. Sex is a dichotomous variable with 0 indicating male and 1 indicating female. Education is a twenty-six-point measure, scaled

TABLE D1. Pairwise Correlations of Measures of Receptivity and Internal Determinants for AME Respondents

	Church Action	Pastoral Action	No Expressing Views If Contrary to Members	Churches Should Be Involved	No Politics in Worship Service	More Church Action	More Pastoral Action
Demographics							
Age	−.064	−.058	.161°°	−.047	.145°°	.064	.090
Female	−.141°°	−.200°°°	.000	−.130°	.108	−.048	−.036
Education	.263°°°	.282°°°	−.359°°°	.254°°°	−.208°°°	.052	.051
Income	.205°°°	.282°°°	−.186°°°	.176°°	−.208°°°	.095	.093
Political Orientation							
Political Interest	.049	.064	−.152°°	.115°	−.086	.146°°	.157°°
Conservative	−.153°°	−.176°°	.094	−.043	−.062	−.125	−.027
Theology							
Orthodoxy	−.009	.118°	.050	−.056	.152°°	−.055	.034
Black Theology	.297°°°	.335°°°	−.160°°	.167°°	−.266°°°	.181°°°	.124°
Socialization							
Pre–Civil Rights Movement	−.077	−.086	.217°°°	−.043	.156°°	−.055	.033
Civil Rights Movement	.010	.019	−.153°°	.021	−.099	.134°	.034
Post–Civil Rights Movement	.096	.097	−.091	.032	−.084	−.116	−.100
Black Organization	.060	.153°°	−.189°°°	.176°°	−.182°°°	−.067	−.085
Historically Black College or University	.059	.076	.023	.175°°	−.002	.142°°	.069
Black Media	.162°°	.183°°°	−.162°°	.039	−.123°	.046	.072

Source: 2004 Religion and Society Survey.
°.1   °°.05   °°°.01 (two-tailed test)

from 0 to 1, indicating the number of years of schooling completed. Income is a nine-point measure based on the reported total family income. The measure is scaled from 0 to 1, with 0 indicating a total family income of ten thousand dollars or less and 1 indicating a family income of seventy-five thousand dollars or more.

Political Interest. The electoral participation measure is a seven-point index (α = .748) comprised of voting in the last presidential election, giving money to a candidate, signing a petition in favor of a candidate, helping in a voter registration drive, giving someone a ride to the polls, attending a fund-raiser, and handing out campaign material. The measure is an additive seven-point index ranging from 0 to 1.

Religious Outlook. The 1993 National Black Politics Study did not ask questions directly related to religious orthodoxy but did ask respondents' level of agreement with the following statement: "Black churches should spend more time on personal salvation." The salvation measure is a four-

TABLE D2. Pairwise Correlations of Measures of Receptivity and Organizational and External Determinants for AME Respondents

	Church Action	Pastoral Action	No Expressing Views If Contrary to Members	Churches Should Be Involved	No Politics in Worship Service	More Church Action	More Pastoral Action
Organization							
Personal Conflict	.006	−.054	−.073	−.085	.0687	−.139°	−.081
Pastor Influence	−.027	.089	−.209°°°	.141°°	−.215°°°	.029	−.008
Serious Conflict	.009	−.057	.055	−.022	.064	−.012	.005
Political Conflict	.007	.006	−.047	.146°	−.131°	.092	−.017
Commitment							
Attendance	−.038	−.037	.056	−.152°°	.136°°	−.165°°	−.131°
Position	−.076	−.095	.141°	−.107	.148°°	−.021	−.021
Environment							
South	−.093	−.033	.067	−.009	.182°°°	−.055	−.036
Inner City	.205°°°	.118°	.026	.068	−.087	.031	.018
Suburb	−.011	.084	−.076	.102	−.065	.119	.062
Small Town	−.152°°	−.150°°	.045	−.154°°	.067	−.092	−.013
Rural	−.122°	−.088	−.016	−.021	.122°	−.064	−.081
Agitation							
Discrimination	.009	.048	−.080	−.014	.044	.137°	.127°

Source: 2004 Religion and Society Survey.
°.1   °°.05   °°°.01

point measure ranging from 0 to 1. Among respondents, 83 percent agreed with this statement. The second measure of theology captures a social theology—specifically Black theology. The measure of Black theology involves the level of importance placed on having Black images of Christ in Black churches. The Black Christ variable is a four-point measure with 0 indicating not important at all and 1 indicating very important. Among respondents, 37.7 percent ranked having Black images of Christ as at least fairly important.

Socialization. As in other analyses, the age cohorts are broken into three categories based on socialization before, during, and after the civil rights movement. The pre-movement generation includes those born before 1944, the movement generation includes those born between 1944 and 1963, and the post-movement generation consists of those born after 1963.

TABLE D3. Pairwise Correlations of Measures of Receptivity and Internal Determinants for NBC Respondents

	Church Action	Pastoral Action	Social Problem	Police Brutality	Racial Discrimination	Abortion Clinic	Gay Rights Laws	More Church Action	More Pastoral Action
Demographics									
Age	.154°°	.072	.034	.183°°	.138°	−.168°°	−.113	.052	.036
Female	.060	−.005	.044	.120°	.104	−.063	−.112	−.129°	−.185°°
Education	.208°°°	.169°°	.065	.130°	−.023	.050	.119	.065	.012
Income	.077	.095	.034	.060	.100	.105	.200°°°	.042	−.013
Political Interest	.250°°°	.205°°°	.304°°°	.231°°°	.210°°°	.068	.105	.177°°	.0354
Conservative	.070	.142°	.036	.133°	.036	.152°	.118	−.009	−.008
Theology									
Orthodoxy	.203°°°	.242°°°	.253°°°	.126°	.227°°°	.155°°	.046	−.056	.004
Black Theology	.270°°°	.339°°°	.152°°	.105	.197°°°	.061	−.060	.0644	.098
Socialization									
Pre–Civil Rights Movement	.231°°°	.070	.082	.170°°	.129°	−.108	−.098	.087	.120
Civil Rights Movement	−.072	−.029	−.054	.009	.043	.043	.011	−.044	−.085
Post–Civil Rights Movement	−.116	−.028	−.012	−.157°°	−.160°°	.047	.074	−.027	−.013
Black Organizations	.266°°°	.192°°°	.044	.053	.065 ·	.058	.050	.069	.051
Black Fraternal Organizations	.152°°	.015	−.003	.052	−.109	−.023	.029	.005	−.081

Source: 2005 Religion and Society Survey.
°.1   °°.05   °°°.01

External Determinants

Organizational Constraints. Denomination is measured the same way as in chapter 4 except that the Holiness/Pentecostal grouping includes those who report membership in COGIC or the Church of God. Organizational commitment is measured using church attendance. Church attendance is a four-point measure ranging from 0 to 1, with 0 indicating never attending church services and 1 indicating attending every week. Among respondents, 85.6 percent attended church services at least once a month.

Environment. Physical environment is measured in two forms, region and community. The region measure is dichotomous, with 0 indicating residence in a state outside of the South and 1 indicating residence in a southern state. The South was home to 52.65 percent of respondents. The community measure captures whether respondents live in large metropolitan areas or suburban areas. Large cities accounted for 56 per-

TABLE D4. Pairwise Correlations of Measures of Receptivity and Organizational and External Determinants for NBC Respondents

	Church Action	Pastoral Action	Social Problem	Police Brutality	Racial Discrimination	Abortion Clinic	Gay Rights Laws	More Church Action	More Pastoral Action
Organization									
Pastor Performance	−.117°	−.115°	.063	.042	.121°	−.002	.070	−.104	−.126°
Serious Conflict	−.070	−.032	.127°	.041	.068	−.073	−.071	.078	−.042
Political Conflict	.023	.051	.003	.069	−.014	.040	.039	.042	.118
Pastor Influence	−.016	−.030	.136°	−.017	−.047	.001	.031	.094	.066
Commitment									
Attendance	.119°	.144°°	.160°°	.097	.171°°	.092	−.027	−.018	.023
Position	.013	−.035	.062	.078	.086	.058	−.071	−.035	−.078
	.849	.598	.382	.272	.226	.425	.326	.625	.286
Environment									
Inner City	.048	.117°	.128°	.066	.034	.012	.083	.018	−.056
Suburb	.025	−.013	−.052	−.145°°	−.047	−.065	−.081	.005	.043
Small Town	.080	.005	−.049	.054	.059	−.047	−.077	−.069	−.013
Rural	−.176°°	−.157°°	−.082	−.041	−.080	.092	.035	.050	.063
South	.004	−.121°	.007	.080	−.030	−.050	−.041	−.110	−.072
Agitation									
Discrimination	−.053	.015	.088	.041	.081	−.042	−.040	.081	.046

Source: 2005 Religion and Society Survey.
° .1   °° .05   °°° .01

TABLE D5. Probit Analysis of Internal and External
Determinants of Receptivity

	Black Churches Should Be Involved in Political Matters	
	B	(S.E.)
Female	−0.158	(0.115)
Education	0.780	(0.478)
Income	−0.483°	(0.190)
Political Activism	1.023°°°	(0.033)
Focus on Salvation	0.426°	(0.167)
Black Christ	0.192	(0.141)
Civil Rights Movement	0.438°°°	(0.125)
Post–Civil Rights Movement	0.218	(0.145)
Baptist	0.166	(0.150)
Methodist	0.168	(0.208)
Holiness/Pentecostal	0.446°	(0.264)
Church Attendance	−0.357	(0.220)
South	0.078	(0.113)
Suburb	0.446°	(0.175)
Large City	0.069	(0.124)
Discrimination	0.517°	(0.220)
Constant	−0.929°	(0.406)
Log-likelihood	−397.471	
Correctly Predicted	71.49%	
N	712	

Source: 1993 National Black Politics Study.
°.1   °°.05   °°°.01

cent of the sample, while suburban areas accounted for 14.7 percent. The remaining respondents resided in small cities, small towns, or rural areas.

Discrimination Scale. The discrimination scale (α = .58) is composed of agreement with the following statements: Blacks have been treated fairly in America; American society has been unfair to Blacks; the American legal system has been unfair to Blacks; and American society owes Blacks. The measure of perceived racial discrimination is a sixteen-point index that ranges from 0 to 1. Overall, respondents ranked high on this scale, with 72.6 percent falling into the fourth quartile.

NOTES

INTRODUCTION

1. To protect the identities of the members, the names of the churches, the pastors, and the respondents have been changed.

CHAPTER 1

1. Along with aggregation, Pratt and Foreman (2000) discuss deletion, integration, and compartmentalization as strategies for managing identities. However, I dismiss these strategies because they are too extreme, compromise the nature of the institution, or require a great deal of resources.

2. Some observers may argue that new members are not socialized in political churches because they deliberately chose to attend such churches. Those who have examined the church selection process, however, have found little evidence to support this belief (McClerking and McDaniel 2005; Roof and McKinney 1992; Wald, Owen, and Hill 1988). For a further discussion of this topic, see chapter 5.

CHAPTER 2

1. For a more detailed description of the methodology, see appendix A.

CHAPTER 4

1. To prevent the overrepresentation of any one church, this analysis of church activity will be limited to the responses of those who report being pastors. The AME sample size is forty-six, while the NBC sample size is twenty-six.

2. For this analysis, the sample size was expanded to include all of the respondents who indicated membership in an AME or NBC Church. The appendix contains the measurement of the variables and correlation matrix.

CHAPTER 5

1. This typology resembles the one used by Sherkat and Ellison (1991), who compare those who benefited from the successes of the civil rights movement and those who preceded it. In this analysis, I add a third category—those who were socialized after the end of the movement—to account for further generational changes.

2. Because several of the predictors of conveyance are attitudes that are related to each other, there is a concern in relation to causality and multicollinearity. Tests for multicollinearity show no reasons for concern; the correlations between the variables, while significant, are not large. In regard to causality, the interviews demonstrate that attitudes such as theology and political interest precede conveyance; however, questions may arise with regard to how theology and political interest shape each other. Following the logic of Miller and Shanks (1996), I conducted an analysis of each of these variables (not shown). The variables were examined in two stages with the belief that theology formed the base for political interest. Theology is informed by stable social, economic, and religious characteristics such as demographics, socialization, denominational affiliation, membership size, member attitudes, and physical environment. Theology, along with the previous measures, informs political interest. The results of this analysis indicate that theological beliefs are informed by demographics and denominational affiliation. The next stage incorporated theology into the model to analyze political interest. The results indicate that political interest is significantly shaped by demographics, theology, denominational affiliation, and member attitudes. These measures have direct effects on conveyance and reinforce each other.

CHAPTER 6

1. The appendix contains the results from the pairwise correlations.

2. Much like the models in the previous chapter, several of the predictors of receptivity are attitudes themselves and can be used to predict each other. Tests for multicollinearity show no reasons for concern; the correlations between the variables, while significant in several cases, are not large. In regard to causality, the interviews demonstrate that attitudes such as theology, beliefs about discrimination, and political interest precede receptivity; however, questions may arise with regard to how these attitudes affect each other. Again, following the logic of Miller and Shanks (1996), I conducted an analysis of each of these variables (not shown). In this case, the variables were examined in three stages because of a broader array of attitudes used to predict receptivity. As in chapter 5, theology is informed by stable social, economic, and religious characteristics such as demographics, socialization, denominational affiliation, church attendance, and physical environment. Theology, along with the previous measures,

informs beliefs about discrimination. Subsequently, beliefs about discrimination inform political interest. The results of this analysis indicate that theological beliefs are informed by demographics, denominational affiliation, church attendance, and physical environment. The second stage incorporated theology into the model to examine beliefs about discrimination, which are informed by demographics, theology, socialization, and physical environment. The final stage incorporated discrimination into the model to analyze political interest. The results indicate that political interest, measured by reported activism, is significantly shaped by demographics, theology, socialization, church attendance, and the physical environment. While several of these measures directly affect receptivity, they also can have indirect effects by shaping attitudes.

3. An argument could also be made for the inclusion of a group consciousness measure in the model. Gurin, Hatchett, and Jackson (1989) as well as Dawson (1994) have shown the importance of linked fate in Black political attitudes. However, the measure of discrimination incorporates issues associated with linked fate and group consciousness. Because the questions used to create the discrimination scale are group-based and because adding the linked fate measures to the model does not boost the explanatory power of the model or affect the explanatory power of the discrimination scale, the model does not include a linked fate measure.

4. These results are the predicted probabilities calculated from a probit regression (see appendix D). The probabilities were calculated with the categorical variables at their mode and continuous variables at their mean.

REFERENCES

Albert, Stuart, and David Whetten. 1985. Organizational Identity. In *Research in Organizational Behavior,* edited by L. L. Cummings and B. M. Staw. Greenwich, CT: JAI.

Alford, Andy. 2005. Seeking a Reason to Stay. *Austin American-Statesman,* December 15, A1.

Allen, Richard L., Michael C. Dawson, and Ronald E. Brown. 1989. A Schema-Based Approach to Modeling an African-American Racial Belief System. *American Political Science Review* 83 (2): 421–41.

Ammerman, Nancy T. 1998. Culture and Identity in the Congregation. In *Studying Congregations: A New Handbook,* edited by N. T. Ammerman, J. W. Carroll, C. S. Dudley, and W. McKinney. Nashville: Abingdon.

Ashforth, Blake E., and Fred A. Mael. 1996. Organizational Identity and Strategy as a Context for the Individual. In *Advances in Strategic Management,* edited by J. A. C. Baum and J. Dutton. London: JAI.

Banerjee, Neela. 2005. Black Churches Struggle over Their Role in Politics. *New York Times,* March 6, 35.

Beatty, Kathleen Murphy, and Oliver Walter. 1989. A Group Theory of Religion and Politics: The Clergy as Group Leaders. *Western Political Quarterly* 42 (1): 129–46.

Becker, Penny Edgell. 1999. *Congregations in Conflict: Cultural Models of Local Religious Life.* Cambridge: Cambridge University Press.

Berelson, Bernard, Paul F. Lazarsfeld, and William McPhee. 1954. *Voting.* Chicago: University of Chicago Press.

Berg, John C. 1994. *Unequal Struggle: Class, Gender, Race, and Power in the U.S. Congress.* Boulder, CO: Westview.

Berry, Jeffrey M. 1977. *Lobbying for the People: The Political Behavior of Public Interest Groups.* Princeton: Princeton University Press.

Beyerlein, Kraig, and Mark Chaves. 2003. The Political Activities of Religious Congregations in the United States. *Journal for the Scientific Study of Religion* 42 (2): 229–46.

Billingsley, Andrew. 1999. *Mighty Like a River: The Black Church and Social Reform.* New York: Oxford University Press.

Bobo, Lawrence, and Franklin D. Gilliam Jr. 1990. Race, Sociopolitical Participation, and Black Empowerment. *American Political Science Review* 84 (2):
377–93.

Brown, Andrew D., and Ken Starkey. 2000. Organizational Identity and Learning: A Psychodynamic Perspective. *Academy of Management Journal* 25 (1):
102–20.

Brown, R. Khari, and Ronald E. Brown. 2003. Faith and Works: Church-Based
Social Capital Resources and African-American Political Activism. *Social
Forces* 82 (2): 617–41.

Brown, Ronald E., and Monica Wolford. 1994. Religious Resources and African
American Political Action. *National Political Science Review* 4:30–48.

Bullock, Charles S., and Harrel R. Rodgers Jr., eds. 1972. *Black Political Attitudes: Implications for Political Support.* Chicago: Markham.

Burroughs, Nannie H. 1999. Report of the Work of Baptist Women. In *African
American Religious History: A Documentary Witness,* edited by M. C. Sernett. Durham: Duke University Press.

Calhoun-Brown, Allison. 1996. African American Churches and Political Mobilization: The Psychological Impact of Organizational Resources. *Journal of
Politics* 58 (4): 935–53.

Calhoun-Brown, Allison. 1998. The Politics of Black Evangelicals: What Hinders
Diversity in the Christian Right? *American Politics Quarterly* 26 (1): 81–109.

Calhoun-Brown, Allison. 1999. While Marching to Zion: Otherworldliness and
Racial Empowerment in the Black Community. *Journal for the Scientific
Study of Religion* 37 (3): 427–39.

Calhoun-Brown, Allison. 2003. No Respect of Persons? Religion, Churches, and
Gender Issues in the African American Community. In *New Day Begun:
African American Churches and Civic Culture in Post–Civil Rights America,*
edited by R. D. Smith. Durham: Duke University Press.

Campbell, Ernest Q., and Thomas F. Pettigrew. 1959. Racial and Moral Crisis:
The Role of Little Rock Ministers. *American Journal of Sociology* 64 (5):
509–16.

Chaves, Mark. 2004. *Congregations in America.* Cambridge: Harvard University
Press.

Childs-Brown, John. 1980. *The Political Black Minister: A Study in Afro-American Politics and Religion.* Boston: Hall.

Chong, Dennis. 1991. *Collective Action and the Civil Rights Movement.*
Chicago: University of Chicago Press.

Clemetson, Lynette. 2004. Both Sides Court Black Churches in the Debate over
Gay Marriage. *New York Times,* March 1, A1.

Cohen, Cathy J. 1999. *The Boundaries of Blackness: AIDS and the Breakdown of
Black Politics.* Chicago: University of Chicago Press.

Cohen, Cathy J., and Michael C. Dawson. 1993. Neighborhood Poverty and

African American Politics. *American Political Science Review* 87 (2): 286–302.

Cone, James H., and Gayraud S. Wilmore, eds. 1993. *Black Theology: A Documentary History.* 2nd ed. Maryknoll, NY: Orbis.

Coppola, Sara. 2004. East Austin Plan: New Life, Old Character. *Austin American-Statesman,* October 5, A1.

Crawford, Sue E. S., Mellisa M. Deckman, and Christi J. Braun. 2001. Gender and the Political Choices of Women Clergy. In *Christian Clergy in American Politics,* edited by S. E. S. Crawford and L. R. Olson. Baltimore: Johns Hopkins University Press.

Crawford, Sue E. S., and Laura R. Olson. 2001. Clergy as Political Actors in Urban Contexts. In *Christian Clergy in American Politics,* edited by S. E. S. Crawford and L. R. Olson. Baltimore: Johns Hopkins University Press.

Crenshaw, Kimberle. 1992. Whose Story Is It Anyway? Feminist and Antiracist Appropriations of Anita Hill. In *Race-ing Justice, Engendering Power: Essays on Anita Hill, Clarence Thomas, and the Construction of Social Reality,* edited by T. Morrison. New York: Pantheon.

Dawson, Michael C. 1994. *Behind the Mule: Race and Class in African American Politics.* Princeton: Princeton University Press.

Dawson, Michael C. 2001. *Black Visions: The Roots of Contemporary African-American Political Ideologies.* Chicago: University of Chicago Press.

Dawson, Michael C., Ronald E. Brown, and James S. Jackson. 1998. 1993 National Black Politics Study [computer file]. Chicago: University of Chicago/ Detroit: Wayne State University.

Deluga, Ronald J. 1998. Leader-Member Exchange Quality and Effectiveness Ratings. *Group and Organization Management* 23 (2): 189–216.

Dillard, Angela D. 2007. *Faith in the City: Preaching Radical Social Change in Detroit.* Ann Arbor: University of Michigan Press.

Downs, Anthony. 1957. *An Economic Theory of Democracy.* New York: Harper Collins.

Du Bois, W. E. B. [1903] 1990. *The Souls of Black Folk.* New York: Vintage.

Du Bois, W. E. B. [1903] 2000. The Problem of Amusement. In *Du Bois on Religion,* edited by P. Zuckerman. New York: AltaMira.

Du Bois, W. E. B., ed. 2003. *The Negro Church.* New York: AltaMira.

Dudley, Carl S. 1998. Process: Dynamics of Congregational Life. In *Studying Congregations: A New Handbook,* edited by N. T. Ammerman, J. W. Carroll, C. S. Dudley, and W. McKinney. Nashville: Abingdon.

Dutton, Jane E., and Janet M. Dukerich. 1991. Keeping an Eye on the Mirror: Image and Identity in Organizational Adaptation. *Academy of Management Journal* 34 (3): 517–54.

Dutton, Jane E., Janet M. Dukerich, and Celia V. Harquail. 1994. Organizational

Images and Member Identification. *Administrative Science Quarterly* 39 (2): 239–63.

Eiesland, Nancy L., and Stephen R. Warner. 1998. Ecology: Seeing the Congregation in Context. In *Studying Congregations: A New Handbook,* edited by N. T. Ammerman, J. W. Carroll, C. S. Dudley, and W. McKinney. Nashville: Abingdon.

Eisenhardt, Kathleen M. 1989. Building Theories from Case Study Research. *Academy of Management Review* 14 (4): 532–50.

Eisinger, Peter K. 1973. The Condition of Protest Behavior in American Cities. *American Political Science Review* 67 (1): 11–28.

Ellison, Christopher G. 1991. Identification and Separatism: Religious Involvement and Racial Orientations among Black Americans. *Sociological Quarterly* 32 (3): 477–94.

Findlay, James F. 1993. *Church People in the Struggle: The National Council of Churches and the Black Freedom Movement.* New York: Oxford University Press.

Fitts, Leroy. 1985. *A History of Black Baptists.* Nashville: Broadman.

Fletcher, Michael A. 2006. Few Black Churches Get Funds: Small Percentage Participate in Bush's Faith-Based Initiative. *Washington Post,* September 19, A19.

Franklin, John Hope, and Alfred A. Moss Jr. 1988. *From Slavery to Freedom: A History of Negro Americans.* New York: Knopf.

Franklin, V. P. 1995. *Living Our Stories, Telling Our Truths: Autobiography and the Making of the African-American Intellectual Tradition.* New York: Oxford University Press.

Frazier, E. Franklin. 1974 [1964]. *The Black Church in America.* New York: Knopf.

Goodstein, Laurie. 2006. Disowning Conservative Politics, Evangelical Pastor Rattles Flock. *New York Times,* July 30, 1.

Greenberg, Kenneth S., ed. 2003. *Nat Turner: A Slave Rebellion in History and Memory.* Oxford: Oxford University Press.

Gurin, Patricia, Shirley Hatchett, and James S. Jackson. 1989. *Hope and Independence: Blacks' Response to Electoral and Party Politics.* New York: Sage.

Guth, James, John C. Green, Corwin E. Smidt, Lyman A. Kellstedt, and Margaret M. Poloma. 1997. *The Bully Pulpit: The Politics of Protestant Clergy.* Lawrence: University of Kansas Press.

Guth, James, Lyman A. Kellstedt, Corwin E. Smidt, and John C. Green. 1998. Thunder on the Right? Religious Group Mobilization in the 1996 Election. In *Interest Group Politics,* edited by A. J. Cigler and B. A. Loomis. Washington, DC: Congressional Quarterly Press.

Hadden, Jeffrey K. 1967. *The Gathering Storm in Churches.* Garden City, NY: Doubleday.

Hamilton, Charles V. 1972. *The Black Preacher in America.* New York: Morrow.

Hamilton, Charles V. 2002. *Adam Clayton Powell, Jr.: The Political Biography of an American Dilemma.* New York: Copper Square.

Hansen, John Mark. 1985. The Political Economy of Group Membership. *American Political Science Review* 79 (1): 79–96.

Harding, Vincent. 1969. Religion and Resistance among Antebellum Negroes, 1800–1860. In *The Making of Black America,* edited by A. Meier and E. Rudwick. New York: Atheneum.

Harris, Fredrick C. 1999. *Something Within: Religion in African-American Political Activism.* New York: Oxford University Press.

Harris, Fredrick C., Valeria Sinclair-Chapman, and Brian D. McKenzie. 2005. *Countervailing Forces in African American Civic Activism, 1973–1994.* Cambridge: Cambridge University Press.

Harris-Lacewell, Melissa Victoria. 2004. *Barbershops, Bibles, and BET: Everyday Talk and Black Political Thought.* Princeton: Princeton University Press.

Harvey, Paul. 1997. *Redeeming the South: Religious Cultures and Racial Identities.* Chapel Hill: University of North Carolina Press.

Hatch, Mary Jo. 1993. The Dynamics of Organizational Culture. *Academy of Management Review* 18 (4): 657–93.

Hatch, Mary Jo, and Majken Schultz. 2002. The Dynamics of Organizational Identity. *Human Relations* 55 (8): 989–1018.

Higginbotham, Evelyn Brooks. 1993. *Righteous Discontent: The Women's Movement in the Black Baptist Church, 1880–1920.* Cambridge: Harvard University Press.

Hoge, Dean R., Charles Zech, Patrick McNamara, and Michael J. Donahue. 1998. The Value of Volunteers as Resources for Congregations. *Journal for the Scientific Study of Religion* 37 (3): 470–80.

Howard, John R. 1999. *The Shifting Wind: The Supreme Court and Civil Rights from Reconstruction to Brown.* Albany: State University of New York Press.

Huckfeldt, Robert, Eric Plutzer, and John Sprague. 1993. Alternative Contexts of Political Behavior: Churches, Neighborhoods, and Individuals. *Journal of Politics* 55 (2): 365–81.

Jackson, Joseph H. 1999. National Baptist Philosophy of Civil Rights. In *African American Religious History: A Documentary Witness,* edited by M. C. Sernett. Durham: Duke University Press.

Jamal, Amaney. 2005. The Political Participation and Engagement of Muslim Americans. *American Politics Research* 33 (4): 521–44.

Jelen, Ted G. 1993. *The Political World of Clergy.* Westport, CT: Praeger.

Jordan, Winthrop D. 1968. *White over Black: American Attitudes towards the Negro, 1550–1812.* Chapel Hill: University of North Carolina Press.

King, Martin Luther, Jr. 1999. Letter from Birmingham Jail—April 16, 1963. In

African American Religious History: A Documentary Witness, edited by M. C. Sernett. Durham: Duke University Press.

Kingdon, John W. 1995. *Agendas, Alternatives, and Public Policies.* New York: Harper Collins.

Kirkpatrick, Shelley A., and Edwin Locke. 1995. Leadership: Do Traits Matter? *Academy of Management Executive* 5 (2): 48–60.

Klinkler, Philip A., and Rogers M. Smith. 1999. *The Unsteady March: The Rise and Decline of Racial Equality in America.* Chicago: University of Chicago Press.

Lee, Shayne. 2003. The Church of Faith and Freedom: African-American Baptists and Social Action. *Journal for the Scientific Study of Religion* 42 (1): 31–41.

Lincoln, C. Eric. 1984. *Race, Religion, and the Continuing American Dilemma.* New York: Hill and Wang.

Lincoln, C. Eric. 1994. *The Black Muslims in America.* Grand Rapids, MI: Eerdmans.

Lincoln, C. Eric, and Lawrence H. Mamiya. 1990. *The Black Church in the African American Experience.* Durham: Duke University Press.

Loguen, Jermain W. 1999. I Will Not Live a Slave. In *African American Religious History: A Documentary Witness,* edited by M. C. Sernett. Durham: Duke University Press.

Marx, Gary T. 1967. Religion: Opiate or Inspiration of Civil Rights Militancy among Negroes? *American Sociological Review* 32 (1): 64–72.

Mays, Benjamin E., and Joseph W. Nicholson. 1969 [1933]. *The Negro's Church.* New York: Russell and Russell.

McAdam, Doug. 1982. *Political Process and the Development of Black Insurgency, 1930–1970.* Chicago: University of Chicago Press.

McClerking, Harwood K., and Eric L. McDaniel. 2005. Belonging and Doing: Political Churches and Black Political Participation. *Political Psychology* 26 (5): 721–34.

McDaniel, Eric L. 2003. Black Clergy in the 2000 Election. *Journal for the Scientific Study of Religion* 42 (4): 533–46.

McDaniel, Eric L. 2007. The Black Church: Maintaining Old Coalitions. In *A Matter of Faith: Religion in the 2004 Presidential Election,* edited by D. E. Campbell. Washington, DC: Brookings Institution Press.

McDaniel, Eric L., and Harwood K. McClerking. 2005. Who Belongs? Understanding How Socioeconomic Stratification Shapes the Characteristics of Black Political Church Members. *National Political Science Review* 10: 15–28.

McKinney, William, Anthony T. Ruger, Diane Cohen, and Robert Jeager. 1998. Resources. In *Studying Congregations: A New Handbook,* edited by N. T.

Ammerman, J. W. Carroll, C. S. Dudley, and W. McKinney. Nashville: Abingdon.

McRoberts, Omar M. 1999. Understanding the "New" Black Pentecostal Activism: Lessons from Ecumenical Urban Ministries in Boston. *Sociology of Religion* 60 (1): 47–70.

McRoberts, Omar M. 2003. *Streets of Glory: Church and Community in a Black Urban Neighborhood*. Chicago: University of Chicago Press.

Mead, Frank S., and Samuel S. Hill. 1995. *Handbook of Denominations in the United States*. Nashville: Abingdon.

Miller, Steve. 2001. NAACP Votes to Fight Bush on His Faith-Based Initiative. *Washington Times,* July 11, A6.

Miller, Warren E., and J. Merrill Shanks. 1996. *The New American Voter*. Cambridge: Harvard University Press.

Montgomery, William E. 1993. *Under Their Own Vine and Fig Tree: The African-American Church in the South, 1865–1900*. Baton Rouge: Louisiana State University Press.

Morris, Aldon D. 1984. *The Origins of the Civil Rights Movement: Black Communities Organizing for Change*. New York: Free Press.

Morris, Milton D. 1975. *The Politics of Black America*. New York: Harper and Row.

Myrdal, Gunnar. 1962. *An American Dilemma: The Negro Problem and Modern Democracy*. New York: Harper Torchbooks.

Nelsen, Hart M., Thomas W. Madron, and Raytha L. Yokley. 1975. Black Religion's Promethean Motif: Orthodoxy and Militancy. *American Journal of Sociology* 81 (1): 139–46.

Olson, Laura R., Sue E. S. Crawford, and James Guth. 2000. Changing Issue Agendas of Women Clergy. *Journal for the Scientific Study of Religion* 39 (2): 140–53.

Olson, Mancur. 1965. *The Logic of Collective Action*. Cambridge: Harvard University Press.

Oppel, Richard A., and Gustav Niebuhr. 2000. Bush Meeting Focuses on Role of Religion. *New York Times*, December 21, 37.

O'Reilly, Kenneth. 1995. *Nixon's Piano: Presidents and Racial Politics from Washington to Clinton*. New York: Free Press.

Owens, Michael Leo. 2006. Which Congregations Will Take Advantage of Charitable Choice? Explaining the Pursuit of Public Funding by Congregations. *Social Science Quarterly* 87 (1): 55–75.

Paris, Peter J. 1991. *Black Religious Leaders: Conflict in Unity*. Louisville: Westminster/John Knox.

Payne, Charles M. 1995. *I've Got the Light of Freedom: The Organizing Tradi-

tion and Mississippi Freedom Struggle. Berkeley: University of California Press.

Payne, Daniel Alexander. 1998. *History of the African Methodist Episcopal Church.* Nashville: AMEC Sunday School Union/Legacy Publishing.

Peters, L. H., D. D. Hartke, and J. T. Pohlmann. 1985. Fiedler's Contingency Theory of Leadership: An Application of the Meta-Analysis Procedures of Schmidt and Hunter. *Psychological Bulletin* 97 (2): 274–85.

Philpot, Tasha S. 2007. *Race, Republicans, and the Return to the Party of Lincoln.* Ann Arbor: University of Michigan Press.

Pinn, Anne H., and Anthony B. Pinn. 2002. *Fortress Introduction to Black Church History.* Minneapolis: Fortress.

Pinn, Anthony B. 2002. *The Black Church in the Post–Civil Rights Era.* Maryknoll, NY: Orbis.

Piven, Frances Fox, and Richard A. Cloward. 1977. *Poor People's Movements: Why They Succeed, How They Fail.* New York: Vintage.

Plohetski, Tony, and Patrick George. 2007. Austin Police to Face Inquiry. *Austin American-Statesman,* June 2, A1.

Pratt, Michael G. 2000. The Good, the Bad, and the Ambivalent: Managing Identification among Amway Distributors. *Administrative Science Quarterly* 45 (3): 456–93.

Pratt, Michael G. 2003. Disentangling Collective Identities. In *Identity Issues in Groups: Research on Managing Groups and Teams,* edited by J. Polzer, E. Mannix, and M. Neale. Stamford, CT: Elsevier Science.

Pratt, Michael G., and Peter O. Foreman. 2000. Classifying Managerial Responses to Multiple Organizational Identities. *Academy of Management Review* 25 (1): 18–42.

Quinley, Harold E. 1974. The Dilemma of an Activist Church: Protestant Religion in the Sixties and Seventies. *Journal for the Scientific Study of Religion* 13 (1): 1–21.

Raboteau, Albert J. 1978. *Slave Religion: The "Invisible Institution" in the Antebellum South.* Oxford: Oxford University Press.

Raboteau, Albert J. 2001. *Canaan Land: A Religious History of African Americans.* Oxford: Oxford University Press.

Randolph, Peter. 1999. Plantation Churches: Visible and Invisible. In *African American Religious History: A Documentary Witness,* edited by M. C. Sernett. Durham: Duke University Press.

Reed, Adolph L., Jr. 1986. *The Jesse Jackson Phenomenon: The Crisis of Purpose in Afro-American Politics.* New Haven: Yale University Press.

Robertson, David. 1999. *Denmark Vesey.* New York: Vintage.

Robinson, Carin. 2006. From Every Tribe and Nation? Blacks and the Christian Right. *Social Science Quarterly* 87 (3): 591–601.

Roof, Wade Clark, and William McKinney. 1992. *American Mainline Religion: Its Changing Shape and Future.* New Brunswick: Rutgers University Press.

Rosenstone, Steven, and John Mark Hansen. 1993. *Mobilization, Participation, and Democracy in America.* New York: Macmillan.

Rowland, Christopher, ed. 1999. *The Cambridge Companion to Liberation Theology.* Cambridge: Cambridge University Press.

Sanders, Cheryl Jeanne. 1996. *Saints in Exile: The Holiness-Pentecostal Experience in African American Religion and Culture.* New York: Oxford University Press.

Schein, Edgar H. 1984. Coming to a New Awareness of Organizational Culture. *Sloan Management Review* 25 (2): 3–16.

Schein, Edgar H. 2004. *Organizational Culture and Leadership.* San Francisco: Jossey-Bass.

Schriesheim, Chester A., Linda L. Neider, and Terri A. Scandura. 1998. Delegation and Leader-Member Exchange: Main Effects, Moderators and Measurement Issues. *Academy of Management Journal* 41 (3): 298–318.

Scott, Susanne G., and Vicki R. Lane. 2000. A Stakeholder Approach to Organizational Identity. *Academy of Management Journal* 25 (1): 43–62.

Scott, W. Richard. 1998. *Organizations: Rational, Natural, and Open Systems.* Upper Saddle River, NJ: Prentice Hall.

Sernett, Milton C., ed. 1999. *African American Religious History: A Documentary Witness.* Durham: Duke University Press.

Shaw, Todd C., and Eric L. McDaniel. 2007. "Whosever Will": Black Theology, Homosexuality, and the Black Political Church. *National Political Science Review* 11:137–56.

Sherkat, Darren E., and Christopher G. Ellison. 1991. The Politics of Black Religious Change: Disaffiliation from Black Mainline Denominations. *Social Forces* 70 (2): 431–54.

Simon, Herbert. 1964. On the Concept of Organizational Goal. *Administrative Science Quarterly* 9 (1): 1–22.

Smidt, Corwin E. 2004. Introduction to *Pulpit and Politics: Clergy in American Politics at the Advent of the Millennium,* edited by C. E. Smidt. Waco, TX: Baylor University Press.

Smith, R. Drew, and Corwin E. Smidt. 2003. System Confidence, Congregational Characteristics, and Black Church Civic Engagement. In *A New Day Begun: African American Churches and Civic Culture in Post–Civil Rights America,* edited by R. D. Smith. Durham: Duke University Press.

Smith, Robert C. 1996. *We Have No Leaders: African Americans in the Post–Civil Rights Era.* Albany: State University of New York Press.

Stanton, Robert. 1998. Floyd Flake. *Headway,* September–October, 10.

Stark, Rodney, and Charles Y. Glock. 1968. *American Piety: The Nature of Religious Commitment.* Berkeley: University of California Press.

Stonebraker, Robert J. 1993. Optimal Church Size: The Bigger the Better? *Journal for the Scientific Study of Religion* 32 (3): 231–41.

Tamney, Joseph B. 1991. Social Class Composition of Congregations and Pastoral Support for Liberal Activism. *Review of Religious Research* 33 (1): 18–31.

Tate, Katherine. 1993. *From Protest to Politics: The New Black Voters in American Elections.* Cambridge: Harvard University Press.

Tocqueville, Alexis de. 1945. *Democracy in America.* Toronto: Vintage.

Troubling Questions about the Use of Force. 2005. *Austin American-Statesman,* October 3, A8.

Truman, David B. 1960. *The Governmental Process: Political Interests and Public Opinion.* New York: Knopf.

Ture, Kwame, and Charles V. Hamilton. 1967. *Black Power: The Politics of Liberation.* New York: Random House.

Turner, Nat. 1999. Religion and Slave Insurrection. In *African American Religious History: A Documentary Witness,* edited by M. C. Sernett. Durham: Duke University Press.

Verba, Sidney, Kay Lehman Schlozman, and Henry E. Brady. 1995. *Voice and Equality: Civic Voluntarism in American Politics.* Cambridge: Harvard University Press.

Wald, Kenneth D. 1997. *Religion and Politics in the United States.* Washington, DC: Congressional Quarterly Press.

Wald, Kenneth D., and Allison Calhoun-Brown. 2007. *Religion and Politics in the United States.* Lanham, MD: Rowman and Littlefield.

Wald, Kenneth D., Dennis E. Owen, and Samuel S. Hill Jr. 1988. Churches as Political Communities. *American Political Science Review* 82 (2): 531–48.

Walker, Clarence E. 1982. *A Rock in a Weary Land: The African Methodist Episcopal Church during the Civil War and Reconstruction.* Baton Rouge: Louisiana State University Press.

Walker, Jack L. 1991. *Mobilizing Interest Groups in America: Patrons, Professions, and Social Movements.* Ann Arbor: University of Michigan Press.

Walton, Hanes, Jr. 1985. *Invisible Politics: Black Political Behavior.* Albany: State University of New York Press.

Walton, Hanes, Jr. 1988. *When the Marching Stopped: The Politics of Civil Rights Regulatory Agencies.* Albany: State University of New York Press.

Walton, Hanes, Jr., and Robert C. Smith. 2003. *American Politics and the African American Quest for Universal Freedom.* New York: Longman.

Walton, Hanes, Jr., and Robert C. Smith. 2008. *American Politics and the African American Quest for Universal Freedom.* 4th ed. New York: Pearson Longman.

Warner, Stephen R. 1988. *New Wine in Old Wineskins: Evangelicals and Liberals in a Small-Town Church.* Berkeley: University of California Press.

Weick, Karl. 1995. *Sensemaking in Organizations.* Thousand Oaks, CA: Sage.

White, James. 1994. Buying and Selling Votes Takes Place in Both Parties. *National Minority Politics,* January, 14–15.

Wilcox, Clyde. 1990a. Blacks and the New Christian Right: Support for the Moral Majority and Pat Robertson among Washington, D.C., Blacks. *Review of Religious Research* 32 (1): 43–55.

Wilcox, Clyde. 1990b. Religious Sources of Politicization among Blacks in Washington, D.C. *Journal for the Scientific Study of Religion* 29 (3): 387–394.

Wilcox, Clyde, and Carin Larson. 2006. *Onward Christian Soldiers? The Religious Right in American Politics.* Boulder, CO: Westview.

Wilson, James Q. 1960. Two Negro Politicians: An Interpretation. *Midwest Journal of Political Science* 4 (4): 346–69.

Wilson, James Q. 1973. *Political Organizations.* New York: Basic Books.

Wood, James R. 1981. *Leadership in Voluntary Organizations: The Controversy over Social Action in Protestant Churches.* New Brunswick: Rutgers University Press.

Woodward, C. Vann. 1971. *Origins of the New South, 1877–1913.* Baton Rouge: Louisiana State Press.

Woodward, C. Vann. [1955] 2002. *The Strange Career of Jim Crow.* Commemorative ed. Oxford: Oxford University Press.

Zaller, John R. 1992. *The Nature and Origins of Mass Opinion.* Cambridge: Cambridge University Press.

INDEX